When people are in a certain mood, whether elation or depression, that mood is often communicated to others. Talking to a depressed person we may feel depressed, whereas talking to someone who feels self-confident and buoyant we are likely to feel good about ourselves. This phenomenon, known as *emotional contagion*, is identified here, and compelling evidence for its effect is offered from a variety of disciplines – social and developmental psychology, history, cross-cultural psychology, experimental psychology, and psychophysiology.

*Studies in Emotion and Social Interaction*

Paul Ekman
University of California, San Francisco

Klaus R. Scherer
Université de Genève

General Editors

*Emotional Contagion*

*Studies in Emotion and Social Interaction*

This series is jointly published by the Cambridge University Press and the Editions de la Maison des Sciences de l'Homme, as part of the joint publishing agreement established in 1977 between the Fondation de la Maison des Sciences de l'Homme and the Syndics of the Cambridge University Press.

Cette collection est publiée co-édition par Cambridge University Press et les Editions de la Maison des Sciences de l'Homme. Elle s'intègre dans le programme de co-édition établi en 1977 par la Fondation de la Maison des Sciences de l'Homme et les Syndics de Cambridge University Press.

# Emotional Contagion

Elaine Hatfield
*University of Hawaii*

John T. Cacioppo
*Ohio State University*

Richard L. Rapson
*University of Hawaii*

 **CAMBRIDGE**
UNIVERSITY PRESS

Editions de la Maison des Sciences de l'Homme
*Paris*

Published by the Press Syndicate of the University of Cambridge
The Pitt Building, Trumpington Street, Cambridge CB2 1RP
40 West 20th Street, New York, NY 10011-4211, USA
10 Stamford Road, Oakleigh, Melbourne 3166, Australia
and
Editions de la Maison des Sciences de l'Homme
54 Boulevard Raspail, 75270 Paris, Cedex 06

First published 1994


Library of Congress Cataloging-in-Publication Data
Hatfield, Elaine.
Emotional contagion / Elaine Hatfield, John T. Cacioppo, Richard L. Rapson
  p. cm. – (Studies in emotion and social interaction)
Includes bibliographical references and index.
ISBN 0-521-44498-5. – ISBN 0-521-44948-0 (pbk.)
1. Emotional contagion. I. Cacioppo, John T. II. Rapson, Richard L.
III. Title. IV. Series.
BF578.H38 1994
152.4 – dc20                                                        93–3921
                                                                       CIP

A catalog record for this book is available from the British Library

ISBN 0-521-44498-5   hardback
ISBN 0-521-44948-0   paperback
ISBN 2-7351-0545-8   hardback   (France only)
ISBN 2-7351-0549-0   paperback   (France only)

Transferred to digital printing 2002

# Contents

# Acknowledgments

We would like to thank Cynthia Clement, our literary editor, for helping us track down quotations that were just right for illustrating the scholarly material. We also appreciate the help of Phil Giammatteo and Vinita Shah, who helped with library research, and Maryann Overstreet, who translated Theodor Lipps's German text.

# Introduction and overview

## Introduction

For over a decade, Richard L. Rapson and I (Elaine Hatfield) have worked together as therapists. Often, as we talk through the sessions over dinner, we are struck by how easy it is to catch the rhythms of our clients' feelings from moment to moment and, in consequence, how profoundly our moods can shift from hour to hour.

One day, for example, Dick complained irritably at the end of a session: "I really felt out on a limb today. I kept hoping you'd come in and say something, but you just left me hanging there. What was going on?" I was startled. He had been brilliant during the hour, and I had not been able to think of a thing to add; in fact, I had felt out of *my* depth and ill at ease the whole time. As we replayed the session, we realized that both of us had felt on the spot, anxious, and incompetent. The cause of our anxiety soon became clear. We had been so focused on our own responsibilities and feelings that we had missed how anxious our client had been. We had been taken in by her calm, cool cover-up. Later, she admitted that she had been afraid the whole hour that we would ask her about her drug use and discover that she had returned to her abusive, drug-dealing husband.

Generally, it is fairly easy to recognize that you are tracking a client's emotion. You quickly learn to recognize the flash of anger that you feel at clients who are seething with hidden anger at you and the rest of the world. Then there is the dead, sleepy feeling you get when talking . . . ever so slowly . . . to a depressed client. I am so prone to the deadening effects of the depressed that it is hard to keep even a minimal conversation going with them; I keep finding myself sinking off into sleep.

1

Dick and I were a bit slower to recognize that we experienced the same emotional contagion in private, personal encounters as well. The clear recognition of how pervasive such automatic emotional resonances are, and the resolution to discover more about this fascinating process, came from a single incident. One of my colleagues at the University of Hawaii, a world-famous scholar and scientist, is arrogant, hard driving, and successful. Although we were close friends and political allies, every time I talked with him I came away from the conversation feeling that I had said something stupid and had bored him. I felt awkward, uncomfortable, and ill at ease, and resolved after each encounter to try harder the next time. After three years of working as a therapist I suddenly realized, in the midst of a particularly painful conversation, what was going on. Here, too, I had been blinded by focusing overmuch on what *I* was doing wrong. I had come up with attributions that dealt entirely with my own contribution to the continuing fiasco, but been oblivious to what was going on with him! In a social interaction, focusing *only* on oneself or *only* on the other can be equally blinding. The most information can be gained by alternately checking one's own reactions and observing one's partners, and now and then moving to a different level of analysis to focus on what is going on in the interaction. As I stepped back and analytically began to assess what *my colleague* was feeling and saying, I realized that he was acutely anxious. I soon observed that although he was a big bear of a man, dominant and forceful, he was *always* ill at ease in conversation. Brief expressions of anxiety crossed his face, his voice rose, he twitched, shifting his weight nervously from foot to foot. The next time we met, I reminded myself that I did not need to focus on being witty and charming, and would do better to spend my energy subtly calming and reassuring my anxious friend. This worked much better; we both settled down.

Once sensitive to the pervasiveness of contagion, Dick and I became fascinated with the topic. How could we have made such self-centered and erroneous attributions of our own feelings for so long? How could we have missed the pervasiveness of primitive emotional contagion? Why hadn't we learned to monitor our own feelings long ago to figure out what others were feeling? How did this contagion work? We set out to explore the process of emotional contagion.

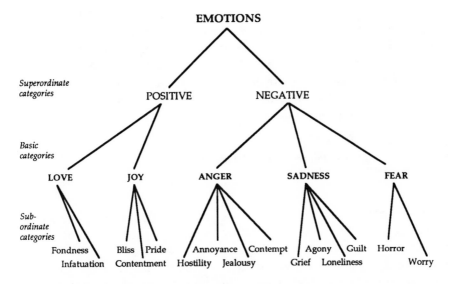

Intro Figure 1. An emotion hierarchy. *Source:* Fischer et al. (1990), p. 90.

## Definitions

Let us begin by defining *emotion* and *primitive emotional contagion*. Emotion differs from attention and memory in that, minimally, emotional stimuli (1) are categorized as being either positive or negative, and (2) predispose people to bivalent behavior (e.g., approach or withdrawal) toward the stimuli. Kurt Fischer, Phillip Shaver, and Peter Carnochan (1990) additionally argue that emotions are

> organized, meaningful, generally adaptive action systems . . . .
> [They] are complex functional wholes including appraisals or
> appreciations, patterned physiological processes, action tenden-
> cies, subjective feelings, expressions, and instrumental behav-
> iors. . . . None of these features is necessary for a particular in-
> stance of emotion. Emotions fit into families, within which all
> members share a family resemblance but no universal set of
> features. (pp. 84–5)

They propose the emotion hierarchy shown in Intro Figure 1.

There is still disagreement as to what, precisely, constitutes an emotion family (Ekman, 1992; Izard, 1992; Ortony & Turner, 1990;

Panksepp, in press). Most theorists, however, probably would agree that emotional "packages" comprise many components, including conscious awareness; facial, vocal, and postural expression; neurophysiological and autonomic nervous system activity; and instrumental behaviors. Different portions of the brain process the various aspects of emotion (Gazzaniga, 1985; Lewicki, 1986; MacLean, 1975; Panksepp, 1986, Papez, 1937).

> There's no limit to how complicated things can get, on account
> of one thing always leading to another.
>
> – E. B. White

Early theorists focused on the question of sequence: Which comes first, the cognitive, somatovisceral, or behavioral aspects of emotion? Recent theorists have moved away from linear, unideterministic reasoning and have decided, instead, that "it depends": Emotional stimuli may well trigger the conversant awareness, somatovisceral, and behavioral aspects of emotion almost simultaneously; which appears first depends on the person and the situation. Thus, theorists are increasingly asking how each of the emotional components acts on and is acted upon by the others (Berscheid, 1983; Candland, 1977; Carlson & Hatfield, 1992). James Laird and Charles Bresler (1992) summarize the position this way:

> All components of the emotional episode are ordinarily generated, more or less independently, by some central mechanism, but activation of any one may increase activity of any other. Their interactive effects might arise because of the way the organism is built . . . or because of classical conditioning, produced by the long history of paired occurrence of emotional responses. (p. 49, orig. MS)

Our definition of emotion, then, stresses the importance of all the elements of the emotional "package" in shaping emotional experience/behavior.

*Emotional contagion*, we believe, is best conceptualized as a multiply determined family of psychophysiological, behavioral, and social phenomena. Because emotional contagion can be produced by innate stimulus features (e.g., a mother's nurturing expressions and actions toward an infant), acquired stimulus features, and/or mental simulations or emotional imagery, we say it is *multiply determined*.

Because it can manifest as responses that are either similar (e.g., as when smiles elicit smiles) or complementary (e.g., as when a fist raised in anger causes a timid person to shrink back in fear, a process sometimes called *countercontagion*), it represents a *family* of phenomena. Emotional contagion is also a *multilevel phenomenon:* The precipitating stimuli arise from one individual, act upon (i.e., are perceived and interpreted by) one or more other individuals, and yield corresponding or complementary emotions (conversant awareness; facial, vocal, and postural expression; neurophysiological and autonomic nervous system activity; and gross emotional behavioral responses) in these individuals. Thus, an important consequence of emotional contagion is an attentional, emotional, and behavioral synchrony that has the same adaptive utility (and drawbacks) for social entities (dyads, groups) as has emotion for the individual.

The focus in this text is on rudimentary or *primitive emotional contagion* – that which is relatively automatic, unintentional, uncontrollable, and largely inaccessible to conversant awareness. This is defined as

> the tendency to automatically mimic and synchronize facial expressions, vocalizations, postures, and movements with those of another person and, consequently, to converge emotionally. (Hatfield et al., 1992, pp. 153–154)

## Organization of the text

In chapters 1 and 2, we discuss three mechanisms that we believe account for emotional contagion in general, and for primitive emotional contagion in particular. We also review evidence for the process that we believe generates primitive emotional contagion: In chapter 1 we show that people do tend automatically to mimic or synchronize with the facial expressions, vocal expressions, postures, and movements of those around them; in chapter 2, that people tend to experience emotions consistent with the facial, vocal, and postural expressions they adopt.

In chapter 3, we review the evidence from a variety of disciplines, including animal research, developmental psychology, clinical psychology, and social psychology, that such emotional contagion is pervasive. We also examine the performing arts and the historical record. The kinds of people who are most able to "infect" others with their own emotions are profiled in chapter 4; those most susceptible to *catching* emotions from others are highlighted in chapter 5, as are the types of situations that foster emotional contagion.

Emotional contagion may well be important in personal relationships: It fosters behavioral synchrony and the tracking of the feelings of others moment to moment, even when individuals are not explicitly attending to this information. In chapter 6 we end by reviewing the implications of our research and outlining some of the broad research questions future researchers might profitably explore over the next decade.

Elaine Hatfield

# 1. Mechanisms of emotional contagion: I. Emotional mimicry/synchrony

I am involved in all mankind.

– John Donne

## Theoretical overview

Emotional contagion is best conceptualized as a multiply determined family of social, psychophysiological, and behavioral phenomena. Theoretically, emotions can be "caught" in several ways. Let us begin by considering a few of these.

### How people might catch the emotions of others

A wise man associating with the vicious becomes an idiot;
a dog traveling with good men becomes a rational being.

– Arabic proverb

*Conscious cognitive processes.* Early investigators interested in how emotions were transmitted from one individual to another focused on complex cognitive processes by which people might come to know and feel what those around them felt. They proposed that conscious reasoning, analysis, and imagination accounted for this transmittal. For example, 18th-century economic philosopher Adam Smith (1759/1976) observed:

> Though our brother is upon the rack . . . by the imagination we place ourselves in his situation, we conceive ourselves enduring all the same torments, we enter as it were into his body, and become in some measure the same person with him, and thence form some idea of his sensations, and even feel some-

thing which, though weaker in degree, is not altogether unlike them. (p. 9)

Such conscious reveries could spark a shared emotional response (Humphrey, 1922; Lang, 1985).

Russian psychophysiologist A. R. Luria (1902/1987), in *The Mind of a Mnemonist*, described S., a subject whose imagination was so powerful that he could alter his emotions and his physiological reactions (heart activity and body temperature) simply by thinking of emotion-producing events:

> The following is the demonstration he gave us of how he could alter his pulse rate. At rest, his pulse was normally 70–72. But after a slight pause he could make it accelerate until it had increased to 80–96, and finally to 100. We also saw him reverse the rate. His pulse began to slow down, and after it had dropped to its previous rate continued to decrease until it was a steady 64–66. When we asked him how he did this, he replied:
>
> What do you find so strange about it? I simply see myself running after a train that has just begun to pull out. I have to catch up with the last car if I'm to make it. Is it any wonder then my heartbeat increases? After that, I saw myself lying in bed, perfectly still, trying to fall asleep. . . I could see myself begin to drop off . . . my breathing became regular, my heart started to beat more slowly and evenly . . .
>
> And here is another experiment he performed for us: . . .
>
> We used a skin thermometer to check the temperature of both hands and found they were the same. After a minute had passed, then another, he said: "All right, begin!" We attached the thermometer to the skin on his right hand and found that the temperature had risen two degrees. As for his left hand, after S. paused for a minute and then announced he was ready, the reading showed that the temperature of his left hand had dropped one and a half degrees.
>
> What could this mean? How was it possible for him to control the temperature of his body at will?
>
> No, there's nothing to be amazed at. I saw myself put my right hand on a hot stove. . . . Oi, was it hot! So, naturally, the temperature of my hand increased. But I was holding a piece of ice in my left hand. I could see it there and began to squeeze it. And, of course, my hand got colder. (p. 139–141)

Of course, conscious rumination may produce what looks like contagion but is not. If an experimenter were to tell two subjects to "think of the saddest event in your life," their ruminations might end up making both of them sad; however, they would not be sharing one another's emotions. There is a yawning gulf between the fact of two people experiencing the same emotions and the assumption that they are somehow sharing one another's feelings. Lauren Wispé (1991) provided an example of how the two processes might differ:

> A wife and a mistress may both feel sadness as they view the body of their loved one. Each knows what the other is probably feeling, but for each, the sadness arises from within as a function of her relationship with the object that they can both perceive. Each is experiencing her own feelings. This is not fellow feeling, as the feelings are not shared; rather, it is a common social-emotional experience. (p. 77)

One mechanism, then, that theorists have highlighted in attempting to explain the transmission of emotions is the conscious processing of information: Individuals imagine how they would feel in another's position and thus come to share their feelings (Bandura, 1969; Stotland, 1969). This mechanism would be expected to be an especially potent determinant of emotional contagion when individuals love, like, or identify with others or share their goals.

*Conditioned and unconditioned emotional responses.* Some researchers have suggested that emotional contagion could result from more primitive associative processes – from conditioned or unconditioned emotional responses. Justin Aronfreed (1970), for example, noted that if a father habitually lashes out at his son when he staggers home from work hot, tired, and upset, soon the sight of the distressed father will come to elicit a stab of anxiety in the son. Through stimulus generalization, the boy might come to feel anxious when *anyone* begins to get upset.

A sender's emotional behavior may also generate an *unconditioned* emotional response in bystanders. When some people are nervous, for example, their shrill, hysterical voices grate on us like chalk screeching on a blackboard. Mary Klinnert and her colleagues (Klinnert, Campos, Sorce, Emde, & Sveida, 1983) observed that

> abrupt, angular movements, shrill, high-pitched voices, loud or otherwise intense vocalizations and movements . . . probably elicit emotional reactions. (p. 79)

Although some people might be aware of the conditioned or unconditioned emotional stimulus and its effects, others may be utterly ignorant of the eliciting stimulus; and all may be powerless against
the emotional forces it unleashes.

Conditioned and unconditioned emotional reactions may act in
concert. For example, the mere sight of facial expressions or postures
previously associated with angular movements, shrill, high-pitched
voices, or intense vocalizations and movements may come to evoke
comparable emotions in observers.

People's conditioned or unconditioned emotional reactions may
be similar to or very different from the emotions of the target. The
sight of a drunken, angry father may enrage his children (an example of primitive emotional contagion), may fill them with fear (an
example of negative or complementary contagion), or may produce
just a generalized feeling of dread – a sense that something is very
wrong. (In this third instance, both father and child are feeling negative, but *not* complementary, emotions.)

*Mimicry/feedback.* A fourth mechanism, involving mimicry and
feedback, has received less attention as a determinant of primitive
emotional contagion; we therefore focus on it in the remainder of
this chapter. This psychological mechanism, which we suspect may
be how emotional contagion generally occurs, can be summarized as
follows:

> *Proposition 1. In conversation, people tend automatically and*
> *continuously to mimic and synchronize their movements*
> *with the facial expressions, voices, postures, movements, and*
> *instrumental behaviors of others.*
> *Proposition 2. Subjective emotional experiences are affected,*
> *moment to moment, by the activation and/or feedback from*
> *such mimicry.*

Theoretically, one's emotional experience may be influenced by either:

1. the central nervous system commands that direct such mimicry/
synchrony in the first place;
2. the afferent feedback from such facial, verbal, postural, or movement mimicry/synchrony; or
3. self-perception processes wherein individuals draw inferences
about their own emotional states based on the emotional expres-

sions and behaviors evoked in them by the emotional states of others (Adelmann & Zajonc, 1989; Izard, 1971; Laird, 1984; Tomkins, 1963).

> *Proposition 3. Given Propositions 1 and 2, people tend to "catch" others' emotions, moment to moment.*

*In sum:* Various mechanisms for emotional contagion have been proposed, several of which are capable of producing the automatic transmission of emotions between individuals. These latter mechanisms range from conditioned and unconditioned emotional responses to interactional mimicry and synchrony. The case for conditioned and unconditioned emotional responses subserving emotional contagion is relatively straightforward; but what evidence is there that primitive emotional contagion occurs via the continuous feedback people receive from interactional mimicry and synchrony? Before examining evidence for Propositions 1–3, let us review several facts about the nature of emotion.

## The nature of emotion

Men's instincts are often wiser than their words.
                                        – C. P. Snow

*Emotional information processing is not always accessible to conversant awareness*

Consciousness and awareness are elusive concepts. Most investigators would say that a person who notices a stimulus – whether only momentarily or sufficiently to subsequently remember being exposed to it – is aware of the stimulus, even if he or she is unaware of the psychological consequences of that exposure (Nisbett & Wilson, 1977). (People often have powerful emotional reactions to others, yet are at a loss to explain just *why* they responded as they did.) At the other end of the spectrum, most investigators would say an individual is unaware of a stimulus if he or she never notices it and it has no effect on that person's cognition, emotion, or behavior. Stimuli falling in the middle ground – those that people cannot report as having detected but that do influence subsequent cognition, emotion, or behavior – are often contested (e.g., Lazarus, 1984; Zajonc, 1984); yet it is these stimuli, not accessible to conversant awareness, that are often the most fascinating by virtue of the subtlety with which they affect behavior. People naturally attend consciously to only a small part of the information being processed moment to moment (Wilson, 1985) – generally, that which is most important, unusual, or difficult. As Roy Lachman, Janet Lachman, and Earl Butterfield (1979) have observed:

> Most of what we do goes on unconsciously. . . . It is the exception, not the rule, when thinking is conscious; but by its very nature, conscious thought seems the only sort. It is not the only sort; it is the minority. (p. 207)

Similarly, much of the processing of emotional information goes on outside of conversant awareness (Ohman, 1988; Posner & Snyder, 1975; Shiffrin & Schneider, 1977).

Despite the subjective experience that information is processed sequentially, the human brain is clearly capable of parallel processing (Gazzaniga, 1985; Le Doux, 1986; Ohman, 1988; Papez, 1937). For example, while we are carrying on a rational conversation, we may also be continuously monitoring our partner's emotional reactions to what we have to say. We may unconsciously and automatically scan her face for second-by-second information as to her emotions. Is she feeling happiness, love, anger, sadness, or fear? We can use a variety of subtle indicators (e.g., facial muscle movements, "micro-expressions," crooked expressions, or the timing of reactions) to decide whether the other person is telling the truth or lying (Ekman, 1985). We may even be able to judge her mood by observing facial muscle movements so minute that they *seem* detectable only in electromyographic (EMG) recordings (Cacioppo & Petty, 1983).

Other types of emotional information are also available. People can listen to the speech of others – to the volume, rhythm, speed, pitch, disfluencies, and word choice, as well as to the length of their pauses. They can observe the way others stand, gesture, or move their hands, legs, and feet. They can also observe instrumental behaviors. Such observations are made so frequently that they tend to become automated; that is, the information is processed quickly, with minimal demand on cognitive resources and minimal impact on conversant awareness.

The great fictional detective Sherlock Holmes could detail consciously the processes of deduction that most of us carry on outside of conscious awareness (Doyle, 1917/1967):

Finding that Holmes was too absorbed for conversation I had tossed aside the barren paper and, leaning back in my chair, I fell into a brown study. Suddenly my companion's voice broke in upon my thoughts.

"You are right, Watson," said he. "It does seem a most preposterous way of settling a dispute."

"Most preposterous!" I exclaimed, and then suddenly realizing how he had echoed the inmost thought of my soul, I sat up in my chair and stared at him in blank amazement.

"What is this, Holmes?" I cried. "This is beyond anything which I could have imagined."

He laughed heartily at my perplexity.

"You remember," said he, "that some little time ago, when I read you the passage in one of Poe's sketches in which a close reasoner follows the unspoken thoughts of his companion, you were inclined to treat the matter as a mere *tour-de-force* of the author. On my remarking that I was constantly in the habit of doing the same thing you expressed incredulity."

"Oh, no!"

"Perhaps not with your tongue, my dear Watson, but certainly with your eyebrows. So when I saw you throw down your paper and enter upon a train of thought, I was very happy to have the opportunity of reading it off, and eventually of breaking into it, as a proof that I had been *en rapport* with you."

But I was still far from satisfied. "In the example which you read to me," said I, "the reasoner drew his conclusions from the actions of the man whom he observed. If I remember right, he stumbled over a heap of stones, looked up at the stars, and so on. But I have been seated quietly in my chair, and what clues can I have given you?"

"You do yourself an injustice. The features are given to man as the means by which he shall express his emotions, and yours are faithful servants."

"Do you mean to say that you read my train of thoughts from my features?"

"Your features, and especially your eyes. Perhaps you cannot yourself recall how your reverie commenced?"

"No, I cannot."

"Then I will tell you. After throwing down your paper, which was the action which drew my attention to you, you sat for half a minute with a vacant expression. Then your eyes fixed themselves upon your newly framed picture of General Gordon, and I saw by the alteration in your face that a train of thought had been started. But it did not lead very far. Your eyes flashed across to the unframed portrait of Henry Ward Beecher which stands upon the top of your books. You then glanced up at the wall, and of course your meaning was obvious. You were thinking that if the portrait were framed, it would just cover that bare space and correspond with Gordon's picture over there."

"You have followed me wonderfully!"

"So far I could hardly have gone astray. But now your thoughts went back to Beecher, and you looked hard across as if you were studying the character in his features. Then your eyes ceased to pucker, but you continued to look across, and your face was thoughtful. You were recalling the incidents of Beecher's career. I was well aware that you could not do this without thinking of the mission which he undertook on behalf of the North at the time of the Civil War, for I remember your expressing your passionate indignation at the way in which he was received by the more turbulent of our people. You felt so strongly about it that I knew you could not think of Beecher without thinking of that also. When a moment later I saw your eyes wander away from the picture, I suspected that your mind had now turned to the Civil War, and when I observed that your lips set, your eyes sparkled, and your hands clenched, I was positive that you were indeed thinking of the gallantry which was shown by both sides in that desperate struggle. But then, again, your face grew sadder; you shook your head. You were dwelling upon the sadness and horror and useless waste of life. Your hand stole towards your own old wound and a smile quivered on your lips, which showed me that the ridiculous side of this method of settling international questions had forced itself upon your mind. At this point I agreed with you that it was preposterous, and was glad to find that all my deductions had been correct."

"Absolutely!" said I. "And now that you have explained it, I confess that I am as amazed as before."

"It was very superficial, my dear Watson, I assure you." (pp. 193–195)

Given this view of emotion, there is really not much mystery to the observations of therapists and others that, though not *consciously* aware that their clients (say) are experiencing joy, sadness, fear, or anger, they "somehow" do sense and react to these feelings. Today, emotion researchers assume conscious awareness of only a small portion of the information we possess about ourselves and others.

## Emotional packages are comprised of several components

As Kurt Fischer, Phillip Shaver, and Peter Carnochan (1990) noted, an emotional package typically includes conscious appraisals, subjective feelings, action tendencies, expressions, patterned physiological processes, and instrumental behaviors. No single feature, not even conscious awareness, is a necessary feature of an emotional episode. James Laird and Charles Bresler (1991), for example, observed that, although some central mechanism ordinarily generated all the components of an emotional episode more or less independently, if any single component was activated, the others tended to be activated as well. For instance, emotional reveries may be read in the resulting facial, vocal, and postural expressions, autonomic nervous system (ANS) activity, and/or instrumental actions. Alternatively, we may come to *feel* an intense emotion as we simulate emotional expressions or behavior (Bower, 1981; Dimberg, 1990).

On occasion, of course, the various components may be desynchronized, since they may be controlled by very different perceptual and reinforcement contingencies and be processed differently in the brain. People passionately in love, for example, are often unaware of the power of that passion: A man may spend the entire hour of his therapy session explaining to us (Hatfield and Rapson) that he has decided to break up with his lover, that all he cares about is his wife and family, and that the other woman means nothing to him. We have had enough experience with those passionately in love to know there is a good chance the besotted client will stop in the waiting room to telephone his paramour, and is likely to suggest that they arrange "one last meeting" so they can say goodbye. We can be equally sure that they will end up spending the night together. Thus people may believe they are ending things as they march steadily and directly into greater involvement. Similarly, in our work with couples, an individual may be convinced that she is feeling calm and cool, discussing issues rationally, being the soul of objectivity, when all the time her hapless mate is all too aware of her sneers, brittle sarcasm, and desire to inflict pain. Such lack of synchrony may be quite disruptive to social exchanges, fostering miscommunication and conflict.

One of the benefits of rudimentary emotional contagion is the synchronizing of social exchanges. Let us examine more closely the evidence for this "synchronization function" of emotional contagion (outlined in Proposition 1).

### Evidence for Proposition 1: Mimicry and synchrony

When people are free to do as they please, they usually imitate each other.

– Eric Hoffer

Mimicry and synchrony are rudimentary and pervasive influences in social interactions, helping to regulate them. People sensitized to the existence of these influences are sometimes startled and amused to discover how pervasive they are. One colleague told me that he had watched in fascination as, a split second after one person at dinner reached for the salt, all the others at the table would reach for a glass of water, the salt, or a napkin. One diner would shift in his seat in an effort to be comfortable; another would almost immediately mirror his new position.

Filmmakers often make visual jokes about the prevalence of mimicry. For example, in Spanish writer-director Pedro Almodóvar's *Women on the Verge of a Nervous Breakdown*, the elegant Carmen Maura steps into a cab. Suddenly tears flood from her eyes; within seconds, the cab driver breaks into a fountain of tears himself. In Japanese director Juzo Itami's film *A Taxing Woman*, the earnest tax collector Nobuki Miyamoto deferentially mimics every move of her superior: patting her hair as he smooths his, leaning forward as he strains to look out the window, twisting to the right as he shifts left. Probably all Americans can recall the Marx Bros.' routines in *A Day at the Races*, in which, during an engrossing poker game, their movements got so intricately intertwined that Groucho, Harpo, and Chico ended up transferring the same cigarette back and forth – one exhaling the smoke that the other had inhaled.

People need not, of course, be consciously aware that they are synchronizing their actions with those of others: Any action continuously performed is likely to become automatic. Nevertheless, the ability to be "in tune" with those around us, to coordinate emotionally and physically with others, is critically important. One of the paradoxes of the human design is that people are much more likely to notice the absence or disruption of synchrony than its presence. It is unsettling when, on an international telephone call, words are delayed a second or two: We begin to trip over our own words, replying too quickly or too slowly. We become extremely angry and frustrated.

Let us now review in more detail the evidence that people synchronize their facial muscle movements, voices, and postural movements with one another.

*Historical    background*

As early as 1759, Adam Smith (1759/1976) observed:

> When we see a stroke aimed, and just ready to fall upon the leg or arm of another person, we naturally shrink and draw back our leg or our own arm; and when it does fall, we feel it in some measure, and are hurt by it as well as the sufferer. The mob, when they are gazing at a dancer on the slack rope, naturally writhe and twist and balance their own bodies as they see him do, and as they feel that they themselves must do if in his situation. Persons of delicate fibres and a weak constitution of body complain, that in looking on the sores and ulcers which are exposed by beggars in the streets, they are apt to feel an itching or uneasy sensation in the correspondent part of their own bodies. The horror which they conceive at the misery of those wretches affects that particular part in themselves more than any other, because that horror arises from conceiving what they themselves would suffer, if they really were the wretches whom they are looking upon, and if that particular part in themselves was actually affected in the same miserable manner. The very force of this conception is sufficient, in their feeble frames, to produce that itching or uneasy sensation complained of. (p. 10)

Smith felt that such imitation was "almost a reflex." Regarding people's ability to understand others' emotional experiences, Theodor Lipps (1903; translated here by Maryann Overstreet) suggested:

> In reality there is only one possible explanation: My understanding of the expressions of life of others has its foundation

in the instinctive impetus (or motor power) of mimicry/imita-
tion on one hand, and instinctive impetus to express my own
inner experiences in a certain way, on the other hand.

This means: Perhaps I see a gesture. Then the same facial expression wakens by virtue of a not further describable adjust-
ment of my natural impulse to such movements, which are
appropriate to call these gestures into existence. These movements in return are the natural expression of an affected inner
condition, i.e., sadness. This condition and the questionable
impulses of movement create a psychic unity. Accordingly, the
impulses of movement that are released by the facial expressions of the unfamiliar gesture close the tendency of experience
of the affected condition in itself. And I also experience it in a
certain way. Only just as such a condition that goes against my
nature. (pp. 193–194)

According to Lipps, the observer automatically imitates the other
person with slight movements in posture and facial expression, thus
creating in himself inner cues that contribute, through afferent feedback, to his understanding and experiencing of the other person's affect. Janet Bavelas and her co-workers (Bavelas, Black, Lemery, &
Mullett, 1987) translate Smith's and Lipps's observations into modern terms:

[T]his is elementary motor mimicry, overt action by an observer that is appropriate to or mimetic of the situation of the other
person, rather than one's own. The observer acts as if in the
other's place to the point of wincing at his pain, smiling at her
delight, or (as Smith described) trying to avoid that person's
danger. (p. 317)

Since the 1700s, researchers have collected considerable evidence
that people do tend to imitate one another's facial expressions,
postures, voices, and behaviors.

## Facial mimicry

The fact that faces mirror the emotional facial expressions of those
around them is well documented. Ulf Dimberg (1982) and Katherine
Vaughan and John Lanzetta (1980), as well as Paul Ekman (cited in
Schmeck, 1983), have documented that people generally tend to
mimic the expressions of those around them. This evidence comes

both from social-psychophysiological research and from studies of overt facial expression. Let us now review some typical work.

*Social-psychophysiological research.* Facial mimicry is at times almost instantaneous: People seem to be able to track the most subtle of moment-to-moment changes. Ernest Haggard and Kenneth Isaacs (1966) observed that emotional experiences and accompanying facial expressions may change with incredible speed. For instance, they reported that unique facial expressions could appear and disappear within a span of 125–200 ms (milliseconds):

> [O]ccasionally the expression on the patient's face would change dramatically within three to five frames of film (as from smile to grimace to smile), which is equivalent to a period of from one-eighth to one-fifth of a second. (p. 154)

Social-psychophysiological investigations have found that individuals' emotional experiences and facial expressions, as measured by EMG procedures, tend to mimic at least rudimentary features of the changes in emotional expression of others that the subjects observe; moreover, this motor mimicry can occur at levels so subtle as to produce no observable facial expressions (e.g., see Cacioppo, Tassinary, & Fridlund, 1990). Ulf Dimberg (1982) measured the facial EMG activity of college students at the University of Uppsala, Sweden, as they looked at pictures of people displaying happy and angry facial expressions. He found that happy and angry faces evoked very different facial EMG response patterns: Subjects observing happy facial expressions showed increased muscular activity over the zygomaticus major (cheek muscle) region; muscular activity in those observing angry facial expressions increased over the corrugator supercilii (brow muscle) region. Subjects also showed an orienting response to both happy and angry faces: Their heart rates decelerated and their skin conductance levels decreased. Similar results were secured by Vaughan and Lanzetta (1980) and Voglmaier and Hakeren (1989).

*ANS responses to others' facial expressions.* Ulf Dimberg (1990) suggested that primates are prewired to respond to emotional faces with a strong ANS response. Dimberg (1982) reported that both happy and angry faces evoked an ANS reaction (as measured by skin conductance response and heart rate deceleration). Gene Sackett (1966), who studied infant monkeys reared in isolation, found results consistent with this reasoning: These monkeys became extremely distressed the first time they were exposed to a picture of an angry adult monkey's face. Sackett concluded that the angry faces triggered an "innate releasing mechanism" for fear. Their responses could not have been learned since these isolated infants had never seen another monkey.

Evolutionary theorists have argued that sad, frightened, and angry faces may trigger powerful emotional reactions, and that it may be difficult to extinguish such innate reactions (see Wispé, 1991, for a review of this research). There is considerable evidence in support of this contention. Researchers (Lanzetta & Orr, 1980, 1981, 1986; Ohman & Dimberg, 1978; Orr & Lanzetta, 1980, 1984) found that it is hard for men and women to learn to associate happy faces with painful experiences, though easy to learn to associate angry faces with them. It is also hard to extinguish the "natural" connections: In these experiments, the researchers' first step was to link a neutral cue (a tone) with electric shock via classical conditioning. Then, in a series of trials, they systematically paired happy, neutral, or angry men's and women's faces with the conditioned stimulus (the tone), but without the subsequent shock. How long did it take subjects to stop showing an ANS response to the happy or angry faces they viewed during extinction trials? As expected, subjects who viewed happy faces (plus the tone) had smaller electrodermal responses than did those who viewed angry faces (plus the tone). In addition, the ANS responses of the happy-face viewers extinguished fairly quickly, whereas those who saw angry faces were much more resistant to extinction. Indeed, John Lanzetta and Scott Orr (1986) found these latter subjects were slow to extinguish their strong autonomic responses to the angry faces even when their shock electrodes were removed and they were assured they would never receive any more shocks! Subjects' *heads* may have known full well that they no longer had to worry about shock, but their guts were far slower to get the message.

*Studies of overt facial expression.* Researchers have found that infants begin to mimic an experimenter's facial gestures shortly after birth. Infants stick out their tongues, purse their lips, open their mouths, and the like soon after the model does so (see Meltzoff, 1988; Meltzoff & Moore, 1977; Reissland, 1988). Jeanette Haviland and Mary Lelwica (1987) further found that 10-week-old infants could and would imitate at least rudimentary features of their mother's facial expressions of happiness and anger. Mothers mimic their infants' expressions of emotion as well: When babies open their mouths, mothers tend to open theirs. This nondeliberate reaction on their part can be one of which the mothers are completely unaware (O'Toole & Dubin, 1968). Other researchers (Termine & Izard, 1988) have demonstrated that when mothers pose the facial expressions of joy and sadness and make appropriate sounds, their 9-month-old infants mirror their expressions. These infants show more expressions of joy to their mothers' posed joy than to posed sadness, and more sadness and anger to maternal posed sadness. Infants may also avert their gaze to the posed sadness.

Other researchers have shown that one's facial expressions mirror those of strangers. Elaine Hatfield and her colleagues (Hsee, Hatfield, Carlson, & Chemtob, 1990) secretly filmed the faces of University of Hawaii students as they viewed a three-minute videotaped interview in which a man recounted either one of the happiest or one of the saddest events in his life. In the happy segment, when he described a surprise birthday party his friends had thrown for him, his facial expression, voice, and gestures conveyed a feeling of happiness. During the sad segment, he described a poignant experience he had had at age 6 at his grandfather's funeral; this time, his facial expression, tones, and gestures conveyed sadness. As subjects viewed each interview (they eventually saw both), their facial expressions were unobtrusively videotaped for later analysis. Judges watching these new tapes rated how happy or sad the subjects' faces seemed to be. As predicted, subjects' faces showed happier expressions when viewing the happy segment and sadder expressions when viewing the sad one. Recently, Harold Wallbott (1991) confirmed that subjects will track facial expressions of the primary emotions of sadness, fear, anger, surprise, disgust, happiness, and contempt; interestingly, evidence of imitation of blends of these emotions was also reported.

Robert Provine (1986) conducted one of the most intriguing studies of facial mimicry. He noted that, in humans, yawning is infectious: "People witnessing or even thinking about yawning often yawn or are tempted to do so" (p. 110). (You may feel like yawning as you read this.) Provine (1989) found clear evidence that, beginning in infancy, yawns are "released" by the witnessing of yawns.

Laugh, and the world laughs with you . . .
– Ella Wheeler Wilcox

In other research, Robert Provine (1992; Provine & Fischer, 1989) demonstrated that laughter is equally contagious – such contagion being one reason networks try to spice up dull TV comedies with riotous laugh tracks. In Thomas Mann's (1965) *Death in Venice*, aging writer Gustav Aschenbach, depressed and overwrought, watches a comedy troupe entertaining in a city decimated by plague; yet, he cannot help but share the comedian's mirthless laughter.

> At the renewal of his professional distance from the audience, he [the comedian] recovered all his boldness again, and the artificial laugh that he directed up toward the terrace was derisive. Even before the end of the articulate portion of the strophe, he seemed to struggle against an irresistible tickling. He gulped, his voice trembled, he pressed his hand over his mouth, he contorted his shoulders; and at the proper moment the ungovernable laugh broke out of him, burst into such real cackles that it was infectious and communicated itself to the audience, so that on the terrace also an unfounded hilarity, living off itself alone, started up. But this seemed to double the singer's exuberance. He bent his knees, he slapped his thighs, he nearly split himself; he no longer laughed, he shrieked. He pointed up with his finger, as though nothing were more comic than the laughing guests there, and finally everyone in the garden and on the veranda was laughing, even to the waiters, bellboys, and house servants in the doorways. (pp. 92–93)

Janet Bavelas and her colleagues (1987) surveyed the research documenting the existence of motor mimicry. They found that people imitate others' expressions of pain, laughter, smiling, affection, embarrassment, discomfort, disgust, stuttering, reaching with effort, and the like, in a broad range of situations. Such mimicry, they argued, is a communicative act, conveying a rapid and precise nonverbal message to another person.

Some researchers have contended that we are especially likely to mimic the facial expressions of those for whom we care (Scheflen, 1964). E. L. Doctorow (1985) in *World's Fair* describes Edgar, a little boy who suffers from his inability to resist mimicking (and catching) the emotional expressions of Donald, the big brother he so admires:*

> In fact, love was what it was all about. However painful it might be, as sure as heat or freezing cold or storms were in the nature of weather, the daily tempest of my life among these

---

* From *World's Fair* by E. L. Doctorow. Copyright © 1985 by E. L. Doctorow. Reprinted by permission of Random House, Inc., and International Creative Management, Inc.

elemental powers – the screams, demands, disagreements – was the nature of love.

. . . But I was coming to rely on my brother in some way that my parents' vehemently intense life together did not allow me to rely on them. Donald was steadfast. He lived his earnest life as one human being, not as half of two. He was still within reach. He taught me card games, easy ones like War and Go Fish, and a hard one, Casino. We played on the floor, where I was comfortable. He held my hand as we walked to the candy store. He was at home when my parents went out at night. The sight of Donald doing his homework suggested to me the clear and purposeful intention of life and its march to a visionary future.

. . . Of course we had our problems. When his friends were around he tended not to want me to be with them, but I understood that, even as I complained and pestered him. It was a matter of principle with me to pester Donald and his friends. Of course they were not without resources in dealing with this. They knew my weaknesses, that, for instance, if anyone around me cried, I cried too. It was true, I caught crying as if it were a communicable disease, I couldn't help it, I was a walking dust mop of emotions. Donald pretended to cry to get rid of me. In fact, he had refined the art of it by only threatening to cry, holding his arm up to his eyes and issuing one preliminary sob and peeking out from under his arm to find me biting my lip, my eyes filling, ready to bawl for no reason, not even knowing what the matter was, the pain, but only that whatever it was, it was overwhelming and impossible to endure. I was burdened with this terrible affliction, just as my friend Herbert from Weeks Avenue had crossed eyes, or a little boy who played in my park had inward-turning feet. There was nothing to do but hope to grow out of it, this awful teariness. First it would hit me in the throat. Then it affected my ability to see, I had to close my eyes. It was a form of shyness or sorrow for the world's hard life. Sometimes my brother and his friends Bernie and Seymour and Irwin would, all together, pretend to cry; and I would be made so tearful by this mass assault that even knowing they were teasing me and even after having them emerge from their pretense laughing and jolly, I would find myself uncontrollably sobbing, as if a substantive wrong had taken place, like a bashed thumb or a cut, or the loss of something precious. And then, of course, it took forever to wind down, a trail of heartbreaking hiccuppy sobs issuing from me for several minutes as I went about my business. (pp. 78–80)

Importantly, an individual's feelings and goals in a social interaction may exert a powerful effect on the shape of emotional contagion. If we dislike someone, the strong antipathetic feelings that sweep over us when we behold their faces may dampen any tendency we might have to mimic their facial expressions. The emotional stimulus may well evoke cognitive appraisals, strong emotions, and conditioned emotional responses inconsistent with those that subjects might normally be expected to mimic. For example, if Jimmy Connors and John McEnroe are locked in a fierce battle at Wimbledon, we may well expect McEnroe to be delighted each time Connors falters. McEnroe may well grin in elation each time Connors mishits a ball and frowns in exasperation. However, even in these instances there seems to be a commonality, an adhesive emotion, that binds two equally matched warriors whose movements are perfectly synchronized. Consistent with these suggestions, Basil Englis, Katherine Vaughan, and John Lanzetta (1981) documented in the laboratory that individuals who were competing in a zero-sum game showed counterempathic facial responses to the other's facial expressions. Interestingly, in other conditions, individuals competed in a game in which they both either won or lost; when the contestants had a shared fate, each showed empathic facial responses to the other's facial expressions. Even though countercontagion was easily accomplished in the zero-sum game, these researchers noted that the subjects' facial reactions tended to be less intense than those of two contestants who shared the same outcomes.

I always smile back at people on television who are smiling at me; I am too eager to please. . . in Italy one doesn't try so hard to please, one is quite naturally pleased and therefore pleasing. I don't want to go home. Imagine smiling back at Miss America.
                                                              – Barbara Harrison

In another series of studies, John Lanzetta and his colleagues (McHugo, Lanzetta, Sullivan, Masters, & Englis, 1985) showed that Republicans and Democrats who watched then-President Reagan express happiness/reassurance, anger/threat, or fear/evasion during a television newscast (Figure 1.1) had very different reactions. When

Figure 1.1. President Reagan displaying happiness/reassurance and anger/threat in a televised news conference.

recalling how they felt when viewing the newscast, supporters and opponents claimed to have had quite different emotional reactions to Reagan's emotional displays. Supporters shared his happiness and were unhappy when Reagan expressed anger or fear; opponents recalled having an overall negative reaction to *all* his emotional displays. When we look at viewers' automatic reactions, however, we find that even the bitterest of enemies could not help but respond to the President's "magic": Both supporters and critics mimicked Reagan's facial expressions, and an analysis of skin resistance levels showed that subjects were most relaxed during happiness/reassurance displays and least relaxed during anger/threat displays, regardless of their attitudes toward Reagan. It would be interesting to see if a less charismatic president would have similar power to transmit his emotions to viewers.

## Vocal mimicry/synchrony

[There is] a species of firefly in Malaysia where, beginning erratically, mutual entrainment develops until all fireflies are flashing in synchrony.

– Eliot Chapple

There is considerable evidence that people mimic and synchronize their vocal utterances. Communication researchers have long argued that communication is as rhythmic as music, dance, or tennis.

*One's own words and movements are normally coordinated.* Recently, we watched British director Jonathan Miller trying to teach diva Susan Bullock, who was singing the part of Violetta in *La Traviata*, to act the part. Violetta was about to die; ideally, the feeble woman was to attempt to raise herself weakly from the bed, in a last effort to say goodbye to Rudolpho. Ms. Bullock kept getting it wrong. She repeatedly bounded up, full of vim and vigor, looking more like a healthy milkmaid than a dying courtesan. Then it occurred to us why it was so difficult for Ms. Bullock to "get it": She was being asked to behave dissynchronyously – to *sing* lustily, so that her voice would reach the rafters, while *acting* as if she was about to expire. Try it yourself. It is very difficult to do.

A number of researchers have argued that self-coordination may be "wired in." Paul Byers (1976) postulated that there is an underlying beat in the nervous system. Eliot Chapple (1982) pointed out that our human biological processes pulse to a natural rhythm. This is true, Chapple suggests, at every level of analysis: from the faint rhythms of DNA and RNA metabolism, through the more pronounced rhythms of CNS and ANS activity, to circadian rhythms, and beyond. Most important, given our interests here, he argues that our speech and interactional rhythms are in synchrony with these biological rhythms. Thus, at any given time, different people will naturally prefer different interaction tempos. At other times or in other settings, these same people will find alternative interactional rhythms most comfortable.

*If partners are to interact smoothly, their speech rhythms must become mutually entrained*

DEVELOPMENTAL RESEARCH. William Condon (1982) argues that such synchrony begins early:

> I think that infants from the first moment of life and even in the womb are getting the rhythm and structure and style of sound, the rhythms of their culture, so that they imprint to them and the rhythms become part of their very being. When they say the baby will babble French or babble Chinese, this may mean that the predominant rhythms are already laid into the neurological system, so that, when the child starts to talk, he incorporates the lexical items of the system right into these rhythms. (p. 66–67)

Presumably, an infant hears his mother speak in a certain pattern; he begins to move with her breathing rhythms, rhythmic heart beats, movements, and so forth. Thus his rhythms become coordinated with hers, early on.

There is some evidence that newborns are capable of vocal mimicry. For example, Marvin Simner (1971) found that 2–4-day-old newborns began crying when they heard the cry of another newborn. The newborns seemed to be responding specifically to the other infant's emotional distress rather than to noise per se: They did not cry when they heard a synthetic cry.

Some researchers have observed that a speaker's sounds and movements "drive" a *synchronous* response in neonates. For example, William Condon and Louis Sander (1974) observed that 1- and 2-day-old neonates synchronize their head, elbow, shoulder, hip, and foot movements with the phonetic speech patterns of American and Chinese adults. Condon and W. D. Ogston (1967) demonstrated such synchrony between a human and a chimpanzee! Condon and Ogston argued that people cannot deliberately produce such cross-modal synchronies; they "just happen." Consistent with this suggestion, there is some evidence to suggest that these movements are mediated by the extrapyramidal system.

RESEARCH WITH ADULTS. Eliot Chapple (1982) contended that social systems tend to be rhythmically organized. An abundance of communication systems research indicates that this is so: People seem capable of mimicking/synchronizing their speech productions with startling rapidity, incorporating an astounding number of speech characteristics simultaneously. For example, William Condon (1982) pointed out that people can mimic and synchronize their speech productions with others within one-twentieth of a second. "For people to match their behaviors within 50 milliseconds," he wrote, "requires some mechanism unknown to man" (p. 70).

The number of characteristics people can mimic simultaneously *is* staggering. There is a good deal of evidence from controlled interview settings to support mutual reciprocal influence on accents (Giles & Powesland, 1975), speech rate (Street, 1984; Webb, 1972), vocal intensity (Natale, 1975), fundamental vocal frequency (Buder, 1991), latency to respond (Matarazzo & Wiens, 1972; Cappella & Planalp, 1981), utterance durations (Matarazzo, Weitman, Saslow, & Wiens, 1963), turn durations (Matarazzo & Wiens, 1972), and pauses (Feldstein & Welkowitz, 1978).

Evidence is also available in more free-wheeling settings. For example, such matching has been found in tightly structured job interviews, presidential news conferences, astronaut-to-ground communications, and young children's conversations (Cappella, 1981). Joseph Cappella and Sally Planalp (1981), for example, studied twelve 20-minute dyadic conversations. They found clear evidence that, over time, partners came to match one another's conversational rhythms, even on a moment-to-moment basis. In most dyads, couples talked about the same amount. (In a very few dyads, partners compensated for one another's shortcomings, some trying to make up for a quiet partner's reticence, others clamming up when confronted with a verbose partner.) Partners also came to match one another's rhythms, as measured by length of vocalizations, mean pause duration, times between turns, length of talkovers, and the probability of breaking silences. The authors noted:

> If the between-turn times are brief, this may be interpreted as interest or involvement by one partner and mimicked by the other in an effort to show similar interest or involvement. When the between-turn reaction times are slow, they may be interpreted as disinterest, distance, or pensiveness by the person, who may mimic this separation from, or thoughtfulness about, the conversation by the slow-reacting partner. (p. 127)

For a recent review of research in this area, see Cappella (1991) or Cappella and Flagg (1992).

*Rapport and vocal mimicry/synchrony.* Researchers generally have assumed that couples should feel more attracted to others and more comfortable in well coordinated interactions – that is, when conversational rhythms are predictably sequenced, rhythmic, and closely coordinated. There is considerable evidence in support of this contention (Cappella & Flagg, 1992; Warner, 1990; Warner, Waggener, & Kronauer, 1983).

Of course, people do not always prefer relationships that are rigidly patterned. Some researchers (Crown & Feldstein, in press), have observed that strangers may feel more constrained to follow conventional patterns of conversational give-and-take than do intimates. (In intimate affairs, one partner may do all the talking in any given conversation; both may feel comfortable with such asymmetries.)

Other theorists point out that strangers may purposely restrain themselves from responding tit for tat, in an effort at "damage control." When people expect an interaction to be cold and unpleasant, they often act in a warm, smiling, and pleasant way themselves in an attempt to keep things from going from bad to worse (Ickes, Patterson, Rajecki, & Tanford, 1982). People who are forced to interact with strangers or with people whose attitudes differ markedly from their own may try to keep their voices and bodies from betraying their antipathy (Cappella & Palmer, 1990).

John Gottman (1979), in his analyses of marital conversations, pointed out that well adjusted couples may be good at resisting getting swept up in angry exchanges. When one gets angry and upset and makes critical statements, the other might react with love and understanding, saying something kind or funny to turn things around. Unhappy couples seem trapped in destructive tit-for-tat exchanges. They are more rigid in their patterning, and anger seems invariably to spark an angry response. Robert Levenson and John Gottman (1983) measured the physiological reactions of couples (including heart rate and skin conductance levels) as they casually discussed events of the day and marital problems. Satisfied couples were less likely to get angry or upset or to catch the anger of their mates during "hot" discussions. Angry exchanges, of course, produced a great deal of ANS physiological activation (as measured by heart rate, skin conductance, pulse transmission time, and general somatic activity). Couples were most likely to show tight ANS linkage when they were engaged in harsh, tit-for-tat exchanges. No surprise, then, that in this situation, dissatisfied, angry couples showed the most physiological linkage. Tight coordination is not always an advantage.

The conclusion that people feel most comfortable in well coordinated exchanges therefore requires some qualification. Although people certainly wish to participate in such interactions, sometimes a bit of spontaneity or novelty – or patience in the face of anger – will be appreciated.

## ANS activity coordination

In the 1950s, researchers conducted a series of studies designed to show that therapists and clients were linked emotionally and physiologically. Early researchers (DiMascio, Boyd, Greenblatt, & Solomon, 1955) found that the heart rates of such subjects "often varied together and at other times varied inversely from each other" (p. 9). Later research (DiMascio, Boyd, & Greenblatt, 1957) found that generally the heart rates of therapists and their clients sped up or slowed down together as things heated up or cooled down during the therapeutic hour. It was only when they were momentarily in an "antagonist" relationship that their heart rates moved in opposite directions.

Recently, Robert Levenson and Anna Ruef (1992) have theorized about the connections among empathy, perceptual accuracy, and physiological linkages between observers and targets. The authors indicated that researchers have failed to agree on a single definition of empathy:

The term "empathy" has been used to refer to at least three different qualities: (a) *knowing* what another person is feeling . . . (b) *feeling* what another person is feeling . . . and (c) *responding compassionately* to another person's distress. (p. 234)

Levenson and Ruef hypothesized that the most basic component of empathy must be the ability to perceive another person's feelings accurately. Unless we know what others feel, we can hardly go on to share their feelings or to respond compassionately to their plight. Knowing and feeling, they argued, might go hand in hand. They tested this in an elegant experiment: Subjects were asked to view videotapes of two 15-minute conversations between married couples. In one, the couple either discussed the events of the day or the events of the past three years. In the second, the couple attempted to resolve a problem in their marriage. Subjects were asked to use a "joystick" device that allowed them to indicate how they thought either the husband or the wife was feeling at the moment. (Subjects were assigned to focus on only one of them.) While subjects were making their ratings, electrodes continuously recorded their physiological responses – their heart rate, skin conductance, pulse transmission time (and amplitude) to the finger, and somatic activity. The researchers, of course, had parallel measures available for the married couple during each 15-minute conversation; they knew what the husband and wife had felt as the conversation progressed and how they had responded physiologically. How accurate were observers in judging the couples' feelings? As might be expected, some subjects were totally accurate (correct 100% of the time) and others completely inaccurate (correct 0% of the time) in judging husbands' and wives' emotions during the continuous stream of behavior. The authors' data gave them some insights into what distinguished accurate from inaccurate perceivers. Using bivariate time-series analyses to determine how tightly linked were observers' and targets' (husbands or wives) physiological reactions, the authors found that subjects were most accurate in assessing targets' *negative* emotions when the subjects' physiological reactions and those of the targets were tightly linked. Accuracy in judging *positive* emotions, on the other hand, did not seem to be related to such linkage. (This should not be too surprising: The husbands and wives discussed not the delights but the problems of marriage. Although the authors suggested that positive emotions may not produce the kinds of patterned autonomic activity necessary for linkage [p. 16], classic research and reviews have found that ANS activation covaries with the intensity rather than the valence of emotions [Dysinger, 1931; McCurdy, 1950].) Levenson and Ruef concluded that people may come to *know* what others feel because they *feel* what the others feel – in "miniaturized form" (p. 14).

## Muscle mimicry

When we daydream about painting a picture or eating an ice cream cone, we can, if we pay careful attention, sometimes notice small muscle movements tracking our thoughts. A demonstration was conducted recently at the University of Iowa's summer program on social psychophysiology: An undergraduate who worked in John Cacioppo's laboratory was wired to electrodes designed to measure facial EMG, heart rate, breathing rate, and skin conductance. The student was instructed to think about anything he wished. Some trainees watched him on a television monitor; all they saw was a blank, relaxed, impassive face. Others watched the monitoring equipment's printout on an eight-channel Grass polygraph recorder, where now and then dramatic changes could be spotted. At one point, for instance, the electrodes connected to the brow (corrugator supercilii) muscle showed a sudden jump. "What are you thinking about?" the trainees asked. "An argument with my roommate." Later, there was a movement around the lips (orbicularis oris) so powerful that it interfered with all the other readings. Several people looked at the television monitor to see what the student was doing but could detect no sign of movement. "What is going on?" they asked. "I've just thought of a great argument," the student answered. "Well, quit it," said the observers. "Just imagine you are listening to what your roommate has to say." When he did so, the pen connected to the electrodes over the brow region remained active while that connected to the electrodes around the lips quieted (Hatfield & Rapson, 1990, p. 11).

If mere thoughts and feelings can generate accompanying muscle activity, perhaps it is not surprising that when we carefully attend to others performing a series of manual activities, we find our own muscles "helping them out." There is some evidence that people do mimic others' muscle activity. Seymour Berger and Suzanne Hadley

(1975), for example, noted that when people perform certain activities, observers tend to "try out" the same activities, flexing or extending the same muscle groups. The authors invited subjects to watch two videotapes (one showing a student stuttering as he read a series of words, the other two men arm wrestling). Electrodes were placed on the observers' foreheads, palms, *lips*, and *arms*. As predicted, subjects showed more EMG activity in the lip area while watching someone stutter through a list of words. They showed more activity in their own right-forearm area (from the lateral epicondyle of the humerus [elbow] to the styloid process of the ulna [wrist]) when they watched two rivals arm wrestle. There was little activity in the muscle groups irrelevant to the videos they were viewing.

## Postural mimicry/mirroring

Wolfgang Kohler (1927) argued that primates are capable of intelligent thought and insight. Figure 1.2 is a photograph of two chimpanzees, Sultan and Grande. Sultan, as he carefully watches Grande strain to reach some bananas, himself reaches up to help the process along.

Humans instinctively engage in the same kind of postural mimicry. In Figure 1.3, we see Gordon Allport's (1937/1961) classic photograph of spectators at the All-Ireland Road Bowls event "helping" the bowler push the ball along.

Thirty years ago, Albert Scheflen (1964) proposed that people often mirror the posture of others. He said that individuals whose postures are "carbon copies" or "mirror images" of each other probably share a common viewpoint. Marianne La France and William Ickes (1981) noted:

> [I]t has been suggested that people who adopt the same posture at the same time may be saying to each other and to those who care to notice that they are sharing a common psychological stance. (p. 139)

Marianne La France (1982) tested these notions in naturalistic observations of instructors' and students' postural configurations. She first coded the arm and torso positions of each at five-minute intervals during a regular class period. (If, say, the instructor's left arm was bent at the elbow across the front of his body, students would be said to be *mimicking* his arm position and posture if their *left* arms

Figure 1.2. Sultan raising a sympathetic left hand to "help Grande along."

Figure 1.3. The All-Ireland Road Bowls championship (an example of postural mimicry).

were in the same configuration, but *mirroring* his arm position and posture if their *right* arms were in that position. If their arms were in any other position, they would be neither mimicking nor mirroring.) Students were then asked how much rapport existed in the class. Surprisingly, the more cohesive groups were *not* more likely to mimic the instructor's arm movements and posture; they *were,* however, more likely to *mirror* these. Similar results were secured by Janet Bavelas and her colleagues in a series of studies (Bavelas, Black, Chovil, Lemery, & Mullett, 1988). They argued that people are attempting to communicate solidarity and involvement when they mimic others' postures.

> Specifically, motor mimicry encodes the message, "I am with you" or "I am like you," by displaying a literal mimesis of the other's behavior. By immediately displaying a reaction appropriate to the other's situation (e.g., a wince for the other's pain), the observer conveys, precisely and eloquently, both awareness of and involvement with the other's situation. (p. 278)

Which kind of mimicry communicates the most solidarity when people are face to face? Is it *rotation symmetry*, where each is leaning, say, to his or her own right, and thus appears to the other to be moving in the opposite direction? Or is it *reflection symmetry* (i.e., mirroring), where one leans to his right and the other to her left, so that both appear to each other to be moving in the same direction? Bavelas and her colleagues created several such pairs of photographs and asked people which one conveyed involvement and "togetherness"; their subjects consistently chose reflection symmetry. They then tested this hypothesis in an ingenious experiment: The experimenter said that she was going to tell the subjects some stories; all they had to do was listen. In the first story, she recounted a tale of nearly drowning in a life-saving class. In the next, she graphically described the perils of a crowded Christmas party, where a tall man had kept coming close to hitting her in the head with his elbow. As she described the incident, she ducked to her *right* to show how she had to lurch to avoid being hit. The authors examined videotapes of the listeners' reactions to see whether they too ducked to their right (rotation symmetry) or to their left (reflection symmetry), or stayed stock still. As predicted, in face-to-face encounters the listeners almost always showed reflection symmetry: When the storyteller leaned right, they leaned left.

Finally, Aron Siegman and Mark Reynolds (1982) studied the effect of an interviewer's warmth on the interviewee's reactions. Interviewers who were to behave warmly were instructed to lean forward as they talked, smile, and nod; the others, who were to be reserved, were told not to do so. Interviewer warmth was reciprocated in kind: Warm interviewers' subjects smiled, nodded, and leaned forward more than their peers did. Warm interviewers also elicited more intimate self-disclosures and less hesitant conversations.

A number of other researchers have documented that rapport and postural mirroring are linked (Charney, 1966; La France, 1979; La France & Broadbent, 1976; Trout & Rosenfeld, 1980); only a few studies have failed to find such a connection. (La France & Ickes, 1981, found that strangers in a waiting room felt self-conscious, as if the conversation were forced, awkward, and strained, when "too much" mirroring occurred. Participants seemed to feel the other was "trying too hard" when others mirrored their every move.)

### Movement coordination

Communication researchers have noted that people often synchronize their rhythms and movements with those with whom they are interacting (Bernieri, 1988). Adam Kendon (1970), for instance, suggested that speakers generally are attuned to their listener's movements:

> As a speaker, we are never indifferent to what the listener is doing. If he drums his fingers, if he frequently shifts in his chair, or looks about the room, or nods his head in an unusual pattern, he may convey the impression that he is bored, improperly attentive, or inattentive, or that he is preoccupied. Sometimes this may throw us off balance to the extent that our flow of talk is brought to a stammering halt. (p. 101)

William Condon and W. D. Ogston (1966) contended that a speaker's speech and movements are mirrored in the listeners' flow of movements:

> Human expression appears to be a function of both speech and body motion inextricably locked together within the flow of behavior, reinforcing and counterpointing one another. (p. 345)

To test some of these notions, Adam Kendon (1970) videotaped the conversations of people in a London pub and carefully analyzed the tapes, word by word and frame by frame. His conclusion: A *speaker's* words typically are coordinated with his or her *own* bodily movements. Kendon described this flow coordination as a series of contrasting waves of movement, where within the larger waves, smaller waves may be contained. The speaker's words and phrases are coordinated with "large movement waves":

> As his arms are lowered, his head may turn to the right, the trunk may bow forward, the eyes shift left, the mouth open, the brows lift, the fingers flex, the feet flex from the ankles and so on. (p. 103)

Syllabic and subsyllabic changes are coordinated with smaller movement waves. Significantly, Kendon also found that speakers' streams of behavior were tightly coordinated with those of listeners. When the speaker spoke and moved, the listener moved as well. Their movement waves coincided. A typical analysis concluded that

> when B is moving, his movements are coordinated with T's movements and speech, and that in their form these movements amount in part to a "mirror image" of T's movements: As T leans back in his chair, B leans back and lifts his head; then B moves his right arm to the right, just as T moves his left arm to the left, and he follows this with a headcock to the right, just as T cocks his head to the left. We might say that here B dances T's dance. (p. 110)

Mark Davis (1985) pointed out that people are probably not able *consciously* to mimic others very effectively: The process is simply too complex and too fast. For example, it took even the lightning-fast Muhammad Ali a minimum of 190 ms to spot a light and 40 ms more to throw a punch in response. Condon and Ogston (1966), however, found that college students could synchronize their movements within 21 ms – half the time of one film frame (42 ms). Davis argues that microsynchrony is mediated by basal brain structures and is either "something you [*sic*] got or something you don't." There is no way that one can deliberately "do" it" (p. 69). People who try consciously to mirror others, he thought, are doomed to look phony.

*Rapport and movement coordination.* Researchers have speculated that people are most likely to coordinate their movements tightly with those whom they like and love. Linda Tickle-Degnen and Robert Rosenthal (1987) argued that rapport and coordinated movement are linked. Adam Kendon (1970) noted that synchrony communicates interest and approval. Frank Bernieri (1988) observed that

> high states of rapport are often associated with descriptive terms such as harmonious, smooth, "in tune with," or "on the same wavelength." Likewise, states of low rapport are often associated with terms such as awkward, "out of sync," or "not getting it together." (p. 121)

If love and attention facilitate the synchronization of the movements of two people, then it seems reasonable that mothers would show evidence of greater synchrony when interacting with their own children than with the children of others. Friends should show more synchrony than enemies, lovers more synchrony than friends. There is considerable evidence that such is the case.

MOTHER–CHILD INTERACTIONS. Beatrice Beebe and her associates (Beebe et al., 1982) pointed out that mothers often consciously vary their interaction rhythms to maintain an optimum level of attention, arousal, and positive affect in their infants. When a mother begins to play rhythmic games with her infant (clapping her own or the baby's hands in rhythm), the infant orients to her and looks at her – at first sober-faced, then with increasingly positive expressiveness. When the mother pauses or moves erratically, the infant quickly loses interest and ceases to smile. Edward Tronick, Heidelise Als, and T. Berry Brazelton (1977) speculated that children may interact in synchrony with their parents if they want a given interaction to continue, but move to dissynchrony if they want to communicate a stop to the interaction.

Frank Bernieri, Steven Reznik, and Robert Rosenthal (1988) measured three kinds of synchrony in parent–child interactions:

1. *Simultaneous movement.* Raters were asked to judge whether a given movement appeared to begin or end in mother and child at the same moment. Did a mother, for example, begin to turn her head at the precise moment her child lifted an arm off the table? If so, it was coded as an instance of simultaneous movement.
2. *Tempo similarity.* Raters were asked to rate the degree to which the two seemed to be "marching to the beat of the same drummer" (p. 246).

3. *Coordination and smoothness.* Raters were told, "Assume you are viewing a choreographed dance rather than a social interaction. How smoothly does the interactants' flow of behavior intertwine, or mesh?" (p. 246).

These researchers found that mothers were more synchronous with their own children than with unrelated children, and that this disparity increased the longer mothers and children interacted. The authors offered three suggestions as to why mother–child interactions might be unusually synchronous:

1. Mothers may be better able to maintain optimal interest and arousal levels with their own children, with whom they are, after all, better acquainted, and to whom they are biologically linked.
2. Mothers may be more attentive to and protective of children who are their own.
3. Mothers doubtless love and like their own children more.

Frank Bernieri's work is especially compelling because it avoids a methodological problem that has plagued researchers: How do you tell if synchrony is in the eyes of the raters or exists in the behavior of the subjects? In the aforementioned study, for example, Bernieri and his colleagues (1988) trained separate cameras on mothers and children. The mothers were always facing right. In *true dyadic interactions*, the interactions of mother and children were displayed on a split screen, mothers to the right and children to the left, and judges were asked to rate how synchronous their movements seemed. In *altered time-frame* interactions, clips of mothers were paired with clips of the child with whom she had interacted at a *different* time. In *switched-partner interactions*, clips of mothers were paired with those of children who had actually interacted with someone else. Finally, in *double-crossed interactions*, mothers were paired with infants who had interacted with someone else at a different point in the experiment. As before, judges were asked to rate how synchronous mother and child movements seemed in these three pseudo-interaction conditions. The authors could thus contrast the amount of synchrony judges saw in true dyadic interactions with that erroneously assumed to exist in the three pseudointeractions. Even in such carefully controlled conditions, they found mothers showed more synchrony with their own children than with the children of strangers.

FRIENDLY INTERACTIONS. Frank Bernieri argued that "the degree to which people's movements seem orchestrated determines how much emotional rapport they will feel" (cited in Goleman, 1991, p. B7). In one study (Bernieri, 1988), young couples spent 10 minutes trying to teach one another a set of made-up words and their definitions. Analysis of videotapes of their interactions documented that those pairs whose movements were in greatest synchrony also felt the most emotional rapport with each other. (Similar results were secured by Bernieri, Davis, Knee, & Rosenthal, 1991, and by Babad, Bernieri, & Rosenthal, 1989.)

Columnist Andy Rooney (1989) pointed out that we cannot help but feel closer to someone, even an enemy, when we share an emotional moment. At the height of the cold war, Vladimir Horowitz played a Mozart piano sonata at a concert he gave in Moscow. Rooney, watching the concert on television, described his own reaction:

> During the latter part of the concert, watching this eighty-one-year-old genius play, I found mist forming in my eyes for some mysterious reason I could not explain. I was not sad. I was exultant. It had something to do with my pride, at that very moment, in being part of the same civilization that this great and endearing man playing the piano was part of.
>
> Almost at the same instant I felt the suggestion of tears in my eyes, the television camera left Horowitz's fingers on the keyboard and dissolved to the face of a Soviet citizen in the audience. He did not look like the enemy. His eyes were closed, his head tilted slightly backward so that his face was up . . . and one lone teardrop ran down his cheek.
>
> It was the same teardrop running down mine. (p. 170)

LOVE RELATIONSHIPS. Timothy Perper (1985), in his *Sex Signals: The Biology of Love*, attempted to describe a typical courtship sequence:

> When the two people are strangers, courtship begins as one person *approaches* or moves next to the potential partner. An approach occurs when a man sits next to a woman in a train. More often, though, the woman makes the approach, for example, by sitting next to a man in a bar. The person approached has two options. He or she can turn slightly, look, move (e.g., make room), or otherwise respond to the other person's pres-

ence. Alternatively, the person approached might simply ignore the person who is approaching.

. . . But if the person approached does turn slightly, or look –
e.g., the man turns and looks at the woman, or she glances up
from her newspaper – then, quite reliably, conversation opens,
usually about banal topics – the bar itself, traveling, trains, and
so on.

As they talk, the two people now *turn* to face each other. Depending on the couple, turning can take anywhere from 10
minutes to two or more hours. However, it is usually slow and
gradual – first the head is turned, then the shoulders and torso,
and finally the whole body. With each turn and shift, again intimacy is increasing. If all goes well, the two people will end up
facing each other and will remain facing for the rest of the interaction.

Simultaneously, two other processes are starting. The first is
*touching*, and again intimacy increases. . . . The person touched
has only two options. He or she can respond positively: by leaning towards the other person, by smiling, or turning more completely, or by reciprocating the touch. Or the person may try to
ignore it. The interaction then typically ceases. But let us assume the touch *is* acknowledged positively, perhaps by a touch
given in reciprocation.

As the two people talk and continue to turn towards each
other, they now touch each other with increasing frequency.
They are now perhaps half- or three-quarters turned towards
each other, and are beginning to look at each other. Such looks
wander over the face, hair, eyes, shoulders, neck, and torso. As
the sequence progresses, the couple will look more and more
frequently at each other until, finally, they virtually never take
their eyes off each other. . . .

The second process is even more remarkable: they start to
move in synchrony with each other. For example, they both
lean forward, reach for their drinks, lift them, sip, place the
glasses back on the bar or table, all simultaneously. Or, if sitting
next to each other on a train, the woman on the right leans her
right arm on the arm-rest and turns to look at the man to her
left, while he leans his left arm on his arm-rest and turns to
look at her on his right. It is as if a mirror had been placed between them.

Synchronization develops throughout the entire sequence. Yet few people spontaneously notice synchronized body movements and postures. Initially, it may involve only a brief (and perhaps accidental) movement made in common and followed by rapid desynchronization of movement. . . . As time passes, more and more movements occur in synchrony, especially after the first exchange of touches. Initially, synchronization involves only arm and head movements, but progresses to a more complex series of simultaneous movements such as drinking in unison. Later, synchronization includes simultaneous shifts of weight and swaying movements that result when the hips, legs, and feet of the two people move in synchrony. This is complete or "full body" synchronization, and involves all movements made by each person.

Full-body synchronization is striking. It is fluid, continuous, and ever changing. . . . I shall stress synchronization, for it is the best indicator that exists of mutual involvement.

The whole sequence, from approach to synchronization, can take from 15 minutes to over three hours. Once synchronized, however, people can stay in synchrony seemingly indefinitely – until the bar closes, until they finish dinner and drinks and must leave, until their train reaches wherever it is going; to put it another way, until the business of the outside world intervenes and causes their interaction to stop. Intimacy has grown stepwise and mutually. (pp. 77–79)

Scientists generally agree that lovers sometimes telegraph their feelings by their close coordination:

Perhaps nowhere is the human dance more evident than in love. Not only do lovers or prospective lovers share a rhythm, but they also make more frequent and more lengthy movements simultaneously than do casual acquaintances. Without realizing it, after a while they actually begin to mirror each other's movements. She, facing him, leans on her right elbow as he leans on his left. They shift postures at the same time. They reach for their wine glasses, raise them and drink simultaneously, an unthinking toast to their closeness. Rhythms may even betray love at first sight to a careful observer before lovers themselves realize what is happening.

Over the course of an evening, a newly acquainted but smit-

ten couple will begin to synchronize first head and arm movements. Then more body parts will join the mating dance, until
the two are dancing as one. . . .

Mirror synchrony is not exclusive to courtship since friends
and established couples display it too, but Perper and other scientists suggest that such exquisite coordination may be an unconscious precondition for further intimacy. (Douglis, 1989, p. 6)

*In sum*. We generally mimic the behavior of those to whom we feel
close, and feel closer to those who mimic our behavior. With this, as
with everything else, however, there are limits: Eventually, enough
is enough. Neurologist Oliver Sacks (1987) portrayed the behavior of
patients afflicted with "super-Tourette's," an "identity-frenzy," and
the equally frenzied reaction it produces in bystanders:*

My eye was caught by a grey-haired woman in her sixties, who
was apparently the center of a most amazing disturbance,
though what was happening, what was so disturbing, was not
at first clear to me. Was she having a fit? What on earth was
convulsing her – and, by what sort of sympathy or contagion,
also convulsing everyone whom she gnashingly, ticcily passed?

As I drew closer I saw what was happening. *She was imitating the passers-by* – if "imitation" is not too pallid, too passive,
a word. Should we say, rather, that she was caricaturing everyone she passed? Within a second, a split-second, she "had"
them all.

I have seen countless mimes and mimics, clowns and antics,
but nothing touched the horrible wonder I now beheld: this
virtually instantaneous, automatic and convulsive mirroring
of every face and figure. But it was not just an imitation, extraordinary as this would have been in itself. The woman not
only took on, and took in, the features of countless people, she
took them *off*. Every mirroring was also a parody, a mocking,
an exaggeration of salient gestures and expressions, but an exaggeration in itself no less convulsive than intentional – a consequence of the violent acceleration and distortion of all her

---

* Copyright © 1970, 1981, 1984, 1985 by Oliver Sacks. Reprinted by permission of Simon
& Schuster, Inc. Reprinted by permission of International Creative Management, Inc.
Copyright © 1970 Oliver Sacks.

motions. Thus a slow smile, monstrously accelerated, would become a violent, milliseconds-long grimace; an ample gesture, accelerated, would become a farcical convulsive movement.

In the course of a short city-block this frantic old woman frenetically caricatured the features of forty or fifty passers-by, in a quick-fire sequence of kaleidoscopic imitations, each lasting a second or two, sometimes less, and the whole dizzying sequence scarcely more than two minutes.

And there were ludicrous imitations of the second and third order; for the people in the street, startled, outraged, bewildered by her imitations, took on these expressions in reaction to her; and those expressions, in turn, were re-flected, re-directed, re-distorted, by the Touretter, causing a still greater degree of outrage and shock. This grotesque, involuntary resonance, or mutuality, by which *everyone* was drawn into an absurdly amplifying interaction was the source of the disturbance I had seen from a distance. This woman who, becoming everybody, lost her own self, became nobody. This woman with a thousand faces, masks, *personae* – how must it be for *her* in this whirlwind of identities? The answer came soon – and not a second too late; for the build-up of pressures, both hers and others', was fast approaching the point of explosion. Suddenly, desperately, the old woman turned aside into an alley-way which led off the main street. And there, with all the appearances of a woman violently sick, she expelled, tremendously accelerated and abbreviated, all the gestures, the postures, the expressions, the demeanours, the entire behavioural repertoires, of the past forty or fifty people she had passed. She delivered one vast, pantomimic regurgitation, in which the engorged identities of the last fifty people who had possessed her were spewed out. And if the taking-in had lasted two minutes, the throwing-out was a single exhalation – fifty people in ten seconds, a fifth of a second or less for the time-foreshortened repertoire of each person. (pp. 122–123)

## Modeling of instrumental behavior

Psychologists have long been interested in the processes of social facilitation. They find that even lower animals imitate one another's instrumental behaviors. Chickens who have eaten their fill begin to

eat again when they are placed with a hungry chicken who is peck-
ing voraciously at a pile of grain (Bayer, 1929). Ants work harder
when paired with other worker ants (Chen, 1937). In a classic experiment, anthropologists documented true imitation in Japanese macaques. One macaque discovered that sweet potatoes tasted better if
they were washed; he began routinely washing his potatoes in a
nearby stream. Other macaques observed him and began to mimic
his potato washing. Soon potato washing became a social norm. In
an early review paper, Robert Zajonc (1965) surveyed evidence that,
at every phylogenetic level, animals tend to imitate one another:
"Monkey see, monkey do" seems to have some validity.

Probably all of us can think of examples when, at a loss as to how
to behave, we simply followed the leader. In 1973, Elaine Hatfield
spent a sabbatical year at the University of Mannheim in Germany.
As a Guest-Worker, Hatfield was required to report to the city hall
and get innumerable documents stamped, collated, and filed. In
1973, however, nearly all the Guest-Workers in Mannheim were
from Turkey. When she arrived at the city hall she found that none
of the processors spoke English and that all the signs routing workers here and there were in Turkish. To her surprise, despite the fact
that no one could give her any directions, the process went off without a hitch. Hatfield simply followed the leaders: She lined up; she
followed endless lines around, dropping off a paper here, following
the line to get it stamped there, sticking out her arm here so a woman in white could give her an innoculation there. At the end of
the day, the line split in two, men to one side, women to the other.
Hatfield followed the women into a small compartment and somehow knew she was supposed to undress. She was examined by a doctor and sent on her way. Not a word had been spoken, but an infi-
nite array of papers had been filed, strictly by the process of monkey
see, monkey do.

Social learning theorists, such as Albert Bandura (1973), have argued that people often learn new behavior by observing the behavior of others and its consequences. Many emotional responses, Bandura admits, are undoubtedly acquired by means of direct classical
conditioning; affective learning, however, frequently occurs through
vicariously aroused emotions. People can develop phobias merely
by witnessing others respond fearfully toward spiders or dogs or
thunderstorms. They can learn to love and hate, or get angry or stay
calm in the presence of others, in the same way. Emotional response

patterns can be extinguished on a vicarious basis as well: If one observes models performing fear-provoking behavior (say, handling snakes) without showing any fear or experiencing any adverse consequences, one's own fears will eventually fade away.

## Summing up

We began this chapter by considering the mechanisms that might account for the process of emotional condition. We advanced three propositions: (1) that people tend to mimic others; (2) that emotional experience is affected by such feedback; and (3) that people therefore tend to "catch" others' emotions. Reviewing evidence for Proposition 1, we found that there is considerable indication that people do tend to mimic and synchronize their movements with the facial expressions, voices, postures, movements, and instrumental behaviors of others. We concluded that people are capable of (1) mimicking/synchronizing their movements with startling rapidity and (2) automatically mimicking/synchronizing an astounding number of characteristics.

Now let us turn to Proposition 2 and the evidence that people's subjective emotional experience is affected, moment to moment, by the activation of and/or feedback from such mimicry.

# 2. Mechanisms of emotional contagion: II. Emotional experience and facial, vocal, and postural feedback

The violinist Itzak Perlman, in trying to play a difficult note raises his eyebrows (if it is a high note) and keeps them raised until the note has been played . . . it is generally believed that these motions are secondary and ancillary. But suppose that a good part of musical memory is in fact lodged in these peculiar movements. Suppose that they are significant.

– Zajonc & Markus (1984, pp. 83–84)

## Introduction

We have defined emotional contagion as a multiply determined family of psychophysiological, behavioral, and social phenomena. In chapter 1, we reviewed evidence that there is a pervasive tendency automatically to mimic and synchronize expressions, vocalizations, postures, and movements with those of another person. This mimicry coordinates and synchronizes social interactions while freeing the interactants to think about other issues, such as what one or both of them are trying to achieve and what each is saying. In this chapter, we focus on another important but often overlooked consequence of mimicry: the tendency for mimicked acts to cultivate a convergence of emotions among the interactants. Thus,

> *Proposition 2. Subjective emotional experiences are affected, moment to moment, by the activation and/or feedback from such mimicry.*

As was outlined in chapter 1, subjective emotional experience could theoretically be influenced by either:

1. the central nervous system commands that direct such mimicry/ synchrony in the first place;
2. afferent feedback from such facial, verbal, or postural mimicry/ synchrony; or
3. conscious self-perception processes, wherein individuals make inferences about their own emotional states on the basis of their own expressive behavior.

Given the functional redundancy that exists across levels of the neuraxis, all three processes may operate to ensure that emotional experience is shaped by facial, vocal, and postural mimicry/synchrony and expression. Thus, research is needed to determine which of these distinctive processes subserves emotional experience and contagion – or, perhaps more likely, under what conditions each underlies emotional experience and emotional contagion.

Researchers have found considerable evidence that emotional experience and somatic expression are tightly linked. Let us begin by reviewing some of the theories as to *why* emotional experience *should be* shaped by changes in the skeletal musculature; later we shall review the voluminous evidence that emotional experience *is indeed* affected by such changes.

## The facial feedback hypothesis

### Historical background

Charles Darwin (1872/1965) argued that emotional experience should be profoundly affected by feedback from the facial muscles.

> The free expression by outward signs of an emotion intensifies it. On the other hand, the repression, as far as is possible, of all outward signs softens our emotions. He who gives way to violent gestures will increase his rage; he who does not control the signs of fear will experience fear in a greater degree; and he who remains passive when overwhelmed with grief loses his best chance of recovering elasticity of mind. (p. 365)

William James (1890/1984a) proposed that people infer their emotions by sensing their *muscular*, glandular, and visceral responses. "We feel sorry because we cry, angry because we strike, and afraid because we tremble" (p. 326). He added:

Everyone knows how panic is increased by flight, and how the giving way to the symptoms of grief or anger increases those passions themselves. Each fit of sobbing makes the sorrow more acute, and calls forth another fit stronger still, until at last repose only ensues with lassitude and with the apparent exhaustion of the machinery. In rage, it is notorious how we "work ourselves up" to a climax by repeated outbreaks of expression. Refuse to express a passion, and it dies. Count ten before venting your anger and its occasion seems ridiculous. Whistling to keep up courage is no mere figure of speech. On the other hand, sit all day in a moping posture, sigh, and reply to everything with a dismal voice, and your melancholy lingers. There is no more valuable precept in moral education than this, as all who have experience know: if we wish to conquer undesirable emotional tendencies in ourselves, we must assiduously, and in the first instance, cold-bloodedly, go through the *outward movements* of those contrary dispositions which we prefer to cultivate. The reward of persistency will infallibly come, in the fading out of the sullenness or depression, and the advent of real cheerfulness and kindliness in their stead. Smooth the brow, brighten the eye, contract the dorsal rather than the ventral aspect of the frame, and speak in a major key, pass the genial compliment, and your heart must be frigid indeed if it do not gradually thaw! (pp. 331–332)

James concluded, "If our hypothesis is true, it makes us realize more deeply than ever how much our mental life is knit up with our corporeal frame, in the strictest sense of the term" (1984b, p. 138).

Recent reviews of the literature on facial feedback show that emotions are influenced *to some extent* by facial feedback (Adelmann & Zajonc, 1989; Matsumoto, 1987). What they disagree about is the relative importance of such feedback – Is it necessary, sufficient, or merely a small part of an emotional experience? – and exactly how the two are linked. Silvan Tomkins (1962, 1963), for instance, proposed that emotional experience depends primarily on naturally occurring facial expression:

Just as the fingers respond both more rapidly with more precision and complexity than the grosser and slower moving arm to which they are attached, so the face expresses affect, both to others, and to the self, via feedback, which is more rapid and more complex than any stimulation of which the slower moving visceral organs are capable. . . . It is the very gross and slower moving characteristic of the inner organ system which provides the counterpoint for the melody expressed by the facial solo. (1962, pp. 205–206)

Tomkins believed that each emotion was associated with a different array of facial expressions. Joy feels different from sadness because smiling feels different from frowning. People know what they are feeling by tuning in to their facial expressions; they know how intensely emotional they are by tuning in to their ANS reactions. In his earliest theorizing, Tomkins wrote as if emotional experience was *necessarily* linked to facial feedback. Over the decades, he has modified his theory, and in his latest writings has contended that facial feedback is a critically important determinant of subjective experience – not necessary perhaps, but certainly sufficient (Tomkins, 1980).

Carroll Izard (1971, 1990) reasoned that emotion results from the interaction of three separate components: subjective experience, neural activity, and voluntary muscle activity (chiefly that of the face). All three components make some contribution to emotion, and all three can augment or attenuate it; however, Izard thought that facial expression was generally of prime importance. Ernst Gellhorn (1964) asserted that the emotional experience is shaped by both facial expression and the balance of ANS sympathetic/parasympathetic activity. He believed that emotions could be controlled by the willed action of the skeletal musculature. An actor playing King Lear, for example, would himself become angry as he enacted his part – cursing Fate, shaking his fists, and thundering at the heavens.

Attribution theorist Daryl Bem (1972) contended that emotional experience is influenced by a variety of factors, facial feedback being only one of them. Bem observed that most theorists assume that we possess a great deal of information about our inner lives. He believed, however, that in real life, we often possess only the foggiest idea as to what we feel. When people are uncertain about their feelings, they must try to read their own emotions in exactly the same way they read others'. Bem argued that people use a variety of clues in deciding what they feel; facial feedback just furnishes one more:

> Individuals come to "know" their own attitudes, emotions, and other internal states partially by inferring them from obser-

vations of their own overt behavior and/or the circumstances in which this behavior occurs. Thus, to the extent that internal cues are weak, ambiguous, or uninterpretable, the individual is functionally in the same position as an outside observer, an observer who must necessarily rely upon these same external cues to infer the individual's inner states. (p. 2)

Most recently, James Laird (Laird & Bresler, 1992) offered a self-perception theory to explain the experience-feedback effects. He proposed that people's conscious feelings of emotion are shaped by self-observation and interpretation of their own emotional behaviors. Emotional experience is shaped by information about one's own facial expressions, postures, instrumental actions, and autonomic responses, as well as by contextual information. Laird has found that great individual differences exist in the extent to which we rely on internal cues versus contextual cues in determining what we feel. Some people seem to rely almost entirely on facial, vocal, and postural feedback in assessing their feelings. Others simply assume that they "must" feel what any reasonable person would feel in such a situation.

Of course, not all theorists agree that the face plays an important role in shaping subjective emotional experience. Carl Lange (1885/1922) and Marion Wenger (1950) argued that emotional experiences and feelings are *not* directly influenced by facial feedback. They believed that emotional experience is entirely dependent upon visceral reactions: Only if facial feedback somehow influenced these reactions could it have any impact on emotion. (If, for example, people snarled in anger and waved their arms around so wildly that it caused their hearts to race and their breathing to become labored, presumably *that* might shape emotion.) For them, then, emotional experience was only influenced *indirectly*, if at all, by facial and other bodily feedback. Ross Buck (1985) stated that expression is merely a "read-out" of underlying experience. Previous to that, George Mandler (1975) contended that if there is any link at all between subjective experience and facial expression, it is merely "epiphenomenal."

Although contemporary theorists disagree on exactly *how* facial feedback influences emotional experience, most do agree that the two are somehow coupled (Adelmann & Zajonc, 1989; Lanzetta & McHugo, 1986). We ourselves take the position that subjective emotional experience is affected by feedback from facial, vocal, and postural muscular movements, as well as by feedback from instrumental emotional activity. We also expect subjective emotional experience to be influenced by feedback from the facial, vocal, and postural movements that are *mimicked* (Proposition 2).

In brief, then, we would argue that the sight of a face that is happy, loving, angry, sad, or fearful can cause the viewer to mimic elements of that face and, consequently, to catch the others' emotions. Paul Ekman, too, observed that emotions may be shaped by such mimicry. He pointed out that this may be one reason why giddy joy or grief are infectious. "The perception of another face is not just an information transfer," contended Ekman, "but a very literal means by which we *feel* the sensations that the other feels" (cited in Schmeck, 1983, p. 1). In chapter 1, we considered evidence for Proposition 1 (including the fact that people tend to mimic facial expressions). Let us now consider the evidence for Proposition 2.

### Evidence in favor of the facial feedback hypothesis

Today, most theorists agree that emotions are tempered to some extent by facial feedback. Researchers have tested the facial feedback hypothesis using three different strategies for inducing subjects to adopt emotional facial expressions. Sometimes experimenters simply ask subjects to exaggerate or to hide any emotional reactions they might have; other times they try to "trick" subjects into adopting various facial expressions. Occasionally, experimenters try to arrange things so subjects will unconsciously mimic others' emotional and facial expressions. In all three types of experiments, scientists have found that the emotional experiences of subjects *are* affected by feedback from the facial expressions they adopt (Adelmann & Zajonc, 1989; Matsumoto, 1987). (For a more critical review of this literature, see Manstead, 1988.)

*Experimental type 1: Subjects are asked to exaggerate or play down their emotional expressions.* Social psychologists occasionally ask subjects simply to exaggerate or inhibit their naturally occurring emotional facial expressions; they then try to find out what effect this has on the subjects' emotional responses. For instance, subjects may be told to try to deceive an observer about what they are really feeling when they are exposed to an amusing movie or given painful electric shocks; later, subjects are asked what they really felt during the movie or the shock. Generally, subjects report that the film was funnier or the shocks more painful when they exaggerated their amusement or pain than when they muted their facial reactions (Kopel & Arkowitz, 1974; Kraut, 1982; Lanzetta, Biernat, & Kleck, 1982; Lanzetta, Cartwright-Smith, & Kleck, 1976; Zuckerman, Klorman, Larrance, & Speigel, 1981). Of course, a few studies have failed to secure such results (Colby, Lanzetta, & Kleck, 1977; Lanzetta et al., 1976; McCaul, Holmes, & Solomon, 1982; Vaughan & Lanzetta, 1980).

In an illustrative series of studies, John Lanzetta and his colleagues (1976) exposed subjects to painful electric shocks. Subjects were instructed either to conceal or to exaggerate their facial reactions to the anticipation and delivery of each shock. Significantly, results from this series of studies revealed that:

1. instructions to inhibit expressive tendencies reduced expressive responses to the electric shocks, whereas instructions to amplify expressive tendencies heightened those responses to the shocks, relative to free-expression (i.e., baseline) conditions; and
2. the inhibition of expressive tendencies led to lower skin conductance response, and the amplification of expressive tendencies to higher skin conductance responses, relative to free-expression conditions.

In an interesting variation on this experimental paradigm, Robert Kleck and his colleagues (Kleck, R. C. Vaughan, Cartwright-Smith, K. B. Vaughan, Colby, & Lanzetta, 1976) found that people, when they knew others were observing them, automatically tried to react "coolly" to impending shock. As a consequence, along with attenuating their expressions of emotion, these subjects seemed to experience less pain and reduced ANS arousal (again, as measured by skin conductance) than did unobserved subjects.

*Experimental type 2: Subjects' facial expressions are surreptitiously manipulated.* In the second type of experiment, experimenters take care to avoid alerting subjects to the fact that they are studying emotions or manipulating emotional expressions. In a classic experiment, James Laird (1984) told subjects he was interested in studying the action of facial muscles. The experimental room contained apparatus designed to convince anyone that complicated multichannel recordings were about to be made of facial muscle activity. Silver cup electrodes were attached to the subjects' faces between their eyebrows, at the corners of their mouths, and at the corners of their jaws. These electrodes were connected via an impressive tangle of strings and wires to electronic hardware (which, in fact, served no function at all). The experimenter then proceeded to arrange the faces of the subjects into emotional expressions, stage-managing them into either smiles or angry frowns by asking them to contract various muscles. In the angry condition, subjects were told to contract the muscles between the eyebrows (to draw them together and down) and to contract the muscles at the corners of the jaw (i.e., to clench their teeth). In the happy condition, the men and women were asked to contract the muscles near the corners of their mouths (to draw the corners of their mouths back and up). Laird found that emotional attributions *were* shaped, in part, by changes in the facial musculature: Subjects in the "frown" condition were angrier, and those in the "smile" condition happier, than their peers. The subjects' comments give us some idea of how this process worked. One man said with a kind of puzzlement:

> When my jaw was clenched and my brows down, I tried not to be angry but it just fit the position. I'm not in any angry mood but I found my thoughts wandering to things that made me angry, which is sort of silly I guess. I knew I was in an experiment and knew I had no reason to feel that way, but I just lost control. (p. 480)

The same experimental manipulations produced differences in recall of sad versus happy memories (Laird, Wagener, Halal, & Szegda, 1982).

Researchers have used a variety of other ingenious techniques to produce smiles or to inhibit them without subjects' awareness. Fritz Strack, Leonard Martin, and Sabine Stepper (1988) led some subjects to smile by requiring them to fill out a series of rating forms with a pen held in their front *teeth*. (With a pen held in the teeth, the facial muscles are eased into a smile.) In other conditions, subjects were inhibited from smiling. (They were required to fill out forms with a pen held in their *lips*.) Still other subjects simply held the pen in their hands. Emotional experiences were shaped by the unconscious tilts of the faces. Students thought a series of cartoons taken from Gary Larson's "The Far Side" were funnier when they held a pen in their teeth (and smiled) than when they held it in their lips (and frowned) or in their hand. In a parallel experiment, other research-

ers (Larsen, Kasimatis, & Frey, 1992) required subjects to move together golf tees taped to their foreheads. This task produced sad feelings as well as sad expressions.

Finally, in two experiments, Joan Kellerman, James Lewis, and
James Laird (1989) investigated the link between love and feedback
from expressions of love. The authors reasoned that "only people in
love exchange those long, unbroken, close-up gazes" (p. 145). (We are
reminded of the line from Rodgers and Hammerstein's [1943] musical *Oklahoma:* "Don't sigh and gaze at me . . . people will say we're
in love.") To test the notion that love would follow gaze, they asked
some men and women to gaze into one another's eyes continuously
for two minutes; then they asked them how romantically they felt
about one another. The authors devised three kinds of control conditions: In one, a subject gazed into the other's eyes, but the other
looked away. In another, both subjects gazed at one another's hands.
In a third control group, subjects gazed into one another's eyes – but
only in order to count how often the other was blinking! How did
experimental subjects' feelings compare to the feelings of couples in
the control conditions? As predicted, the mutual gaze subjects reported greater feelings of romantic love, attraction, interest, warmth,
and respect for one another than did control condition subjects. In a
second experiment, the authors found that passionate and romantic
feelings were most powerfully stimulated when subjects were required to gaze at one another in a romantic setting: a room that was
dimly lit and had romantic music playing softly in the background.

Using such procedures, a variety of researchers have found that
subjects' emotional feelings and/or behaviors are tempered by facial
feedback. Subjects feel the specific emotions (love, joy, anger, fear, or
sadness) consistent with the facial expressions they adopt and have
trouble experiencing emotions incompatible with those poses. These
emotional effects seem to be quite specific. If subjects are made to
look angry, for example, they feel angry but not anxious or sad
(Duclos et al., 1989; Laird, 1974). (For additional research in support
of these contentions, see also Duncan & Laird, 1977; Kellerman et al.,
1989; Kleinke & Walton, 1982; Laird, 1984; Laird & Bresler, 1992; Laird
& Crosby, 1974; Laird et al., 1982; Larsen et al., 1992; McArthur, Solomon, & Jaffee, 1980; Rhodenwalt & Comer, 1979; Rutledge & Hupka,
1985; Strack et al., 1988.) Only a few researchers have failed to secure
such results (Tourangeau & Ellsworth, 1979; see also Matsumoto,
1987).

*Experimental type 3: Studying the effects of emotional mimicry.*
Some experimenters have manipulated the facial expressions by inducing subjects to mimic those of the targets. In a series of studies,
Elaine Hatfield and her Hawaii colleagues (Hsee, Hatfield, Carlson, &
Chemtob, 1990, 1991; Hsee, Hatfield, & Chemtob, 1991) asked college
students to watch interviews in which a fellow student described
one of the happiest or saddest events in his life. In one of these
studies (Hsee et al., 1990) students were asked how happy or sad they
felt while viewing the films. (See the section "Studies of Overt Facial
Expression" in chapter 1 for a fuller description of this experiment.)
As predicted, subjects' own emotions were influenced by the emotional faces they viewed (and mimicked). Subsequent research has
confirmed that subjects' emotions are tempered by the emotional
expressions they mimic. This is true whether the faces they view are
happy (Bush, Barr, McHugo, & Lanzetta, 1989; Hsee et al., 1990, 1991;
Hsee, Hatfield, & Chemtob, 1991; Uchino, Hatfield, Carlson, & Chemtob, 1991), sad (Hsee et al., 1990, 1991; Hsee, Hatfield, & Chemtob,
1991; Uchino et al., 1991), angry (Lanzetta & Orr, 1986), or fearful
(Lanzetta & Orr, 1981).

For example, John Lanzetta and his colleagues (Bush et al., 1989)
speculated that people watching a televised comedy routine should
find the routine even funnier if the camera pans the audience now
and then, pausing to focus on faces of audience members, which are
convulsed with laughter. Subjects' amusement, they argued, should
be heightened by the facial feedback subjects feel as they mimic the
faces of people in the audience. To test this hypothesis, the authors
invited college students to participate in an experiment concerned
with subjective and bodily reactions to a variety of comedians. Students were told they would watch three comic routines and, after
each one, would be asked what they thought of it. Electrodes were
also attached to their faces to measure their "brain waves," that is,
their involuntary reactions to the trio of comedians. To get used to
the procedure, all subjects then watched the first skit. They were
then assigned one of two conditions: inhibition or spontaneity. Subjects in the former were warned to inhibit all facial movement:

> [T]hese sensors are very sensitive to any external body and
> muscle movement, so it is very important that you keep your
> body still and try not to move any of the muscles under the
> sensors while you are watching the video segments. Move-

ment will interfere with the proper recording of neural activity. (p. 37)

Subjects in the spontaneous (control) condition, in contrast, were told just to relax and enjoy the routines. Half the subjects in each condition saw the second routine interspersed with shots of the studio audience that focused on their laughing faces; the other half saw no audience reaction. The third bit of comedy was also shown with and without audience reactions, but to the *reverse* moieties. Thus each subject in each condition saw both types of presentation.

Subjects in the spontaneous condition judged the comedy routines that were intercut with audience reactions to be funnier than those that did not show the audience; inhibited condition subjects exhibited no such preference. (Spontaneous condition subjects also found the intercut routines more amusing than did inhibited condition subjects.) Also, as predicted, subjects in the spontaneous condition showed an increase in zygomaticus major (cheek) and orbicularis oculi (lower eyelid) activity, as well as an elevated heart rate, while viewing the audience's facial reactions; subjects in the inhibition condition did not. (Moreover, spontaneous condition subjects had stronger facial muscle reactions to viewing the intercut routines than did inhibited condition subjects.) This can be explained by the fact that, as anticipated, subjects in the spontaneous condition mimicked the audience's happy facial expressions, whereas those in the inhibition condition self-consciously refrained from moving their facial muscles, as instructed. Thus, Bush and his colleagues (1989) found clear evidence for Proposition 2.

### Emotional experience, ANS activity, and facial expression

Thus far we have considered evidence that emotional experience and posed or spontaneous facial expression are tightly linked. There are also some controversial data suggesting that emotional experience, ANS activity, and facial expression may be linked as well.

Until the 1980s, had psychologists been asked, "Is each basic emotion linked to a specific pattern of ANS response?", most would probably have answered "No." The accepted orthodoxy was that ANS reactions did not affect what emotion people felt, only how intensely they felt. Today, scientists are not so sure about the "right" answer. In the earlier days of psychology as a discipline, William

James (1890/1984a), Albert Ax (1953), and others speculated that perhaps the prototypic emotions were linked to characteristic patterns of ANS activity. Bits and pieces of evidence supported this contention (Beaumont, 1833); however, later researchers were unfortunately unable to find a one-to-one correspondence between the basic emotions and ANS activity (Lacey, 1967). By the 1960s, most researchers agreed with Walter Cannon (1929), Stanley Schachter and Jerome Singer (1962), and others who concluded that the various emotions did not have specific ANS signatures.

Recently, however, Paul Ekman, Robert Levenson, and Wallace Friesen (1983) made a surprising proposal: On the basis of their research, they concluded that each emotion is indeed associated with a distinct pattern of facial expression and with a distinct pattern of ANS activity. Although no one knows whether their speculations will prove to be correct, let us review their intriguing research. The authors asked scientists and professional actors to produce six emotions – surprise, disgust, sadness, anger, fear, and happiness. They were asked to do this in one of two ways: sometimes (1) by trying to relive times when they had experienced such emotions, other times (2) by following instructions as to how to arrange their expressions, muscle by muscle. The muscular instructions for fear, for instance, were only, "Raise your brows and pull them together. Now raise your upper eyelids. Now stretch your lips horizontally back toward your ears." Subjects were required to hold these poses for 10 seconds. During both tasks, the authors assessed second-by-second responses on five physiological measures: heart rate, left- and right-hand temperatures, skin resistance, and forearm flexor muscle tension. Based on this research, the authors came to the following conclusions.

1. When people were asked to relive earlier emotional experiences, their feelings were reflected on their faces, and they experienced the inner turmoil characteristic of these emotions. When actors simply followed orders and mechanically moved their muscles, they apparently still experienced these emotions, for their ANS arousal levels were even stronger.
2. The act of reliving emotional experiences or flexing facial muscles into characteristic emotional expressions both produced effects on the ANS that would normally accompany such emotions. Thus facial expressions seemed to be capable of generating appropriate ANS arousal.

3. The most startling finding, however, was that the six basic emotions Ekman has identified seemed to be associated with distinctive patterns of both facial activity and autonomic activity. The researchers found a clear link between these emotions and the type of ANS arousal subjects displayed (Figure 2.1). Positive and negative emotions produced very different patterns of autonomic activity. (For example, heart rate increased more in anger and fear than it did in happiness; left- and right-finger temperatures increased more in anger than in happiness.) Important differences were also measured among the negative emotions. When subjects were asked to relive an earlier emotional experience, psychologists could distinguish among sadness, fear, anger, and disgust on the basis of changes in skin resistance. When subjects were asked to arrange their muscles in certain ways, the researchers were able to distinguish three subgroups of emotions on the basis of heart rate and finger temperature differences (Figure 2.2).

In subsequent research using the directed facial actions test, Levenson and his colleagues (Levenson, Carstensen, Friesen, & Ekman, 1991; Levenson, Ekman, & Friesen, 1990) have found four pairwise comparisons to be replicable:

1. Fear is associated with higher heart rates than disgust.
2. Anger is associated with higher heart rates than disgust.
3. Sadness is associated with higher heart rates than disgust.
4. Anger is associated with higher finger temperatures than fear.

This line of research may ultimately challenge emotion theories that have assumed autonomic activity to be undifferentiated.

If classic theories are correct and ANS activity does not signal emotional types – only their intensity – we might expect that one's *specific* emotional experiences and *general level* of ANS arousal would be shaped by facial feedback. However, if Ekman and his colleagues are correct and both type and degree of emotion can be predicted by observing ANS activity, then we might expect one's *specific* emotional experiences and *specific* type of ANS arousal to be shaped by facial feedback. A third, intermediate, possibility is that facial, postural, and vocal actions provide feedback closely tied to specific emotions, whereas ANS activity provides some feedback that is specific and a good deal that could fit multiple emotions. John Cacioppo, David Klein, Gary Berntson, and Elaine Hatfield (1993) have

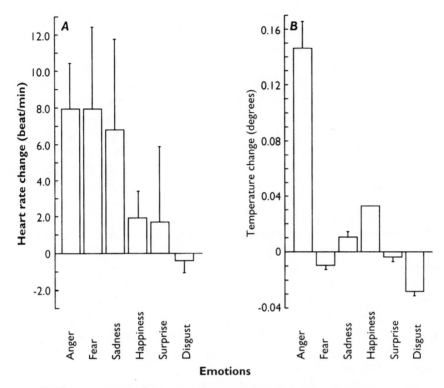

Figure 2.1. The link between subjective experience and ANS activity. Changes in (a) heart rate and (b) right-finger temperature during the directed facial action task. For heart rate, the changes associated with anger, fear, and sadness were greater than those for happiness, surprise, and disgust. For finger temperature, the changes associated with anger were significantly different from those for all other emotions. *Source:* Ekman et al., 1983, p. 1208. Copyright 1983 by the AAAS.

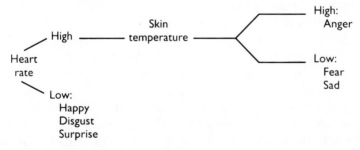

Figure 2.2. Decision tree for discriminating emotions in facial action task. *Source:* Ekman et al., 1983, p. 1209. Copyright 1983 by the AAAS.

noted that this admixture of somatovisceral afference shares a number of features with the visual afference stemming from ambiguous visual figures, such as that depicted in Figure 2.3. Top–down processes make it possible for a person looking at this picture to see or experience two very different perceptual images: the face of an Egyptian woman who is located behind a candlestick, and the profiles of identical twins looking at one another. Once these images have been identified, the viewer finds that he or she may alternate quickly between seeing one or the other of these discrete images, but cannot see both at once. Cacioppo and co-workers suggested that rudimentary cognitive appraisals in combination with this somatovisceral feedback may be sufficient to give rise to spontaneous, discrete, and indubitable emotional perceptions.

*In sum:* In a variety of studies then, we find that people tend to feel emotions consistent with the facial expressions they adopt and, conversely, have trouble feeling emotions inconsistent with those poses. Furthermore, the link between emotion and facial expression appears to be quite specific: When people produced a facial expression of fear, anger, sadness, or disgust, they were more likely to feel the emotion associated not just with any unpleasant emotion but with that *specific* expression; those who made a sad expression felt sad, not angry (Duclos et al., 1989).

Of course, emotions are not solely or perhaps even primarily shaped by facial feedback. If you spill a glass of water while dining with a revered individual in an expensive restaurant, you will likely *feel* embarrassed even if you and your dinner partner *show* little overt evidence of expressing embarrassment. Strong, emotionally evocative events are magnets for attention and thought, and produce enduring episodic memories. If such events may be compared to the images on a painter's canvas, spontaneous facial mimicry and the emotions they cultivate, in contrast, are more like the background and shading on the canvas. Their effects are both subtle and profound. Their subtlety comes from their unfolding automatically and, hence, their sparing of an individual's limited cognitive capacity for processing information; their profundity derives from their effect on a person's moment-to-moment feelings. Thus, although they may not be salient features of an individual's episodic memory, they represent the ground against which the images and events of social interactions are perceived and remembered.

Figure 2.3. An ambiguous figure constructed from overlapping unambiguous elements. Shepard, 1990. p. 58. *Source: Mind Sights* by Roger Shepard. Copyright © by Roger N. Shepard. Reprinted by permission of W. H. Freeman and Company.

## The vocal feedback hypothesis

Vocal feedback can also influence emotional experience. Elaine Hatfield and her colleagues (Hatfield, Hsee, Costello, Schalenkamp, & Denney, in press) conducted a series of experiments designed to test the vocal feedback hypothesis. Subjects were men and women from the University of Hawaii. The sample, representative of Hawaii's multiethnic population, included individuals who were of Japanese, Chinese, Korean, Filipino, Hawaiian, Pacific Island, Hispanic, Caucasian, African, or mixed ancestry.

The first experiment studied the moods of individuals who read joyous, loving, angry, or sad passages. The experimenter told subjects that he was conducting applied social psychological research for the Bell Telephone Company. He was interested in finding out how well various kinds of telephone equipment could transmit the complex sound patterns of emotional communications. Subjects were asked to read, as realistically as possible, short typescripts of a joyous, loving, sad, or angry telephone conversation into the headset. The emotional texts the subjects were to record were as follows:

*Joy and happiness*
Today is the happiest day of my life. It's my 20th birthday. Some buddies of mine decided to throw a surprise birthday party for me. They rounded up a bunch of my friends, snuck into my apartment, decorated it, and waited for me to come in from work. When I walked in the door there they were! I couldn't believe it. There was screaming and shouting and I could hardly stop laughing. I can't imagine I'll ever have a day like that again.

*Love*
Well, let me tell you. Now that I'm in love, I think about John (Susan) constantly. I can twist any conversation around in my mind so that it's really about him (her). I imagine what he (she) would say to me and how I might tell him (her) things I have never told anyone else before. When I see him (her), POW!, my heart takes a leap, my cheeks flush, and I can't help smiling. At night before I go to bed, I think of how adorable he (she) is and how much I love him (her).

*Sadness*
I feel terrible, like the wind has just been knocked out of me. Today was a nightmare. . . . I just heard my little brother has leukemia and has to have chemotherapy. I am in shock. I didn't realize I cared so much for him. . . . I just always thought of him as sort of a pest. I never thought he might die. I spent all day crying. When we went to the hospital, I tried to hide my feelings so that he wouldn't see how terrible I felt, but it is awful. I just feel terrible.

*Anger*
I hate you. Do you understand? You have ruined all that we had together. I hope she's (he's) worth all this to you. What

about us? What about the kids? Where do I go from here? All those times I asked you if anything was wrong. You just said "Oh no, hold on a little longer. I'm just working late to earn a little money." And all the time you were out with him (her). Don't tell me not to yell. You are the one who decided to have the affair, not me. You've ruined everything.

The authors assessed subjects' emotional experience (and the impact of vocal feedback on it) in two ways. First, the subjects described their own emotional states (via a series of self-report measures) at the end of the experiment. Second, although subjects believed themselves to be unobserved as they delivered the emotional messages, their faces were, in fact, surreptitiously videotaped as they spoke into the telephone; judges later rated these secret recordings. The authors found that subjects' emotions, whether conveyed by self-report or by facial expressions, were shaped by feedback from the emotional messages they delivered. Subjects reported feeling happier (and judges rated their faces as looking happier) when they had tried to express the happy message in appropriate tones; they felt more love (and were rated as looking more loving) when they had recited the loving message in a loving voice; and so forth.

In a second experiment, the scientists made every effort to hide the fact that they were interested in the subjects' emotions. This time they claimed that Bell Telephone was testing the ability of various kinds of telephone systems to reproduce the human voice faithfully. Subjects were then led to private rooms, where the experimenter gave them a cassette tape containing one of six sound patterns (joy, love/tenderness, sadness, fear, anger, or a neutral control pattern). Subjects were asked to listen to the sound pattern, practice reproducing its elements, and, once they felt comfortable, reproduce it as exactly as possible into a telephone, which would automatically record the sounds they made.

Communication researchers (Clynes, 1980; Scherer, 1982) have documented that the basic emotions are linked with specific patterns of intonation, vocal quality, rhythm, and pausing. Klaus Scherer (1982) found, for example, that when people were happy they produced sounds with small amplitude variation, large pitch variation, fast tempo, a sharp sound envelope, and few harmonics. The five non-neutral tapes in the Hatfield study were therefore designed to possess the sound patterns appropriate to their respective emotions:

Subjectively, the joyous sounds had some of the qualities of merry laughter; the sad sounds possessed the qualities of crying; the companionate love tape consisted of a series of soft "ooohs" and "aaahs"; the angry tape comprised a series of low growling noises from the throat; and the fearful sounds contained a set of short, sharp cries and gasps. Finally, the neutral tape was one long monotone, a hum, without any breaks.

At the end of the experiment, subjects were asked for "one last favor." The experimenter claimed it would help her in analyzing the data if she had a check on what sort of mood the subjects were in just at the moment. Subjects then indicated how happy, loving, angry, sad, and fearful they felt, right at the moment. Subjects were told that this check would be helpful because moods might affect the ability to reproduce various sounds. Results revealed that subjects' emotions were powerfully affected by the specific sounds they produced. Thus, this experiment, too, provided support for the vocal feedback hypothesis.

In another series of studies, Robert Zajonc, Sheila Murphy, and Marita Inglehart (1989) asked subjects to mimic either the long "e" sound in "cheese" (which required them to smile) or the German "für" (which required them to pucker their lips, mimicking a negative emotional expression). Subjects tended to feel the emotions their voices and faces were induced to express; thus, here too, subjective emotional experiences matched vocal expressions.

Some researchers have tried to put such findings to practical use. For example, Aron Siegman and his colleagues (Siegman, Anderson, & Berger, 1990) wondered whether participants in an angry interchange could calm themselves down if they forced themselves to speak in a reasonable voice. They tested this hypothesis by asking men and women to talk in a variety of vocal styles about topics that made them furious. Some subjects were asked to speak soft and slow, others to speak normally, and still others to speak loud and fast. They found that both men and women felt less angry and had slower heart rates and lower blood pressure when they carefully modulated their voices. Subjects got angrier and more physiologically aroused when they allowed themselves to speak harshly.

*Gender differences in the importance of vocal feedback*

Gerald Cupchik and Howard Leventhal (1974) speculated that men and women might differ in the extent to which their emotional experiences are shaped by vocal feedback. When individuals are asked how funny a joke, a television sitcom, or a film is, they might assume either that they are being asked to make an analytic, abstract judgment *or* that they are being asked how much it made them laugh; the two need not always go together. The dissociation between emotional reports and emotional behavior was quite clear in an early study by Stanley Schachter and Ladd Wheeler (1962) on the effects of epinephrine (which increases ANS activity), chlorpromazine (which reduces ANS activity), and a placebo on emotion. The authors measured people's emotional reactions to humorous films in two ways: (1) by asking subjects to rate how "funny" they thought a film was and (2) by quantifying how much a film made subjects laugh. They found that although subjects' analytic ratings of the films were completely unaltered by the drugs, their laughter was markedly affected by drug-induced ANS levels: Epinephrine increased laughter and chlorpromazine decreased laughter, relative to a placebo. Similiarly, Richard Young and Margaret Frye (1966) asked subjects to listen to jokes when they were alone or in groups. Although the jokes were rated as equally funny in all conditions, subjects laughed aloud far more when they were in large groups.

On the basis of the preceding logic, Howard Leventhal and William Mace (1970) conducted two experiments to test the hypothesis that boy's and girl's subjective, analytic ratings of a humorous film would be differentially shaped by vocal feedback. In the first, they showed boys and girls a humorous film and either encouraged or forbade laughter during the film. In the second study, boys and girls viewed a film that either did or did not contain canned laughter. In both studies, the authors found that ratings by the girls of the film's funniness were consistent with the extent to which they had laughed during it; their judgments and behavior were in accord with the vocal feedback hypothesis. The ratings of the boys, however, were not influenced by how much they laughed: In the first study, boys rated the film as *less* funny when they had been encouraged to laugh than when they had been forbidden to do so; in the second, boys who viewed the film accompanied by canned laughter valued it less than those who saw the non-laugh-tracked version.

Cupchik and Leventhal (1974) proposed that men and women may well differ in how they go about making abstract judgments. Perhaps men tend to be more analytic: They make fairly abstract judgments as to the humorousness of movies or cartoons, and their judgments may be less influenced by their own individual emotional reactions, whether by constitution or by socialization. Women may be more likely to synthesize abstract information with information concerning their own and others' emotional behaviors; that is, they may treat "the situation as a whole" (Arnold, 1960, p. 80). The authors attempted to test this hypotheses in a series of careful experiments. In one, men and women were asked to judge the funniness of 100 cartoons from *Punch*, *Playboy*, and *The New Yorker*. They were told either to aim for as much objectivity as possible or else just to sit back, relax, and have fun.

When women in this experiment were asked to be objective, they had no trouble doing so: They used abstract standards for judging how funny the cartoons were, and their judgments were not affected by how much *they* had laughed at them. When women were asked to "just relax and have fun," their judgments were influenced by their own emotional reactions: They judged the cartoons to be funnier when they had laughed more (in the canned-laughter conditions); they reacted, in short, as the vocal feedback hypothesis says they should. Men's reactions were far more complex: Their judgments and laughter depended on how sensitive they were to internal cues, whether the cartoons were funny or dull, whether it was in the first half or second half of the trials, whether they were trying to be objective or to just relax and enjoy themselves, and whether or not they had heard canned laughter.

It is worth emphasizing that results have *not* differed for men and women in most of the more recent studies on the effects of vocal feedback on emotions (e.g., Hatfield et al., 1991). Thus, whether gender differences are receding as the socialization of boys and girls becomes more uniform, or are only manifest in selected contexts (e.g., when rendering judgments of the emotional impact of a stimulus), the spontaneous emotional reactions of both men and women appear to be influenced by vocal feedback.

### The postural feedback hypothesis

I was uncomfortable with her . . . because her melancholy
could turn from thoughtful pessimism to bleak sadness. I knew
when: sadness gave her bad posture.

– Paul Theroux

Theorists have long noticed that people's attitudes are reflected in their postures. In fact, the term "attitude" comes originally from the

Latin words *apto* (aptitude or fitness) and *acto* (postures of the body) (Bull, 1951). Sir Francis Galton (1884) suggested that one could gauge whether or not guests at a dinner party were attracted to one another by measuring their bodily orientations:

> When two persons have an "inclination" to one another, they visibly incline or slope together when sitting side by side, as at a dinner table, and they then throw the stress of their weights on the near legs of their chairs. It does not require much ingenuity to arrange a pressure gauge with an index and dial to indicate changes in stress, but it is difficult to devise an arrangement that shall fulfill the three-fold condition of being effective, not attracting notice, and being applicable to ordinary furniture. I made some rude experiments, but being busy with other matters, have not carried them on, as I had hoped. (p. 184)

Nina Bull (1951), too, observed that attitudes comprise both mental and motor components and that the two are tightly linked. To test this notion, she conducted a series of 53 experiments. In the first set, she found that when men and women were hypnotized and were instructed to experience certain emotions (joy, triumph, disgust, fear, anger, and depression), they automatically adopted appropriate bodily postures. In the second set, she required subjects to adopt a series of emotional postures. Some examples:

> *Depression:* "You feel heavy all over. There is a slumping sensation in your chest."
> *Fear:* "Your whole body feels stiffened up. You can't catch your breath. You want to run away but you can't."
> *Anger:* "Your hands are getting tense and your arms are getting tense. You can feel your jaw tightening."
> *Joy:* "There is a feeling of relaxation and lightness in your whole body." (p. 79)

When subjects were required to adopt these postures, they soon came to experience the emotions associated with them. When instructed to try to experience emotions incompatible with these postures, they had great difficulty in doing so.

John Riskind and Carolyn Gotay (1982) conducted four experiments designed to discover whether emotion and motivation are changed by postural feedback. They placed some subjects in confident, expansive, upright physical postures, and others in slumped, depressed postures. Although the two groups did *not* come to differ in how sad they felt, the former (upright) group felt more confident, was more persistent on standard learned-helplessness tasks, and experienced less stress than did the latter (slumped) group. Similar results were subsequently secured by John Riskind (1983, 1984).

Sandra Duclos and her co-workers (1989) arranged subjects into sad, angry, and fearful postures. Their instructions were as follows:

> *Fearful:* Please scoot to the front edge of your chair, and draw your feet together and under the chair. Now turn your upper body toward the right, twisting a little at the waist, but keeping your head facing me (front). Now please dip your right shoulder a bit and, while keeping the twist and the dip, lean your upper body slightly back as you raise your hands to about mouth level, arms bent at the elbow and palms facing front.
>
> *Sad:* Please sit back in your chair, resting your back comfortably against the chair back, and draw your feet loosely in under the chair. You should feel no tension in your legs or feet. Now fold your hands in your lap, just sort of loosely cupping one hand in the other. Now please drop your head, letting your rib cage fall and letting the rest of your body go limp. You should feel just a slight tension up the back of your neck and across your shoulder blades.
>
> *Angry:* Please put your feet flat on the floor directly below your knees, and put your forearms and elbows on the chair arms. Now please clench your fists tightly and lean your upper body slightly forward. (p. 105).

They found that subjects' feelings came to match precisely those associated with the postures they had adopted. When, for instance, they were placed in sad postures, they came to feel sad, not angry or fearful.

The secret to being a good actor is honesty. If you can fake
*that*, you've got it made.

– George Burns

Psychophysiologist Susana Bloch and her colleagues (Bloch, Orthous, & Santibanez, 1987) trained actors at the Theater School of the Universidad de Chile to experience and project the basic emotions

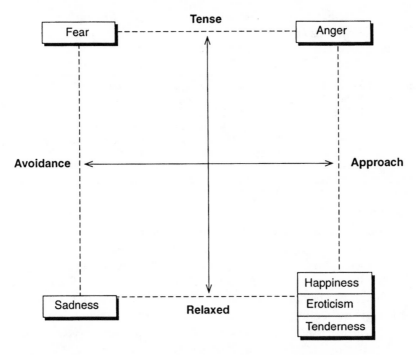

Figure 2.4. Representations of the six basic emotions in terms of postural tension–relaxation and approach–avoidance parameters. *Source:* Bloch et al., 1987, p. 4.

(happiness, eroticism, tenderness, sadness, anger, and fear) by relying on facial, breathing, and postural feedback. She proposed that

> each basic emotion can be evoked by a particular configuration composed of: (1) a breathing pattern, characterized by amplitude and frequency modulation; (2) a muscular activation characterized by a set of contracting and/or relaxing groups of muscles, defined in a particular posture; (3) a facial expression or mimicry characterized by the activation of different facial muscle patterns. (p. 3)

She pointed out that the basic emotions (and the postures associated with them) can be represented on two axes: tension–relaxation and approach–avoidance (Figure 2.4).

Actors were thus taught to feel the basic emotions by being taught to perform the respiratory–postural–facial effector patterns associated with these emotions (Table 2.1). (Eventually, with extensive prac-

Table 2.1. *Schematic representation of posture, body direction, and breathing style for the basic emotions*

| Emotion | Posture | Direction | Main breathing trait (and mouth aperture) |
|---------|---------|-----------|-------------------------------------------|
| Happiness | Relaxed | Approach | Saccadic expiration (mouth open) |
| Eroticism | Relaxed | Approach | Small amplitude, low frequency (mouth open) |
| Tenderness | Relaxed | Approach | Small amplitude, low frequency (mouth closed in a relaxed smile) |
| Sadness | Relaxed | Avoidance | Saccadic inspiration (mouth open) |
| Fear | Tense | Avoidance | Inspiratory apnea (mouth open) |
| Anger | Tense | Approach | Hyperventilation (mouth closed tight) |

*Source:* Based on Bloch et al., 1987, p. 5.

tice, she argued, actors would no longer need to experience emotions; they would simply be able to express the packages of emotion at will.) They were instructed to begin by adopting a particular pattern of breathing; then add the postural component; and, finally, put on the facial expression. They were then asked to describe the emotions they were feeling. As expected, their subjective experience was altered by facial, vocal, and postural feedback patterns. Actors were also taught that they could feel and express emotions more intensely, simply by varying the intensity of their emotional expressions.

### The muscular contraction feedback (proprioception) hypothesis

While shivering in my shoes / I strike a careless pose
And whistle a happy tune, / And no one even knows I'm afraid.
The result of this deception / Is very strange to tell,
For when I fool the people I fear / I fool myself as well!
        – "I Whistle a Happy Tune," from *The King and I* *

Some evidence that feedback from our muscular contractions affects emotions comes from yet other sources. Robert Zajonc and Hazel Markus (1982) have observed:

> In general, we should not be terribly surprised that it is so difficult to change attitudes and preferences by cognitive methods. These methods do not reach the motor system and other somatic representational systems of the organism. They only deal with one representational system – the one that exists in the

form of associative structures, images, and other subjective states. Since attitudes contain such a substantial affective component, they are likely to have multiple representations – and somatic representations are probably among the more significant ones. (p. 130)

Recently, John Cacioppo, Joseph Priester, and Gary Berntson (in preparation) have argued that one way to shape attitudes toward, or preferences for, novel objects is to manipulate collateral somatic activity. One of the most primitive discriminations people make is between stimuli that are positive (warrant approach) and those that are negative (warrant withdrawal). When attracted to someone or something, we tend to approach it or bring it toward us; when we dislike someone or something, we tend to withdraw or push the object away. John Cacioppo and his colleagues (Cacioppo, Klein, Berntson, & Hatfield, 1993) proposed that the relationship between attitude and approach–avoidance should work the other way as well:

Our aim here is to explore a complementary perspective: that certain patterns of collateral somatic activation can subtly influence a person's perception of and attitudes toward novel stimuli in focal attention. (p. 4)

If, for example, while looking at a Chinese ideograph, we somehow find ourselves performing a static flexion of the arms and torso (associated with approaching, acquiring, or ingesting certain classes of stimuli), the ideograph may gain in appeal from the fortuitous pairing. If, in contrast, we are led to perform a static extension of the arms and torso (associated with withdrawing from, avoiding, or rejecting certain classes of stimuli) while regarding the ideograph, it may begin to lose some of its appeal.

The authors tested this hypothesis in three experiments. In the first, subjects were told that since prior research had linked tension to a variety of problems in thinking and health, this experiment was designed to explore the effects of muscle tension on thinking and judgment. Subjects were shown 24 Chinese ideographs and asked simply to indicate whether they "liked" or "disliked" them. (This was done to ensure that subjects' evaluative processes were engaged during the presentation of the ideographs.) While they made their ratings, they performed a flexion or extension task, to achieve a mild but noticeable level of tension in their arms. (All subjects performed *both* somatic tasks, alternating when instructed, while viewing subsets of the ideographs.) In the flexion condition, subjects were told that their task while they made their ratings was to place their palms on the bottom of the table and to lift lightly. In the extension condition, subjects were told to press their palms down on the table lightly. At the end of the experiment, subjects' attitudes toward the ideographs were assessed by asking them to sort them into six bins, four per bin. The labels on these bins ranged from *extremely pleasant* (+3) to *extremely unpleasant* (–3). Based on a pretest, the ideographs presented during isometric arm flexion and extension had been selected to be equivalent and neutral in affective tone; as expected, however, by the conclusion of the experiment subjects were expressing differentially more positive attitudes toward ideographs associated with flexion than toward those associated with extension.

The authors replicated these findings in two subsequent experiments. In Experiment 2, subjects rated the ideographs while pressing down, relaxing, or lifting up on an exercise bar. Then they sorted the ideographs into bins. As before, although their initial attitudes toward the ideographs did not differ, their later attitudes toward them were more positive if they had been paired with arm flexion, and more negative if they had been paired with arm extension.

In Experiment 3, subjects were again to rate the appeal of Chinese ideographs while engaged in flexion, relaxation, or extension. Once again, in spite of the fact that their initial judgments did not differ, flexion led to more positive attitudes, and extension to more negative attitudes, than did relaxation. This trio of experiments provides clear evidence that affective reactions toward neutral, nonassociative stimuli can be influenced by patterns of collateral somatic activity as rudimentary as flexor or extensor contractions that suggest approach or withdrawal orientations. It appears that we come to like things we approach or bring toward us and to dislike things we avoid or push away (as well as the other way around) even when we are not focused on the association between our somatic disposition and these objects.

Similar results were secured by Gary Wells and Richard Petty (1980). These authors asked subjects to listen to an editorial while shaking their heads either vertically or horizontally (as previously instructed), ostensibly to test the quality of the headphones. Subjects heard either an editorial that argued for a tuition hike or one calling for a reduction. As predicted, those who had been instructed to make vertical head movements agreed more strongly with the editorial they heard than did those who made horizontal head movements.

Sabine Stepper and Fritz Strack (1992) also reported evidence that feelings are determined in part by collateral somatic activity. In one experiment, subjects were led to believe that the authors were studying the influence of different ergonomic working positions on the performance of different tasks. Subjects were then induced to sit in an upright or slumped posture while performing an achievement task. Stepper and Strack found that subjects felt more pride in their successful performance when their postures were upright rather than slumped. Conceptually similar results were found in a second experiment, in which subjects were led to contract the corrugator supercilii (which draws the brows down and together, as during hard concentration) or the zygomaticus major (which draws the mouth into a smile) while they recalled autobiographical episodes.

In yet another experiment, Daniel Wegner and his colleagues (Wegner, Lane, & Dimitri, 1991) explored the allure of secret liaisons:

> This experiment was designed in an attempt to capture some of what happens at the height of intrigue in a secret affair. Picture this: The couple have just brushed ankles under the table, and a look flashes between them as they both recognize instantly the precarious situation they have encountered. Others at the table do not know of their relationship – the one that is just now forming as their contact lingers – and they obviously cannot know. But the touch continues. The partners must put on a show of indifference to each other and feign interest in the above-board conversation, all the while trying not to let their continuing covert activities seep into their minds and actions. Our prediction is that this prototypical secret liaison has the effect of producing in each partner a preoccupation with and attraction toward the other. (p. 18)

They tested this notion in a simple experiment: College men and women at the University of Virginia, who were strangers to one another, were invited in to play a card game. One team was told (privately) that it was their job to play the game using "natural nonverbal communication." They were to keep their feet in contact with those of their partner for the entire game, so they could send secret signals to one another. Half of the time, in the secret condition, men and women were told that they should not let the other team know they were playing "footsie"; in the nonsecret condition, everyone knew what was going on. The other team was not allowed to touch.

As predicted, men and women felt more romantic attraction for one another if they had been allowed to play a secret game of "footsie." Their competitors, on the other hand, became most romantically aroused when they had been tipped off to what was going on. Once again, subjects' passionate feelings seemed to fall in line with the passionate behaviors they performed.

### Emotional experience and dramatic presentations

A character can invade your body and take over like a virus.
When the movie making ends, it's like getting over a sickness.
You slowly but surely get well and come back to yourself.
                                        – Jennifer Jason Leigh

Theorists such as Konstantin Stanislavski (Moore, 1960) have observed that actors sometimes "catch" the emotions of those they portray. By extension, critics have noted that Robin Williams has an unusual ability to "gobble-up" the characters he is asked to portray. One critic (Morgenstern, 1990) reported:

> He loves to play with abstract ideas, and he's a good listener. Sometimes he's so good that you get the impression of an emotional mirror: if you're calm, he's calm; if you're up, he's up – way up. (p. 34)

Neurologist Oliver Sacks said that, when Williams played him in the film *Awakenings,* it was like walking into a three-dimensional mirror:

> Sacks discusses this surreal experience with great humor, but he makes no bones about his misgivings. "I was a little scared when I learned that someone with such powers of apprehension as Robin was getting me as a subject," Sacks recalls, "because he does have this extraordinary, at times involuntary, power of mimicry. No, mimicry is the wrong word. He just sort of takes in the entire repertoire of a person; their voice, gestures, movements, idiosyncrasies, habits. He gets you."
>
> The subject's misgivings grew as Williams worked on the exterior aspects of his character. "It was like a twin," Sacks says, "like encountering someone with the same impulses as one's own. I'd see his hand on his head in a strange way, then I'd realize that was my hand. But I hasten to add that this was an

early and transient stage, a mirroring that gave way to much deeper and richer and unexpected development." (Morgenstern, 1990, p. 96)

Often, this close mimicry means that actors like Robin Williams come to share the feelings of those they portray.

Kirk Douglas (1988) reported that once while he was driving to Palm Springs, California, he offered a lift to a young sailor, who, when he recognized Douglas, exclaimed in shock: "Hey! Do you know who you are?" Douglas admits, upon reflection, that sometimes actors do come close to getting lost in their parts:

> I was close to getting lost in the character of Van Gogh in *Lust for Life*. I felt myself going over the line, into the skin of Van Gogh. Not only did I look like him, I was the same age he had been when he committed suicide. Sometimes I had to stop myself from reaching my hand up and touching my ear to find out if it was actually there. It was a frightening experience. That way lies madness. . . . The memory makes me wince. I could never play him again. (Lehmann-Haupt, 1988, p. B2)

Afterward, following a private screening of *Lust for Life*, fellow actor John Wayne berated him:

> Kirk! How can you play a part like that? There's so goddamn few of us left. We got to play strong, tough characters. Not those weak queers. I tried to explain. "Hey, John, I'm an actor. I like to play interesting roles. It's all make-believe, John. It isn't real. You're not really John Wayne, you know." (Douglas, 1988, p. 243)

He says he's not quite sure when he's acting and when he's not
. . . and I can't always tell. It's a bit eerie, really.
  – Joan Plowright speaking of her husband, Laurence Olivier

Konstantin Stanislavski (Moore, 1960) speculated as to how this process might work: People's emotional experiences might be stored in an "emotional memory." There they remain as distilled essences of emotion. In his view:

> Emotional memory stores our past experiences; to relive them, actors must execute indispensable, logical physical actions in

the given circumstances. There are as many nuances of emotions as there are physical actions. (pp. 52–53)

Thus, Stanislavski proposed we may relive emotions anytime we engage in a variety of small actions that were once associated with those emotions.

## Summing up

There is an impressive array of evidence supporting Proposition 2: People's subjective emotional experience does seem to be affected, moment to moment, by the activation and/or feedback from facial, vocal, postural, and movement mimicry.

In the next chapter we consider evidence, from a variety of disciplines, for Proposition 3: that people do indeed tend to catch the emotions of others.

# 3. Evidence that emotional contagion exists

## Introduction

In chapter 1, we proposed the following:

> *Proposition 3. Given Propositions 1 and 2, people tend to "catch" others' emotions, moment to moment.*

Researchers from a variety of disciplines have provided evidence in support of this contention.

## Animal research

Ethologists believe that the imitation of emotional expression constitutes a phylogenetically ancient and basic form of intraspecies communication. Such contagion appears in many vertebrate species (Brothers, 1989).

In the 1950s, a great deal of research documented that animals do seem to catch others' emotions. Robert Miller and his Pittsburgh colleagues (Miller, Banks, & Ogawa 1963; Miller, Murphy, & Mirsky, 1959; Mirsky, Miller, & Murphy, 1958) found that monkeys can, through their faces and postures, transmit their fears. The faces, voices, and postures of frightened monkeys serve as warnings; they signal potential trouble. Monkeys catch the fear of others and thus are primed to make appropriate instrumental avoidance responses.

Some scientists (Miller et al., 1963) tested these hypotheses by means of a cooperative conditioning paradigm. In such a paradigm, one monkey is shown the CS; a second monkey possesses the power to make an appropriate avoidance response. The question is, "Can the monkeys learn to communicate?" In this cooperative conditioning experiment, each time rhesus monkeys spotted the illuminated face of the target monkey on a television monitor, it was their task quickly to press a lever to avoid electric shock. Sometimes monkeys were shown a calm CS face, sometimes a frightened or pained face. What did the frightened face look like?

> The jaw was clenched, drawing the corners of the mouth downward and visibly tightening the loose skin of the chin and neck. The nostrils were flared, perhaps reflecting changes in respiration. The expressive change in the eyes was more difficult to describe. The eyes were opened more widely upon stimulus presentation and appeared to have an unfocused quality in contrast to the appearance between trials when the animal was looking at objects in the test room. If the CS was not quickly terminated by an avoidance response, the stimulus animal became increasingly apprehensive as the shock period approached. It would move its head in short, jerky thrusts and sometimes appeared to be vocalizing though the sound-deadening quality of the test room prevented the sound from being perceived in the control room or in the responder's test room. (p. 29)

Not surprisingly, monkeys found it far easier to learn that, compared to a calm face, a frightened face signaled danger. Subjects immediately picked up the fear of the target monkey. (They displayed heart rate changes, piloerection, etc.) They also found it easier to learn a conditioned avoidance response. Researchers (Mirsky et al., 1958; Miller et al., 1959) then conducted a series of extinction trials. Subject monkeys sometimes were suddenly shown photographs of target monkeys (or of themselves) who were calm; sometimes they were shown monkeys who were frightened or in pain. Here too, the frightened or suffering target monkeys were especially effective in triggering previously extinguished avoidance responses. This was true even when the calm monkeys had originally been the CS for avoidance learning and had been paired with painful shocks!

Robert Miller and his colleagues (Miller et al., 1959; Miller, 1967) found that *Macaca mulatta* monkeys can easily learn to perform "altruistic" acts. For example, if monkeys observed a fellow monkey in pain, experiencing electric shock, they could easily learn to press a series of levers to turn off *his* shocks. Presumably, they read the pain in their fellows' face, shared his distress and physiological arousal, and thus learned to act to reduce his suffering. In fact, monkeys learned to save themselves *and* others from electric shock with equal alacrity!

These classic studies seem to indicate that even animals lower on the phylogenetic scale are capable of emotional contagion.

## Developmental research

I watched my grandmother's choking fits at the kitchen table,
and my own throat would feel narrow.
　　　　　　　　　　　　　　　　　　　　　　　　– John Updike

Child psychologists have long been interested in primitive emotional contagion, empathy, and sympathy (Eisenberg & Strayer, 1987). Originally, the German term *Einfühlung* meant "to feel one's way into" another person's experience – or, in our terms, to experience emotional contagion (Stein, 1917/1964). Edward Titchener (1909) argued that people could never *know* what another felt by reasoning; they could only know by *feeling themselves into* the other's feelings. He observed:

> Not only do I see gravity and modesty and pride and courtesy and stateliness, but I feel or act them in the mind's muscle. (p. 21)

Later researchers speculated about how this process might work. Gordon Allport (1937/1961) thought that it involved "the imaginative transposing of oneself into the thinking, feeling, and acting of another" (p. 536) and "the imitative assumption of the postures and facial expressions of other people" (p. 530). Gardner Murphy (1947) speculated that people came to feel as others feel because of *motor mimicry* – "his muscles tighten as he watches the tug of war; his larynx tires and his heels rise as the soprano strains upward" (p. 414).

Today, theorists make clear distinctions between the process in which we are interested, primitive empathy or emotional contagion, and empathy or sympathy. As you'll recall from the Introduction, we have defined *primitive emotional contagion* as

> the tendency to automatically mimic and synchronize facial expressions, vocalizations, postures, and movements with those of another person and, consequently, to converge emotionally. (Hatfield et al., 1992, pp. 153–154)

Nancy Eisenberg and Paul Miller (1987) defined *empathy* as

> an affective state stemming from apprehension of another's emotional state or condition and which is congruent with it. (p. 292)

Lauren Wispé (1991), in defining *sympathy*, observed:

> The definition of sympathy has two parts: first, a heightened awareness of the feelings of the other person and, second, an urge to take whatever actions are necessary to alleviate the other person's plight. (p. 68)

Developmental researchers acknowledge that the most primitive, basic process is emotional contagion (Eisenberg & Strayer, 1987; Zahn-Waxler & Radke-Yarrow, 1990). The sequence of development seems to look like this:

> From a few months after birth through the first year of life, studies have shown, infants react to the pain of others as though it were happening to themselves. Seeing another child hurt and start to cry, they themselves begin to cry, especially if the other child cries for more than a minute or two.
>
> But around one year of age, infants begin to realize that the distress is being felt by someone else. "They recognize it's the other kid's problem, but they're often confused over what to do about it" . . .
>
> During this phase, toddlers often imitate the distress of someone else – apparently, researchers say, in an effort to better understand what the other person is feeling. . . .
>
> "From around 14 months to 2 or 2½ years, you see children feel their own fingers to see if they hurt when someone else hurts their fingers," said Marion Radke-Yarrow, chief of the Laboratory of Developmental Psychology at the National Institute of Mental Health.
>
> . . . "By 2½, though, toddlers clearly realize that someone else's pain is different from their own, and know how to comfort them appropriately." (Goleman, 1989, pp. B1, B10)

Unfortunately for our purposes, researchers have been less interested in the rudimentary process of emotional contagion, and have devoted most of their attention to understanding the development of the more cognitive, sophisticated, and "socially beneficial" processes of empathy and sympathy. Nonetheless, child psychologists and developmentalists have collected some evidence that, from the start, both parents and children are powerfully "enmeshed"; both show evidence of emotional contagion (Thompson, 1987).

Nothing was more enjoyable than mimicry. I was about the
height of my father's back pocket, from which his
handkerchief always hung out, and for years I pulled the
corner of my handkerchief out exactly the same distance.
                                        – Arthur Miller

If you live with a cripple, you will learn to limp.
                                        – Plutarch

There is considerable evidence that parents and children are able to communicate emotionally with one another from birth. They mimic one another's faces, voices, and movements and, in that way, can come to know and/or feel what the other is feeling.

## Evidence that children catch their parents' emotions

There is evidence that even neonates may match others' sounds and movements from the moment of birth. In one study, a woman put on a happy, sad, or surprised face for a group of preterm neonates or a group of full-term infants. Researchers found that for both groups of infants, happy faces elicited more widened lips, the sad faces more pouting lips, and the surprised faces more wide-open mouths (Field, Woodson, Cohen, Garcia, & Greenberg, 1982). Their data suggest that infants possess the ability to imitate facial expressions *at birth*. Other researchers have demonstrated that newborns are capable of movement synchrony. Rresearchers walked up to neonates who were only 30–56 hours old, placed their faces 19 cm from those of the infants, and talked. All the infants displayed movement synchrony (Berghout-Austin & Peery, 1983).

Martin Hoffman (1978) observed that neonates commonly engage in contagious crying in hospital nurseries. Infants also appear to match the pitch levels of the voices they hear (Webster, Steinhardt, & Senter, 1972). Martin Hoffman (1973) has suggested that caretakers may teach their infants to feel what they feel by means of physical handling (see Figure 3.1). When a mother is distressed, if her body stiffens, the infant in her stiffened arms will also experience distress. Subsequently, Hoffman speculated, the facial and verbal expressions that initially accompanied the mother's distress would serve as conditioned stimuli that evoke distress in the child. Stimulus generalization ensures that, eventually, even distressed strangers will begin to evoke distress in the child. In summarizing such research, Hoffman (1987) wrote:

> Infants may experience empathetic distress through the simplest arousal models . . . long before they acquire a sense of others as distinct from the self. Distress cues from the dimly perceived other are confounded with unpleasant feelings empathetically aroused in the self. Consequently, infants may at times act as though what happened to the other happened to themselves. Infants also seem to catch their parents' fears and anxiety. (p. 51)

Hoffman cited as examples such cases as that of a toddler who buries his face in his mother's lap upon seeing another child fall and cry, or who strikes his doctor in anger when he sees another child receiving an injection.

In any case, there is accumulating evidence that depressed mothers communicate their depression to their infants and toddlers, who are then at risk for depression themselves (Downey & Coyne, 1990). Children who observe angry adults become unusually aggressive toward their peers (Cummings, 1987).

Novelist Anita Brookner (1987) visited a friend and was struck by the powerful anxiety that father transmitted to son:

> I felt that mingling of pity and distaste as I contemplated the vistas of his childhood, the father's frantic and many ministrations, all lacking in conviction because of his overriding anxiety. And the anxiety passed from one to the other, like the parcel in a game that used to be played at the children's parties of my youth. (p. 102)

The operation of a rudimentary form of emotional contagion is also believed to underlie what Joseph Campos and Craig Sternberg (1981) have called "social referencing." They reported that, in ambiguous situations, infants scan their parents' faces, pick up the happiness, anger, surprise, or fear they find there, and use that information in deciding how to proceed. The facial expressions of the

Figure 3.1. Father wincing as he anticipates his son's shot. Reprinted by permission of the photographer, Anita Henderson.

parents are thought to instill confidence or fear in the infants, and the specific emotion aroused in the infants is thought then to determine the infants' behavior.

> There is something about an abject person that rouses cruelty in
> the kindest breast.
>                                        – Elizabeth Bowen

Children don't always, of course, catch others' emotions; they don't always empathize with their anxiety or suffering. Novelist John Updike (1989) described that peculiar blend of emotional resonance punctuated by occasional cruelty that characterizes early childhood:

> As a child, I had tortured my toys, talking aloud to them, fascinating and horrifying myself. In some spasm of indignation I had slit my rubber Donald Duck's neck, halfway only, losing my nerve, so that the cut was there, opening and closing like a little lipless mouth when I moved Donald's head. . . . On the other hand, I cringed when other children fished, or trapped a

toad, or caught a grasshopper and proceeded to pull off its legs until just an immobile staring torso of living tissue remained. Whenever animals or insects were placed at the mercy of my fellow children, a sensation of dread led me to turn away, to shut my eyes and turn my back. (pp. 156–157)

### Evidence that parents catch their children's emotions

Parents seem to catch the feelings of newborns as well. Ann Frodi and her colleagues (1978) found that parents who were asked to observe a sad or angry newborn reported feeling more "annoyed, irritated, distressed, disturbed, indifferent, and less attentive and less happy" than those who viewed a smiling infant. When parents viewed a sad or angry child, their diastolic blood pressure rose and their skin conductance increased. Although mothers were most likely to catch and mimic their newborns' positive emotions (interest, enjoyment, and surprise), they also mimicked, to some extent, their negative emotions (pain, sadness, and anger) (Malatesta & Haviland, 1982).

It has long been known that adult eye contact and vocalization (whether contingently or randomly uttered) are powerful elicitors of infant vocalization (Bloom, 1975). What is less well known is that mothers' reactions are shaped by their infants as well. In an ingenious experiment, researchers found that infants' vocalizations and head turns would increase the likelihood of mothers' vocalizations and smiles (Gewirtz & Boyd, 1976, 1977). Mothers and infants (from a variety of ethnic and socioeconomic groups, with infants varying from 1 week to 2 years of age) have been found to match both the timing and the duration of their vocalizations and to coordinate their movements (Cappella, 1981).

Although these interesting lines of research do not speak definitively to the hypothesis that parents and children are genetically predisposed to take on one another's emotional reactions, the potential adaptive significance for a species of synchronizing the attention, emotions, and behaviors of caretaker and newborn is undeniable.

*Cross-cultural restrictions on emotional contagion.* Parents don't always share children's emotions. Societies may teach people not to respond to children's emotional displays; they may even instruct adults to mock such outbursts. Paul Theroux (1988), in his travels through rural China, observed the following incident:

[S]oon after, we saw a child being beaten by its mother in a yard. I was riveted by it. The child was smacked so thoroughly that he became hysterical and could not be calmed. He went around hitting his mother and wetting himself and howling. He was about seven years old. The usual Chinese reaction to someone in distress is laughter, and soon Mr. Wei and the others watching began to find the tormented child an object of amusement. (pp. 411–412)

*Children's emotions may provoke complementary emotions.* Parents may respond with a complementary rather than an identical emotion. They may, for example, find their children's self-centered and exaggerated anger amusing, or frightening, or embarrassing.

*Children's physical problems may make contagion difficult.* Parents' emotional reactions are also tempered by the ability (or inability) of their children to send and receive emotional messages. Selma Fraiberg (1974), who had studied blind babies for 12 years, described some of the difficulties of working with them:

Sometimes when we have professional visitors at the project to look at films or videotapes, I steal glances at their faces when the child is seen on the screen. With sighted children it is always interesting to see the resonance of mood on the viewer's face. We smile when the baby on the film smiles; we are sober when the baby is distressed. We laugh sympathetically when the baby looks indignant at the examiner's sneakiness. We frown in concentration as the baby frowns when the toy disappears. When he drops a toy, we look below the movie screen to help him find it.

But the blind baby on the screen does not elicit these spontaneous moods in the visitor. Typically, the visitor's face remains solemn. This is partly a reaction to blindness itself. But it is also something else. There is a large vocabulary of expressive behavior that one does not see in a blind baby at all. The absence of differentiated signs on the baby's face is mirrored in the face of the observer.

One afternoon recently our staff devoted a session to the discussion of self-observations in relation to blind infants. Our consensus, as a team of researchers and clinicians who have worked with blind children for several years, was that we have never overcome this sense of something vital missing in the social exchange. And yet our rewards from blind children have been very great. All the staff members have strong attachments to children we have known since the first year of life. With rare exceptions the babies have grown into preschool children who are healthy, active, freely mobile, talkative and mischievous, surely a group of highly personable and attractive youngsters. Among ourselves we talk about them the way proud parents do. We are never aware that something is missing in our response until a sighted child comes to visit.

When a sighted child comes to visit, there is spontaneous rapport and we trot out our repertoire of antics with babies. We are back in the tribal system where the baby plays his social game and we play ours. If one has worked very largely with blind babies for many years, as we have, the encounter with a sighted baby is absurdly like the experience of meeting a compatriot abroad after a long stay in a country where the language and customs are alien. The compatriot, who can be a perfect stranger asking for directions, is greeted like a friend, his regional accent and idiom are endearing, and with nothing more in common than a continent two strangers can embark upon a social exchange in which nearly all the tribal signs are understood and correctly interpreted.

What we miss in the blind baby, apart from the eyes that do not see, is the vocabulary of signs and signals that provides the most elementary and vital sense of discourse long before words have meaning. (p. 217)

Finally, even if parents do catch their children's emotions, that does not always ensure that they will treat their children as they would wish to be treated. Researchers find, for example, that parents generally do suffer when their newborns are disagreeable or sickly (e.g., colicky). Tragically, this may lead caretakers to abuse or neglect their children (Bugental, Blue, & Lewis, 1990).

## Clinical research

### Therapists' reactions to clients

In the early days, Sigmund Freud (1912/1958) sternly warned therapists to keep their distance, emotionally, from clients:

I cannot advise my colleagues too urgently to model themselves during psychoanalytic treatment on the surgeon, who
puts aside all his feelings, even his human sympathy. (p. 115)

Nonetheless, therapists have long observed that clinicians tend to
catch the feelings of their clients. Clinicians point out the difficultly
of working with depressed clients; one keeps nodding off. Something about their slow sentences, sad facial expressions, or the endless, hopeless details they recite, keeps putting one to sleep. It is hard
to concentrate and attend long enough to be helpful. Carl Gustav
Jung (1968) observed:

Emotions are contagious. . . . In psychotherapy, even if the doctor is entirely detached from the emotional contents of the patient, the very fact that the patient has emotions has an effect
upon him. And it is a great mistake if the doctor thinks he can
lift himself out of it. He cannot do more than become conscious of the fact that he is affected. If he does not see that, he
is too aloof and then he talks beside the point. It is even his
duty to accept the emotions of the patient and to mirror them.
(p. 155)

Theodor Reik (1948), in *Listening with the Third Ear*, noted that
therapists and others possess a great deal of information, conscious
and unconscious, about others:

Psychical data are not uniform. We have, of course, in the first
place the considerable portion that we seize upon through conscious hearing, sight, touch, and smell. A further portion is
what we observe unconsciously. It is permissible to declare that
this second portion is more extensive than the first, and that far
greater importance must be ascribed to it in the matter of psychological comprehension than to what we consciously hear,
see, etc. Of course, we seize upon this, also, by means of the
senses that we know but, to speak descriptively, it is precon-
scious or unconscious. We perceive peculiarities in the features
and bearing and movements of others that help to make the
impression we receive without our observing or attending to
them. We remember details of another person's dress and peculiarities in his gestures, without recalling them; a number of
minor points, an olfactory nuance; a sense of touch while shaking hands, too slight to be observed; warmth, clamminess,
roughness or smoothness in the skin; the manner in which he

glances up or looks – of all this we are not consciously aware, and yet it influences our opinion. The minutest movements accompany every process of thought; muscular twitching in face or hands and movements of the eyes speak to us as well as words. No small power of communication is contained in a glance, a person's bearing, a bodily movement, a special way of breathing. Signals of subterranean motions and impulses are being sent silently to the region of everyday speech, gesture, and movement. (p. 135)

While we have no idea consciously of the hidden purposes and impulses of another person, unconsciously we may react to them as sensitively as a seismograph to a faint subterranean vibration. (p. 480)

We are reminded of Freud's view that mortals are not so made as to retain a secret. "Self-betrayal oozes from all our pores." . . . That statement clamors for a sequel. What sequel, may easily be guessed when we reflect that we react to the unconscious with all our organs, with our various instruments of reception and comprehension. *The self-betrayal of another is sucked in through all our pores.* (pp. 142–143)

Reik described four aspects of the process by which clinicians move in close enough to glimpse the emotions of their clients and then move back far enough to deal with them:

1. *Identification* – paying attention to another and allowing oneself to become absorbed in contemplation of that person.
2. *Incorporation* – making the other's experience one's own by internalizing the other.
3. *Reverberation* – experiencing the other's experience while simultaneously attending to one's own cognitive and affective associations to that experience.
4. *Detachment* – moving back from the merged inner relationship to a position of separate identity, which permits a response to be made that reflects both understanding of others as well as separateness from them. (Marcia, 1987, p. 83)

A shy man often makes other people shy, too. A person who adopts a masochistic attitude in his social relations often stirs an unconscious sadistic instinctive reaction in another. Is it not his unconscious desire to stir it?

– Theodor Reik

Recently, clinicians have begun to speculate about how the process of "countertransference" may operate and how such emotional information might be used therapeutically (Emde, Gaensbauer, & Harmon, 1981; Tansey & Burke, 1989). Michael Tansey and Walter Burke (1989), for instance, suggest that therapists may respond to clients' emotions in two different ways: by feeling exactly what the client feels (*concordant identification*) or by feeling emotions that are *complementary* to those of the clients (e.g., feeling hurt at a client's angry attack). The authors assume that therapists are generally provoked to feel what clients *wish* them to feel. (Presumably, in concordance, the clients wish the therapists to share their experiences; in complementarity, to fall into a very different, but facilitative, role – playing, say, stern disciplinarian to the client's child.)

Wilhelm Reich (1933/1945) hypothesized that therapists can gain insight into the thoughts, feelings, and characters of their clients by careful observation and imitation of their expressive movements.

> The patient's expressive movements involuntarily bring about *an imitation* in our own organism. By imitating these movements, we "sense" and understand the expression in ourselves and, consequently, in the patient. (p. 362)

Therapists can read clients' character structures and psychological conflicts in their patterns of chronic muscular tension (their "armor"). The angry, who would like to "chew up" their subordinates, might telegraph their rage by their chronically clenched jaws. Those who feel the weight of the world pressing upon them might signal their sadness and exhaustion by their bent necks and stooped shoulders. People who are desperately trying to suppress thoughts, memories, emotions, and sensory awareness tense their muscles. Tension, then, signals conflict. Reich adds:

> The armoring, its nature, the degree of its rigidity, and the inhibition of the body's emotional language can be easily assessed once the analyst has mastered the language of biological expression. The expression of the armored organism is one of "holding back." The meaning of this expression is quite literal: *the body is expressing that it is holding back.* Pulled-back shoulders, thrust out chest, rigid chin, superficial, suppressed breathing, hollowed-out loins, retracted, immobile pelvis, "expressionless" or rigidly stretched-out legs are the essential attitudes and mechanisms of total restraint. (p. 363)

People who adopt a rigid armor become insensitive not only to their own feelings, but those of others as well. Highly neurotic people, he claims, generally lack empathy.

Frieda Fromm-Reichmann (1950) took the process one step further. She advised young therapists, when they were uncertain as to what their clients were feeling, purposely to imitate their physical experiences and postures in order to gain some insight into their unconscious thoughts and feelings. Interestingly enough, Edgar Allan Poe (1915), in "The Purloined Letter," contended that if people consciously imitate others' facial expressions, they will soon come to feel as they do:

> When I wish to find out how wise, or how stupid, or how good, or how wicked is any one, or what are his thoughts at the moment, I fashion the expression of my face, as accurately as possible, in accordance with the expression of his, and then wait to see what thoughts or sentiments arise in my mind or heart, as if to match or correspond with the expression. (p. 100)

*Clinicians' assessments of clients' emotional states: Conscious judgments versus emotional contagion.* Clinical researchers, then, have pinpointed two very different ways in which they can gain knowledge about their clients' emotional states. First, they may *consciously* process emotional information. They can carefully weigh clients' statements; their facial, vocal, and postural expressions of emotion; their ANS reactions; their instrumental behaviors; and the context in which these reactions occur. Second, therapists may monitor *their own* emotional reactions, moment to moment.

Generally, therapists' conscious perceptions and emotional reactions will be in synchrony; but what happens when they are not? Sometimes, clients may claim they are feeling "just fine," but their faces, voices, and postures convey a different story. Their therapists certainly feel that something is amiss. How do therapists deal with such conflicting information? Elaine Hatfield and her colleagues (Hsee, Hatfield, & Chemtob, 1991) hypothesized that psychotherapists would have a complex reaction, tending to *think* one thing and *feel* another. Their conscious assessments would be unduly swayed by what the clients have to *say*, but their own *feelings* would be more influenced by what clients are really feeling.

To test these hypotheses, 87 University of Hawaii students were recruited for an experiment. The sample was representative of Hawaii's multiethnic population: 25% of the subjects were Japanese, 10% Chinese, 4% Korean, 12% Filipino, 7% Hawaiian, 2% Pacific Islander, 5% from other Asian groups, 2% Hispanic, 13% Caucasian, 2% African-American, 10% from other backgrounds, and 8% of mixed ethnic background.

When the subjects arrived, they were seated in front of a television monitor. The experimenter began by explaining the purpose of the experiment. He said that modern-day cinematographers use a wide array of techniques to adapt foreign films for the American market. Major studios might dub in English voices or add subtitles to foreign films. (Two film clips, from *Betty Blue* [a German film] and *Z* [a Greek movie], were shown to illustrate these procedures.) Sometimes, however, filmmakers had to rely on cheaper techniques. Recently, he claimed, the University of Hawaii had developed a special computer translation program: One simply fed the foreign dialogue into the computer and then into a voice synthesizer, and an English translation would emerge. It was true that the resulting English "voices" sounded a bit odd (similar to the the flat, halting voices on telephone answering machines), but the technique seemed to work nonetheless.

Now the students were to evaluate this process. They would be asked to view a three-minute clip of a Polish educational film, in which they would see a Polish factory worker chatting with an interviewer at the worker's tenth high-school reunion. In a voice-over, they would hear the worker describe what he had been thinking and feeling at the time of the interview. In fact, both the videotape and the subsequent audiotaped translation had been carefully prepared in two versions. On the *videotapes*, an actor simply expressed his honest feelings of either joy or sadness. (One could presumably guess his feelings by observing his honest facial, postural, and gestural expressions.) On the *audiotapes*, a computer voice claimed that the actor was feeling either happy or sad at the time the film was made. (It was, of course, critically important that the audio contain no paralinguistic cues: Neither rhythm, stress, rate, pitch, nor amplitude should provide any information as to the worker's real feelings.)

CONSTRUCTING THE AUDIOTAPES: WHAT THE TARGET *SAID* HE FELT: An actress (a college student) was hired to make the audiotapes. (A woman's voice was used instead of a man's to make it clear to subjects that they were listening to a computer, not to the man whose face appeared on the videotape.) This actress made every effort to duplicate a computer's vocal simulation – her voice was unfailingly flat, machinelike, and unemotional. Half of the time the computerlike voice claimed that [s]he had been extremely happy during the initial interview, half of the time that [s]he had been extremely sad. The target's appraisals were designed to be plausible, regardless of whether they were paired with the film of a Polish worker who was actually happy or actually sad at the time the videotape was shot. Thus, in the happy condition, the audiotape said:

> When I look at my film, I am surprised at the look on my face. Although I did not look that happy, I was actually extremely happy at the time the film was shot. The reunion was really a pleasant event. Here, I was telling the interviewer that I met many old friends and that we talked about how our lives have become better and better since high school, how happy our families are, and how filled with hope for the future we feel. I had a great time at the reunion, and I was really happy at the time I was interviewed.

In the sad condition, the audiotape said:

> When I look at the film, I am surprised at the look on my face. Although I did not look that sad, I was actually extremely sad at the time the film was shot. The reunion was really an unpleasant event. Here, I was telling the interviewer that I met many old friends and that we talked about how our lives have gone downhill since high school, how miserable our families are, and how hopeless we feel for the future. I had a miserable time at the reunion, and I was really sad at the time I was interviewed.

CONSTRUCTING THE VIDEOTAPES: WHAT THE TARGET *ACTUALLY* FELT. The videotapes contained an interview with a man who was recounting either one of the happiest or one of the saddest events of his life. His spontaneous facial expressions and gestures clearly conveyed his feelings.

Four tapes were constructed by merging the two audio and the two video tracks (Table 3.1). After subjects had viewed one of the four videotapes, they were asked to (1) guess how happy the *target*

Table 3.1. *Resultant four interview videotape combinations*

|  | Target's appraisal of his own emotions | Target's actual emotional experience/ facial expression |
|---|---|---|
| 1. | Happy | Happy |
| 2. | Happy | Sad |
| 3. | Sad | Happy |
| 4. | Sad | Sad |

*Source:* Based on Hsee et al., 1991b.

had been at the time the film was shot and (2) report how happy or sad *they* had felt while viewing the film. As predicted, the authors found that what subjects *thought* and what they *felt* were two different things, differentially influenced by various kinds of information. Subjects' appraisals of the target's emotions were most influenced by the target's self-reports and, to a lesser extent, by the evidence of their own senses (i.e., their observations of the target's facial expressions). Subjects' own emotions were influenced by both the target's self-reports and his actual expressions of emotion.

Clinicians have long observed that therapists rely on both their conscious analytic skills and their own emotions for information as to what their clients are feeling second to second. The preceding research provides some evidence that both sources of information can provide unique and valuable information as to the feelings of others. In part, therapists must place some weight on what targets say about their inner lives. (Only clients can guide them through their emotional landscapes.) However, therapists may well want to know more than what their clients say about their own inner lives. Sometimes clients don't know or are unwilling to admit what they feel. Here, therapists' realization that emotions are contagious may give them a source of additional information. Understanding that their own emotions may well be affected by their clients' moment-to-moment, more-or-less nonconscious, emotional expressions – their fleeting facial expressions, the way they tilt their heads, the grace of their gestures, their tones and cadences, the sharpness of their phrases – gives therapists a unique additional source of information.

*Do therapists' expectations subtly affect emotional contagion?* One problem therapists naturally face in trying to use their own emotions as a guide to clients' feelings lies in separating out their own reactions from the feelings they are catching from their clients. Therapists might worry, for example, that what they *expect* to see is shaping what they *do* see. There is some evidence from social cognition research that peoples' expectations *do* affect their perceptions (Goldfried & Robins, 1983; Hirt, 1990; Markus, 1977; Swann & Read, 1981; Wilson, 1985). Our beliefs influence the types of information to which we attend and actually remember (Snyder, 1984). We tend to process carefully information that is consistent with our beliefs and to ignore information that says we are wrong (Jelalian & Miller, 1984).

Recently, Elaine Hatfield and her colleagues (Uchino et al., 1991) set out to assess what role, if any, the expectations of therapists have in shaping their emotional reactions to clients: Do therapists "catch" the emotions they *assume* clients must be feeling, or the emotions clients actually *are* feeling? To answer this question, students at the University of Hawaii were told that they would soon be viewing men and women who were happy or sad, or they were given no information as to the targets' emotional states. Then subjects were shown a series of happy or sad target faces. Subjects' emotional reactions to the faces were assessed in two ways: First, subjects were asked how happy or sad they felt as they observed the faces. Second, subjects' faces were secretly videotaped as they viewed the target faces; judges viewing the tapes rated how happy or sad subjects' faces appeared to be. In this experiment, there was no evidence that the subjects' expectations influenced their susceptibility to emotional contagion: Regardless of what subjects expected to see, they caught the emotions actually expressed by the targets.

Clinicians know emotions are contagious, but sometimes they forget. Irvin Yalom (1989), in *Love's Executioner*, describes one of his most frustrating cases. Marvin, shortly after his retirement, began to be possessed by terrible nightmares. He dreamed of Victorian undertakers:

> The two men are tall, pale, and very gaunt. In a dark meadow they glide along in silence. They are dressed entirely in black. With tall black stovepipe hats, long-tailed coats, black spats and shoes. . . . Suddenly they come upon a carriage, ebony black, cradling a baby girl swaddled in black gauze. (p. 242)

He dreamed the ground liquefied under his feet. He suffered from severe migraine headaches and impotence. Not surprisingly, the therapist at first concluded that the reason these symptoms had erupted now was that Marvin had recently retired: He was experiencing "existential anxiety" about his inevitable death. That was the explanation, until Marvin's wife, Phyllis, appeared.

> But Phyllis supplied additional explanations for "Why now?"
> "I'm sure you know what you're talking about and that Marvin must be more upset than he knows at the idea of retiring. But, frankly, *I'm* disturbed at the idea of his retirement – and when I get upset, upset about anything, Marvin gets upset. That's the way our relationship works. If I worry, even if I keep it completely silent, he senses it and gets upset. Sometimes he gets so upset, he takes my upsetness away from me." (p. 266)

## Psychopathic clients

People who have been severely abused in childhood, who suffer brain damage, or who have a genetic defect may end up profoundly insensitive to the feelings of others.

Researchers (Harlow & Harlow, 1965) provide dramatic evidence that if monkeys are isolated from their mothers and their peers for 6–12 months, they lose forever their capacity to form social relationships. When they are in the presence of others, they are first frightened and then aggressive. Robert Miller (1967) found that monkeys kept in isolation during the first years of their lives permanently lost the ability to communicate their own pain and suffering to others. Hence, neither isolates nor normally raised monkeys came to their aid when they were given electric shocks. Isolates were equally unable to read other monkeys' feelings; hence, although they could learn to save themselves, isolates never learned to come to the aid of their comrades.

Forensic psychologists have observed that psychopathic killers are sometimes stunningly insensitive to their victims' emotions. The casual reactions of serial killers often stun reporters, investigators, and jurors. Gary Gilmore was interviewed on death row by Larry Schiller, a sympathetic reporter who tried to understand why Gary had killed so casually and suggested some possibilities:

> I believe you had rough breaks. . . . You got into trouble, and had a temper and were impatient, but you weren't a killer.

Something happened. Something turned you into a man who could kill Jensen and Bushnell, some feeling, or emotion, or event. (Mailer, 1979, p. 934)

Gilmore replied, chillingly:

I was always capable of murder. . . . There's a side of me that I don't like. I can become totally devoid of feelings for others, un-emotional. I know I'm doing something grossly fucking wrong. I can still go ahead and do it. (p. 934)

Cousins Angelo Buono and Kenny Bianchi kidnapped a number of young women, raping, torturing, and killing them. During inter-rogation, the serial killers coolly, without feeling, recounted how they conducted the torture. They described, for example, "playing" with Lissa Kastin:

The murder itself went as before, except that Angelo added one new twist, tightening and then slackening the cord, bringing her to the brink of death and back again several times over, de-lighting in the absolute power of it. (O'Brien, 1985, p. 48)

The police interrogators, Sergeants Frank Salerno and Peter Finni-gan, were stunned by this lack of feeling for their victims:

Salerno and Finnigan concealed their revulsion as Kenny re-counted every detail of the killing with no more emotion than someone talking about what he had eaten for lunch. The cool, inflectionless voice; the way Bianchi said "Judy Miller" over and over again, running the syllables together, indifferently, with utter detachment, as though the girl had been a thing, a toy of no consequence – it was chilling and, at last, incompre-hensible. (O'Brien, 1985, p. 285)

One young woman, however – Veronica Compton, a playwright and a poet – found the idea of a killing spree sexually and romanti-cally arousing.

He [Kenny Bianchi] confided to her his pride in having killed so many women. He said that he believed in living for the mo-ment and that his ideal would be to be at one with nature, free as a jungle beast. What was it like, she wanted to know, just to pick out girls at random and have sex with them and kill them?

"Well," Kenny said, "it's kind of like this, Veronica. It's like a kid going down the street and you see all these candy stores and you can pick any candy that you want and you don't have to pay for it and you just take it. You just do what you want. It's the greatest."

They discussed how delightful it would be to go on a killing spree together. Veronica suggested that they live together, kill dozens of people, keep the bodies in the basement, and then commit double suicide. "I know what we could do," she said. "We could cut off their parts and have a collection of cunts, clits, and cocks! We could keep them in jars and take them out to look at them!" (O'Brien, 1985, p. 309)

Compton, Buono, and Bianchi were not without feeling; they took simple delight in the suffering of others. However, they did not share their victims' suffering. The inner "pleasure" of power overrode all possibility of contagion in these monsters.

*Peoples' reactions to the anxious, depressed, or angry*

When you're smiling
When you're smiling
The whole world smiles with you.
  – From a popular song by Fisher, Goodwin, & Shay

It is easy to love people who are cheerful and enthusiastic. Historian Geoffrey Ward (1989), in *A First-Class Temperament*, noted President Franklin Roosevelt's contagious enthusiasm and he recounted Commandant Wilson Brown's memories of the young FDR visiting Brown's barge:

I can see to this day the new assistant secretary-to-be as he strode down the gangplank to the club float with the ease and assurance of an athlete. Tall . . . smiling, Mr. Roosevelt radiated energy and friendliness.

. . . Once aboard the barge [Roosevelt] showed immediately that he was at home on the water. Instead of sitting sedately in the stern sheets as might have been expected, he swarmed over the barge from stem to stern during the passage to the Navy Yard. With exclamations of delight and informed appreciation he went over every inch of the boat from the coxswain's box to the engine room. When she hit the wake of a passing craft and he was doused with spray, he just ducked and laughed and pointed out to his companions how well she rode a wave. Within a few minutes he'd won the hearts of every man of us on board, just as in the years to come he won the hearts of the crew of every ship he set foot on. . . . He demonstrated . . . the invaluable quality of contagious enthusiasm. (pp. 221–222)

Anxiety, of course, is equally contagious (Figure 3.2) – as Somerset Maugham found in his visits with the high-strung Henry James:

When Maugham dined with the Jameses . . . James insisted on walking him to the corner, where he could catch a streetcar back to Boston. This was more than courtesy on the part of James, he thought, for "America seemed to him a strange and terrifying labyrinth in which without his guidance I was bound to get hopelessly lost."

. . . [T]he streetcar came into view. Afraid it would not stop, James began waving frantically when it was still a quarter of a mile away. He urged Maugham to jump on with the greatest agility of which he was capable, and warned him that if he were not careful he would be dragged along, and if not killed, at least mangled and dismembered. Maugham informed him that he was quite accustomed to boarding streetcars. Not American streetcars, James said. They were of a savagery and ruthlessness beyond conception. James' anxiety was contagious, and when the car pulled up Maugham jumped on, and felt that he had miraculously escaped serious injury. He looked back and saw James standing on his short legs, in the middle of the road, still watching the streetcar, until he faded out of sight. (Morgan, 1980, p. 167)

It is probably not surprising that people enjoy being with those who are cheerful: Not only are such people rewarding in themselves, but we tend to catch their emotions. One of our clients, a shy, slightly depressed Japanese woman, noted that when she went to Mills College, she was going to be on the lookout for friends who were "pretty boisterous." "Somehow, I can always play off other people's energy," she noted. Clinical researchers have collected considerable evidence as to the impact that manic, depressed, anxious, and angry people have on those around them. In some of these research reports we find clear evidence of contagion.

Figure 3.2. Cartoon by Feiffer. *Source:* Jules Feiffer, Introduction to *Jules Feiffer's America: From Eisenhower to Reagan,* by Jules Feiffer, edited by Steven Heller. Copyright © 1982 by Jules Feiffer. Reprinted by permission of Alfred A. Knopf, Inc.

An isolated individual does not exist. He who is sad, saddens
others.

                    – Antoine de Saint Exupéry

James Coyne (1976) invited men and women to participate in a
study of the acquaintance process. They were simply to call a woman, located somewhere in Ohio, and chat with her on the telephone for 20 minutes. The woman with whom they chatted was,
unbeknownst to them, either depressed or nondepressed. Dealing
with someone's depression took a toll: Those who spoke with a depressed woman became aware that she was sad, weak, passive, and
in a low mood. They came away from the encounter feeling more
depressed, anxious, and hostile than before, and were not eager to
talk to her again. Subjects who talked to a nondepressed woman naturally did not have such disagreeable reactions.

Mary Howes, Jack Hokanson, and David Lowenstein (1985) investigated how people react to the depressed. Students entering Florida
State University for the first time were assigned a roommate. Before
they entered college, the students took the Beck Depression Inventory; they took it again periodically over the three months they lived
together. Those who had been assigned to live with a mildly depressed roommate themselves became more and more depressed
over time. These findings are a bit unsettling. They suggest that depressed physicians, nurses, and teachers, for example, might have a
depressing effect on their charges, at a time when they are especially
vulnerable.

Novelist Margaret Drabble (1939/1972) depicted the difficulty of
dealing with the depressed:

> When the meal was over, Mrs. Brayanson retired immediately
> to bed. Her lack of interest in life had afflicted them all: it was a
> disease, a mildew, which oppressed even strangers. Simon no-
> ticed that even Christopher had more or less given her up,
> though he had managed to get a faint flicker of a smile once or
> twice during the meal. . . . Her withdrawal from the scene had
> the immediate effect of cheering everybody else up. (p. 312)

Sometimes we see clients who underestimate how vulnerable
people are to contagion. Some who feel they have failed their parents when they were children resolve to "go home" for Christmas
and make it all up to their parents. They plan a long trip to their

parents' home. Once they get there, things may go well for a day or two; then the clients find their resolve fading. They are swept up into the old family pattern again. They find themselves getting furious and shouting at their parents ("Don't tell me to have a good day. I'll have a good day if I feel like it!"), and/or getting depressed, unable to drag themselves out of bed. They leave, feeling that they have done more harm than good, owing their parents even more than before. Vivian Gornick (1987) detailed a typical exchange with her mother. Both began with the best of intentions.

That space. It begins in the middle of my forehead and ends in the middle of my groin. It is, variously, as wide as my body, as narrow as a slit in a fortress wall. On days when thought flows freely or better yet clarifies with effort, it expands gloriously. On days when anxiety and self-pity crowd in, it shrinks, how fast it shrinks! When the space is wide and I occupy it fully, I taste the air, feel the light. I breathe evenly and slowly. I am peaceful and excited, beyond influence or threat. Nothing can touch me. I'm safe. I'm free. I'm thinking. When I lose the battle to think, the boundaries narrow, the air is polluted, the light clouds over. All is vapor and fog, and I have trouble breathing.

Today is promising, tremendously promising. Wherever I go, whatever I see, whatever my eye or ear touches, the space radiates expansion. I want to think. No, I mean today I really want to think. The desire announced itself with the word "concentration."

I go to meet my mother. I'm flying. Flying! I want to give her some of this shiningness bursting in me, siphon into her my immense happiness at being alive. Just because she is my oldest intimate and at this moment I love everybody, even her.

"Oh, Ma! What a day I've had," I say.

"Tell me," she says. "Do you have the rent this month?"

"Ma, listen . . ." I say.

"That review you wrote for the *Times*," she says. "It's for sure they'll pay you?"

"Ma, stop it. Let me tell you what I've been feeling," I say.

"Why aren't you wearing something warmer?" she cries. "It's nearly winter."

The space inside begins to shimmer. The walls collapse inward. I feel breathless. Swallow slowly, I say to myself, slowly.

To my mother I say, "You *do* know how to say the right thing at the right time. It's remarkable, this gift of yours. It quite takes my breath away."

But she doesn't get it. She doesn't know I'm being ironic. Nor does she know she's wiping me out. She doesn't know I take her anxiety personally, feel annihilated by her depression. How can she know this? She doesn't even know I'm there. Were I to tell her that it's death to me, her not knowing I'm there, she would stare at me out of her eyes crowding up with puzzled desolation, this young girl of seventy-seven, and she would cry angrily, "You don't understand! You have never understood!" (pp. 103–104)

Things seem to go best in situations such as these if people recognize how much effort it takes to behave well while resisting getting swept up into a whirlpool of anxiety, anger, or depression. People can usually be on their best behavior for an hour or two a day; after that they have to go back to their hotel and rest up. Having recharged themselves, there is a small prayer of things going well . . . for another hour or two.

## Social-psychological research

### Cross-cultural research: Hysterical contagion

Sentiments, emotions, and ideas possess in crowds a contagious power as intense as that of microbes.
— Gustav Le Bon

Pure truth cannot be assimilated by the crowd; it must be communicated by contagion.
— Henri-Frédéric Amiel

Early sociologists such as Gustav Le Bon (1896) sparked an interest in the "group mind" and the "madness" of crowds. Novelists such as Victor Hugo (1831/1928), in *The Hunchback of Notre-Dame*, reflected their vision of the group mind as a single, sinister entity.

It was no easy matter on that day [the Epiphany and the Festival of Fools] to get into this great hall, though it was then reputed to be the largest room in the world. To the spectators at the windows the palace yard crowded with people had the appearance of a sea, into which five or six streets, like the mouths of so many rivers, disgorged their living streams. . . . Great were the noise and the clamour produced by the cries of some, the laughter of others, and the trampling of the thousands of feet. . . . (p. 12)

The crowd increased every moment, and, like water that rises above its level, began to mount along the walls, to swell about the pillars, to cover the entablatures, the cornices, all the salient points of the architecture, all the rilievos of the sculpture. Accordingly, the weariness, the impatience, the freedom of a day of license, the quarrels occasioned every moment by a sharp elbow or a hobnailed shoe, and the tediousness of long waiting, gave . . . a sharp, surly note to the clamor of the populace, kicked, cuffed, jostled, squeezed, and wedged together almost to suffocation . . . (p. 16)

At this moment the clock struck twelve.

"Aha!" said the whole assembled multitude with one voice . . . Profound silence succeeded; every neck was outstretched, every mouth open, every eye fixed on the marble table; but nothing was to be seen. . . .

They waited one, two, three, five minutes, a quarter of an hour; nothing came. Not a creature appeared either on the platform or on the stage. Meanwhile impatience grew into irritation. Angry words went round, at first, it is true, in a low tone. "The mystery! the mystery!" was faintly muttered. A storm, which as yet only rumbled at a distance, began to gather over the crowd. It was Jehan du Moulin who drew down the first spark.

"Let us instantly have the mystery . . . or I recommend that we should hang the Bailiff of the Palace by way of comedy and morality."

"Well said!" cried the people; "and let us begin with hanging the sergeants!"

. . . The four poor devils turned pale, and began to look at each other. The crowd moved toward them, and they saw the frail wooden balustrade which separated them from the people already bending and giving way to the pressure of the multitude.

The moment was critical. "Down, down with them!" was the cry, which resounded from all sides. (pp. 21–3)

In a second example, Victor Hugo described the excited levity that took over the crowd, as revelers began to compete in making the funniest faces.

> The grimaces began . . . A second and a third grimace succeeded – then another and another, followed by redoubled shouts of laughter and stampings and clatterings of glee. The crowd was seized with a sort of frantic intoxication, a supernatural kind of fascination . . . every human expression, from rage to lechery; all ages . . . a human kaleidoscope.
>
> The orgies became more and more uproarious . . . The great hall was one vast furnace of effrontery and jollity; where every mouth was a cry, every eye a flash, every face a contortion, every individual a posture; all was howling and roaring . . . The lucky Pope of Fools was brought out in triumph . . . the populace instantly recognized him . . . and cried out with one voice: "It is Quasimodo the bell-ringer!" . . . There was no end to their applause. (pp. 46–50)

Since then, sociologists have explored the process of hysterical contagion in a variety of societies. Wen-Shing Tseng and Jing Hsu (1980) defined mass hysteria as

> a sociocultural-psychological phenomenon in which a group of people, through social contagion, collectively manifest psychological disorders within a brief period of time. (p. 77)

In Malaysia, to take one example, epidemic hysteria has been endemic from time immemorial. Schoolchildren in rural secondary schools often fall prey to hysterical laughter and depression. In 1971, 30 men and women suddenly became delirious, laughing and shouting at intervals. Governmental authorities concluded that the spirits had possessed the victims to punish them for failing to offer thanks at a *keramat* (shrine), where they had sought winning numbers in a four-digit lottery. *Bomohs* (Malay native healers) were summoned, sacrifices and mass prayers were offered, and the offended spirits were pacified; the contagious laughing stopped. Unfortunately, local newspapers had dramatically publicized the outbreak, so the infection quickly spread to nearby schools (Teoh, Soewondo, & Sidharta, 1975).

In East Africa, tribesmen were infected with hysterical laughter and crying (Ebrahim, 1968). In the New Guinea Highlands, settlers fell prey to anger, giddiness, and sexual acting out (Reay, 1960). In Singapore in 1973, workers at a large television factory suddenly became hysterical. Some had seizures – they fell into a trance state, screamed and cried, sweated, and struggled violently (swinging their upper limbs and kicking about). More became frightened; they complained of dizziness, numbness, and faintness. Physicians gave the workers Valium and chlorpromazine and sent them home. They calmed down, but the hysteria quickly spread to other factories (Chew, Phoon, & Mae-Lim, 1976).

Wen-Shing Tseng and Jing Hsu (1980) argued that people are most vulnerable to hysterical contagion when they are under stress. Such acting out allows them to solve certain cultural problems. Collective emotional outbursts may bring drama and excitement into otherwise monotonous lives. They may allow people to express their simmering resentments, provide a cultural "time-out" when they can take a vacation from ordinary life, and help them adapt to a new culture (as during religious conversions). (We wish to thank Lois Yamuchi for sharing her research on this topic with us.)

Mass hysteria does not only occur in third-world countries and "primitive" tribes. Novelist Katherine Anne Porter had a lifelong interest in modern-day forms of hysteria. Her biographer wrote:

> Although Porter said publicly that her part of Texas was an ironclad Protestant region still untainted by "petty middle class puritanism" and that "the petty middle class of fundamentalists who saw no difference between wine-drinking, dancing, card-playing and adultery had not yet got altogether the upper hand," in private she admitted that it was "poxed with teetotalitarians who seemed to hold that every human activity except breathing was a sin."
>
> The atmosphere affected her profoundly and she was haunted always by her childhood memories – by the tangible devil, whom she thought of as a creature dressed in red who lived in her grandmother's closet; by the revival meetings with the "singing and praying and shouting and tears and sacred joy" and the mourners' bench for repentant sinners. She remembered one old lady . . . . who came from the meetings so overwrought that she used to throw the silver candlesticks around. Such occasions left Porter with a deep interest in mass hysteria and became her touchstone for political and religious frenzy.

When she watched a Hitler rally in Berlin, she said it reminded her of a Methodist revival meeting. (Givner, 1982, pp. 184–185)

The now legendary radio broadcast by Orson Welles of H. G. Wells's *The War of the Worlds* caused a wave of panic across America. An estimated 32 million Americans heard this CBS broadcast of October 30, 1938. Thousands telephoned family and friends to warn them of the attack from Mars, fell to their knees in prayer, or packed up their families and drove aimlessly for miles, not knowing where they were headed (Cantril, 1940).

In the crowd, herd, or gang, it is a mass-mind that operates – which is to say, a mind without subtlety, a mind without compassion, a mind, finally, uncivilized.

– Robert Lindner

In 1962, Alan Kerckhoff and Kurt Back (1968) watched a drama unfold. The first reports on the six o'clock news suggested that a mysterious epidemic had hit Montana Mills:

Officials of Montana Mills shut down their Strongsville plant this afternoon because of a mysterious sickness.

According to a report just in from Strongsville General Hospital, at least ten women and one man were admitted for treatment. Reports describe symptoms as severe nausea and breaking out over the body.

Indications are that some kind of insect was in a shipment of cloth that arrived from England at the plant today. And at the moment the bug is blamed for the outbreak of sickness. (p. 3)

The mysterious illness soon raced through the plant. In a few weeks, more than 59 women and 3 men in the 965-person plant were stricken with the mysterious illness, characterized by panic, anxiety, nausea, and weakness. Experts from the U. S. Public Health Service Communicable Disease Center and University entomologists were brought in. The vast textile plant was vacuumed for specimens. The total catch consisted of one black ant, a housefly, a couple of gnats, a small beetle, and one mite (a chigger). Nonetheless, the plant was fumigated. In the end, scientists concluded that hysterical contagion had sparked the epidemic.

To find out which workers had been susceptible to hysterical contagion, and why, Kerckhoff and Back conducted a series of interviews. They talked to those who had fallen ill, to those who had not, and to those who had witnessed the epidemic; they also studied medical records. Their conclusions were as follows:

1. Workers were most likely to catch the "disease" if they had been under severe stress at the time the "epidemic" struck. Women were most susceptible if their marriages were in trouble, if they were responsible for supporting their families, felt trapped, and were overworked and exhausted at the time the epidemic hit. Workers were especially vulnerable if they lacked coping skills. Women did not catch the disease if they were under stress, but did not have the "luxury" of falling ill. Women who had job security quickly succumbed. Women who reported they needed a job badly, who felt insecure about their abilities, were straining to produce, who felt obligated to keep their job at any cost, and were worried about being laid off did not get sick.

2. Initially, five of the six earliest victims were social isolates; they had a history of "nervousness" and fainting. Once the panic began to spread, however, workers were most likely to catch the disease if they had close emotional ties with the other "infected" workers. Women who were members of other social groups, social isolates, or outsiders (either because they were black, new at the plant, or because their workstations separated them geographically from the victims) did not get sick. Many such women, in fact, were often so little touched by the epidemic that they were skeptical that an "epidemic" had ever existed.

*Mimicry mania.* Anthropologists have also observed "arctic hysteria" or "mimicry mania" in northern Asia. M. A. Czaplicka (1914), for example, summarizes several reports:

> In a Middle Vil[yui River] village Maak [1883] knew many Yakut women suffering from a very common disease which shows itself in the patients imitating all the gestures and words of bystanders, whatever their meaning, which was sometimes quite obscene.
>
> During the early days of his travels in the Yakut province, Jochelson [1900] was disagreeably struck by the fact that, when he was stopping in certain *yurta* ('houses'), the women, whom he knew could not speak Russian, would repeat in broken language what he and his companions had been saying. When he

showed his displeasure by severe glances, he was told that he should not mind, for the women were only *omüraks*.

Unintentional visual suggestion shows itself in cases in which, when some of the younger people begin to dance, all the villagers, even the oldest, follow their example. Jochelson reports an instance of an old woman quite unable to stand alone, who on such an occasion stood up and began to dance without assistance until she fell exhausted. (p. 810)

Priklonski [1890] describes some instances of this mimicry mania in the Yakutsk territory. One was the case of a barber in Verkhoyansk, and another occurred on an Amur steamer, where all the people on board were amusing themselves at the expense of a *merak* (a man suffering from *ämürakh*). They pretended to be throwing things overboard into the water, and the *merak* divested himself of all his property to do the same. A third case was observed in Olëkminsk on the Lena. A hysterical woman, who at ordinary times was quite modest and even shy, was being tormented during an attack of *ämürakh* by a number of people who made indecent gestures, all of which she imitated. He quotes also an episode which was related to him by Dr. Kashin, who was much interested in this disease. Once, during a parade of the 3rd Battalion of the Trans-Baikal Cossacks, a regiment composed entirely of natives, the soldiers began to repeat the words of command. The Colonel grew angry and swore volubly at the men; but the more he swore, the livelier was the chorus of soldiers repeating his curses after him. (p. 313)

Relief may be equally contagious. Lyall Watson (1976) describes the case of an Indonesian man who runs *amok* once or twice a month. He would be seized by a sudden vision and run through the village, his eyes bulging and his hair standing on end. In the temple he would alternately scream defiance, hack at the air in panic, or crouch, whimpering in pain. Finally, he was emotionally spent. There was a sudden stillness, and then:

Naum stood and looked at the crowd on the beach. He smiled tentatively. The people smiled back. Naum giggled, and a wave of response moved through the crowd. Naum grinned. The people beamed. Naum offered a laugh, and it came out rather high and shaky, as though it were something he had never tried before. . . . Then Naum burst into a great roar of laughter, a huge sound that flooded out on a tide of release, and suddenly all the others were laughing together, holding on to each other, staggering around the beach, collapsing in heaps, laughing until the tears ran down their cheeks. (p. 132)

## Experimental social-psychological research

As Louis XVI said, when surrounded by a fierce mob, "Am I
afraid? Feel my pulse." So a man may intensely hate another,
but until his bodily frame is affected, he cannot be said to be
enraged.
                                          – Charles Darwin

Surely the best known study of emotional contagion by social psychologists is the classic work by Stanley Schachter and Jerome Singer (1962). The authors argued that both mind and body make a critical contribution to emotional experience: Cognitive factors determine the specific emotion that people feel; the level of ANS arousal determines how intensely they feel what they feel. Schachter and Singer argued that when people become aroused, they search for an appropriate label for their feelings. A quick appraisal of the situation allows them to label their feelings. Interestingly, Thomas Mann (1969), in his story of *The Magic Mountain,* anticipated such a link between emotion and physical symptoms when describing Hans Castorp's reactions to some symptoms he thought signaled tuberculosis. (In actuality, Castorp was undoubtedly experiencing the effects of high altitude at the sanitorium in Switzerland where he was residing.)

> "If I only knew," Hans Castorp went on, and laid his hands like a lover on his heart, "if I only knew why I have palpitations the whole time – it is very disquieting; I keep thinking about it. For, you see, a person ordinarily has palpitations of the heart when he is frightened, or when he is looking forward to some great joy. But when the heart palpitates all by itself, without any reason, senselessly, of its own accord, so to speak, I feel that's uncanny. . . . You keep trying to find an explanation for them, an emotion to account for them, a feeling of joy or pain, which would, so to speak, justify them." (pp. 71–72)

Schachter and Singer (1962) tested their theory in an ingenious series of experiments.

1. *Manipulating physiological arousal.* Presumably, people experience emotion only when they are physiologically aroused. Thus, the authors' first step was to inject some subjects with the drug "Suproxin" (actually adrenalin), which produced a pounding heart, trembling hands, and accelerated breathing. They injected other subjects with a placebo.

2. *Manipulating an appropriate explanation.* According to the authors, people only feel what it is appropriate to feel. If they are surrounded by others who are euphoric – say, caught up in a wild, abandoned water fight – they will assume it is appropriate to feel happy. If they are surrounded by people who are furious, it is appropriate to be angry. On the other hand, if they are in a doctor's examination room and he asks them to describe their symptoms, they will probably tend to think about them in physical terms. In the second phase of the experiment, then, Schachter and Singer attempted to manipulate subjects' explanations of any arousal they might experience. Subjects were assigned to one of three experimental conditions: In the informed condition, they were alerted to exactly what they would feel physiologically and why; in the ignorant condition, they were given no explanation for whatever feelings they were to experience; and in the misinformed condition, they were told they would experience symptoms very different from those they in fact were to experience (i.e., that their feet would feel numb, they would have an itching sensation over parts of their body, and they would get a slight headache). In the first condition, then, subjects had a perfectly good explanation for what was about to happen to them; in the other two conditions, they did not. They had to look to their own thoughts and to the external setting for clues.

3. *Producing an emotion.* Next, the experimenters arranged for the subjects to be placed in a setting in which it was easy to catch either a euphoric or an angry emotion at the time the drugs or placebo began to take effect. They did this in the following way. In the euphoria condition, subjects were assigned to interact with an actor who acted giddy and silly. In the angry condition, they interacted with one who acted angry and resentful. The authors, then, assumed that, under the right conditions, *subjects might "catch" the targets' emotional reactions.*

4. *Assessing emotion.* Schachter and Singer measured their subjects' emotional states in two ways. First, they asked subjects to complete a standard self-report measure, and asked them how euphoric or angry they felt and whether they had experienced heart palpita-

tions or tremor. Second, while all this was going on, observers watched the subjects from behind a one-way mirror and rated how euphoric or angry the subjects acted.

Schachter and Singer's results supported their two-component theory. The subjects who had everything going for them – those who were in a setting in which it was appropriate to feel euphoria or anger *and* who were physiologically aroused – were most likely to catch the confederates' emotions. The authors could have interpreted these data in a relatively conservative way, arguing that:

1. both cognitive and physiological factors may contribute to emotion;
2. sometimes, cognition may *follow* physiological arousal; and
3. people may assess the intensity of their feelings, in part, by observing how stirred up they are physiologically.

Had they stopped with these conclusions, their theory would have been subject to very little criticism; however, they went further, making a number of controversial assertions. They argued, for example, that:

1. cognition *always* follows physiological arousal;
2. cognition and physiological arousal are *indispensable* aspects of an emotional experience;
3. neurochemical differences between emotions are nonexistent or unimportant; and
4. *any* emotional label can be attached to a given state of arousal – which one is attached depends on the situation.

Additional evidence for the two-component theory of emotion comes from Stanley Schachter and Ladd Wheeler (1962) and from George Hohmann (1966).

Two decades later, of course, critics have pointed out a series of flaws in Schachter and Singer's bold proposals. (See Carlson & Hatfield, 1992, for a review of the critics' arguments; see also Marshall & Zimbardo, 1979; Maslach, 1979.) What interests us here is not the controversy, but rather the evidence in this experiment that people do tend to catch euphoria and anger, plus its clues as to how this process of contagion might operate.

More recently, social psychologists have explored the process of emotional contagion in a romantic setting (Snyder, Tanke, & Berscheid, 1977). Men and women at the University of Minnesota were invited to participate in a study of the acquaintance process. Couples-to-be were always directed to different rooms so they would not bump into one another before the experiment began. The experimenter explained that they would be getting acquainted with one another over the telephone. Before the conversation began, each man was given a Polaroid snapshot of his partner, along with some biographical information; in truth, however, the snapshot was *not* of his partner but of either a good-looking or a homely woman. Each man was then asked for his first impression of his intended partner. Men who thought they were paired with an attractive woman expected her to be sociable, poised, humorous, and socially adept; those who thought they were paired with a homely woman anticipated that she would be unsociable, awkward, serious, and socially inept. Such results are not surprising: It has long been known that good-looking people make more positive first impressions than homely ones (Hatfield & Sprecher, 1986).

What was startling was that the men's expectations had a dramatic impact on the *women's* behavior – in the short space of a telephone call. Men thought their partners were unusually good-looking or unattractive; in fact, of course, the women on the other end of the line varied greatly in appearance. Nonetheless, within the space of a telephone conversation, women became what men expected them to be. After the telephone conversation, judges were asked to listen to tapes of the women's portion of the conversation and to guess what the women were like. Women who had been addressed as if they were beauties soon had begun to sound like them, becoming unusually "animated," "confident," and "adept." Those spoken to as though they were homely soon began acting that way, becoming withdrawn, lacking in confidence, and awkward. Men's expectations were now reflected in women's behavior.

How did this happen? What had transpired? When the men's portion of the conversation was analyzed, it was found that those who thought they were talking to beautiful women were more sociable, sexually warm, interesting, independent, sexually permissive, bold, outgoing, humorous, and socially adept than the men who thought they were talking to a homely woman. The men assigned to "attractive" women were also more comfortable, enjoyed themselves more, liked their partners more, took the initiative more often, and used their voices more effectively. In a nutshell, the men who thought they had attractive partners tried harder. Undoubtedly, this behavior caused the women to try harder in return. If the stereotypes held by the men became reality within only 10 minutes of a telephone conversation, one can imagine what happens over several years.

Ladd Wheeler (1966) and other social psychologists have found that group members seem particularly susceptible to catching the laughter (Leventhal & Mace, 1970), fear, and panicky behavior of others (Schachter & Singer, 1962). Wheeler (1966) attempted to distinguish "true" contagion (the rapid transfer of emotion from one person to others in the group) from other types of social influence, such as conformity, conscious imitation and responsiveness to social pressure, and social facilitation. He took the position that contagion was distinct from these other forms of influence in that it required a preexisting approach–avoidance conflict. Presumably, person $X$ was conflicted between the instigation to perform $B_n$ (say, to get angry and yell at a noisy neighbor) and the internal restraints against the performance of $B_n$. When $X$ saw person $Y$ yell at the inconsiderate neighbor, $X$ was likely to quickly catch $Y$'s emotion and imitate $Y$'s hostile actions; that is, person $Y$'s behavior disinhibited person $X$'s hostility toward the inconsiderate neighbor.

An example of this process: When Elaine Hatfield first began teaching at the University of Minnesota, she, Elliot Aronson, and Dana Bramel team-taught a huge Introductory Social Psychology course. Now and then, shortly after the lecturer began to shout out his lecture in the large hall, one student, A. G., would realize he was uncomfortable, stand up, and painstakingly begin to rearrange his underwear. A few students would usually titter in embarrassment for A. G. as the inevitable happened. One week, after the lecture, the three professors, carried away by silliness, built joke upon joke on speculations as to what A. G. had in mind by his performance. The next week, shortly after Hatfield began her lecture, A. G. again stood up. A few students began to giggle, anticipating his next move. Elaine was horror-struck: All the jokes of the previous week came back to her, and she became terrified she would begin to giggle. She began to give herself a stern lecture as she tried to continue her lecture. "This is unprofessional! It would be horrible to humiliate a student in front of 500 other students by laughing! Elliot and Dana would never behave so heartlessly." Elaine looked over to catch the stern gazes of Elliot and Dana, in hopes of keeping her smiles in check – only Elliot wasn't behaving "professionally": Tears of laughter were running down his cheek at the recognition of Elaine's attempts at suppressed merriment. That was too much. Now Elaine began to laugh uncontrollably and the class followed suit. Only A. G. remained unperturbed, carefully tugging his wayward underwear from various cracks and crevices.

Wheeler's disinhibition model of emotional contagion is an interesting variation on the notion espoused here that contagion is a normal, coordinating component of a wide variety of social interactions. Thus, the disinhibition model alerts us to the fact that socialization can lead to a masking or suppression of the normal or rudimentary behavioral and cognitive effects of emotional contagion.

We see, then, that there is considerable evidence that in a variety of cultures, as well as our own, people do tend to catch the emotions of others.

**Historical research**

Were our forebears as sensitive to others' emotions and as likely to catch them as we are? Theorists are divided. Before the Enlightenment of the 18th century most people neither read nor wrote; thus, it is not easy for historians to answer such questions. Some argue that emotional sensitivity, compassion, and empathy were very scarce commodities before the modern age. Lawrence Stone (1977), in his trailblazing *The Family, Sex, and Marriage: In England 1500–1800*, argued that even the closest of family relationships involved little ability to feel oneself into the emotions of others. The English of that era, he insisted, tended to display "suspicion towards others, proneness to violence, and an incapacity to develop strong emotional ties to any one individual" (p. 409). Stone's challenging explorations have generated lively debates among historians and many other scholars. Were people as remote, their emotions as crude and ugly, as he said? Some historians insist that there was more preindustrial compassion than Stone admits (Gadlin, 1977; Ladurie, 1979; Taylor, 1989).

The idea that kindness to others, emotional closeness, and warmth may be quite new goals in human history has been given further weight by the great art historian Kenneth Clark. Lord Clark (1969) singled out as "the greatest achievement of the nineteenth century" – a moment ago in historical time – an idea often assumed to have been around forever: that feeling of responsibility to other people we call "humanitarianism." Clark, in his *Civilisation*, went on to indicate how new a notion it was:

> We are so much accustomed to the humanitarian outlook that we forget how little it counted in earlier ages of civilisation. Ask any decent person in England or America what he thinks matters most in human conduct: five to one his answer will be 'kindness'. It's not a word that would have crossed the lips of any of the earlier heroes of this series. If you had asked St. Francis what mattered in life, he would, we know, have answered 'chastity, obedience and poverty'; if you had asked Dante or Michelangelo they might have answered 'disdain of baseness and injustice'; if you had asked Goethe, he would have said 'to live in the whole and the beautiful'. But kindness, never. Our ancestors didn't use the word, and they did not greatly value the quality. (p. 329)

The development of kindness in human life was inhibited by the ghastly conditions under which most humans labored before the coming of the Industrial Revolution – conditions that led to early death, nearly constant misery, and a dark view of earthly existence. It is small wonder that promises of the afterlife seemed so appealing to the poor people who lived like the peasants of early modern France, portrayed in Robert Darnton's (1984) *The Great Cat Massacre*. Noting that family size was kept down by the ubiquity of death – of the mother and of her babies during childbirth and infancy – Darnton offered this general picture of rural life in the 17th and early 18th centuries:

> Stillborn children, called *chrissons*, were sometimes buried casually, in anonymous collective graves. Infants were sometimes smothered by their parents in bed – a rather common accident, judging by episcopal edicts forbidding parents to sleep with children who had not reached their first birthdays. Whole families crowded into one or two beds and surrounded themselves with livestock in order to keep warm. So children became participant observers of their parents' sexual activities. No one thought of them as innocent creatures or of childhood itself as a distinct phase of life, clearly distinguishable from adolescence, youth, and adulthood by special styles of dress and behavior. Children labored alongside their parents almost as

soon as they could walk, and they joined the adult labor force as farm hands, servants, and apprentices as soon as they reached their teens.

The peasants of early modern France inhabited a world of step-mothers and orphans, of inexorable, unending toil, and of brutal emotions, both raw and repressed. The human condition has changed so much since then that we can hardly imagine the way it appeared to people whose lives really were nasty, brutish, and short. (pp. 27–29)

Darnton and Stone may have a somewhat bleaker view of the crudity of emotional life as the norm for the premodern past than some other historians; yet it is quite clear that there exists precious little evidence of kindness as a social standard before 1700 – again, historically only yesterday. Kindness is a relatively new idea in history, and it may require the capacity to empathize with the suffering of others and to pick up their sorrow. Were people of the preindustrial West, partly because of the ubiquity of early death, perhaps encouraged to numb themselves to the hardships of others and to turn down their emotions of sympathy?

In any case, there is evidence that, during many historical periods, people were fairly insensitive to suffering around them and relatively immune to that kind of emotional contagion. For example, in 1466 in Rome, Pope Paul II initiated the February Carnival, a race run on the Corso, a narrow ribbon of road that ran from the Piazza del Popolo to the Piazza Venezia in the Holy City. To our eyes, the Carnival may seem a barbaric celebration:

The Carnival was, even after its most barbarous customs were suspended by fiat, a peculiar mixture of glamour and cruelty. Even some of its participants were terminally divided between believing the Carnival was an occasion of innocent vivacity and condemning it as the epitome of masked wickedness. Horses were at one time whipped by little boys, and donkeys and buffaloes viciously goaded by men on horseback; and cripples and hunchbacks, naked old men, and despised Jews were made to run for sport. (Harrison, 1989, pp. 227–228)

Four centuries later, in the same city, Charles Dickens attended a public execution. He reported that, at the beheading, the crowd "counted the drops of blood that spurted out of the neck of the executed man in order to bet that number on the lottery; [Dickens] was naturally appalled" (Harrison, 1989, p. 325). In cases like this – as in lynchings, cat massacres (Darnton, 1984), and guillotinings – contagion becomes complex! Spectators, though not catching the suffering of the executed, may well be picking up the pleasure, excitement, and anger of the mob around them. As the preceding examples suggest, if people lacked empathy for the woe of others, contagion seemed plentiful enough when it came to the rougher and wilder emotions of fear, anger, and hatred.

We are not, unfortunately, limited to the years before the beginnings of the material advances of the modern era (usually located by historians at the birth of the Industrial Revolution in mid-18th-century England) to discover the ways in which tyrannies, religious paranoias, general repression, and group hatreds have blighted human existence. In our own time, in all corners of the world (including some glittering, advanced, and sophisticated symbols of Western "civilization"), we have seen one horrifying instance after another of the ways in which the nightmarish conditions of the external world can overwhelm ideas of human compassion and emotional sensitivity, unleashing pestilences of hatred and fear. Consider the testimony of Hermann Friedrich Graebe, sworn on November 10, 1945, at Wiesbaden, Germany.

On 5 October 1942, when I visited the building office at Dubno, my foreman Hubert Moennikes of 21 Aussenmuehlenweg, Hamburg-Haarburg, told me that in the vicinity of the site, Jews from Dubno had been shot in three large pits, each about 30 meters long and 3 meters deep. About 1500 persons had been killed daily. All of the 5000 Jews who had still been living in Dubno before the pogrom were to be liquidated. As the shootings had taken place in his presence he was still much upset.

Thereupon I drove to the site, accompanied by Moennikes, and saw near it great mounds of earth, about 30 meters long and 2 meters high. Several trucks stood in front of the mounds. Armed Ukrainian militia drove the people off the trucks under the supervision of an SS-man. The militia men acted as guards on the trucks and drove them to and from the pit. All these people had the regulation yellow patches on the front and back of their clothes, and thus could be recognized as Jews.

Moennikes and I went directly to the pits. Nobody bothered us. Now I heard rifle shots in quick succession, from behind one of the earth mounds. The people who had got off the trucks – men, women, and children of all ages – had to undress upon the order of an SS-man, who carried a riding or dog whip. They had to put down their clothes in fixed places, sorted according to shoes, top clothing and underclothing. Without screaming or weeping, these people undressed, stood around in family groups, kissed each other, said farewells and waited for a sign from another SS-man, who stood near the pit, also with a whip in his hand. During the 15 minutes that I stood near the pit I heard no complaint or plea for mercy. I watched a family of about 8 persons, a man and woman, both about 50 with their children of about 1, 8 and 10, and two grown-up daughters of about 20 to 24. An old woman with snow-white hair was holding the one-year-old child in her arms and singing to it, and tickling it. The child was cooing with delight. The couple were looking on with tears in their eyes. The father was holding the hand of a boy about 10 years old and speaking to him softly; the boy was fighting his tears. The father pointed toward the sky, stroked his head, and seemed to explain something to him. At that moment the SS-man at the pit shouted something to his comrade. The latter counted off about 20 persons and instructed them to go behind the earth mound. Among them was the family, which I have mentioned. I well remember a girl, slim and with black hair, who, as she passed close to me, pointed to herself and said, "23." I walked around the mound, and found myself confronted by a tremendous grave. People were closely wedged together and lying on top of each other so that only their heads were visible. Nearly all had blood running over their shoulders from their heads. Some of the people shot were still moving. Some were lifting their arms and turning their heads to show that they were still alive. The pit was already $2/3$ full. I estimated that it already contained about 1000 people. I looked for the man who did the shooting. He was an SS-man, who sat at the edge of the narrow end of the pit, his feet dangling into the pit. He had a tommy gun on his knees and was smoking a cigarette. The people, completely naked, went down some steps which were cut in the clay wall of the pit and clambered over the heads of the people lying there, to the place to which the SS-man directed them. They lay down in front of the dead or injured people; some caressed those who were still alive and spoke to them in a low voice. Then I heard a series of shots. I looked into the pit and saw that the bodies were twitching or the heads lying already motionless on top of the bodies that lay before them. Blood was running from their necks. I was surprised that I was not ordered away, but I saw that there were two or three postmen in uniform nearby. The next batch was approaching already. They went down into the pit, lined themselves up against the previous victims and were shot.

. . . On the morning of the next day, when I again visited the site, I saw about 30 naked people lying near the pit – about 30 to 50 meters away from it. Some of them were still alive; they looked straight in front of them with a fixed stare and seemed to notice neither the chilliness of the morning nor the workers of my firm who stood around. A girl of about 20 spoke to me and asked me to give her clothes, and help her escape. At that moment we heard a fast car approach and I noticed that it was an SS-detail. I moved away to my site. Ten minutes later we heard shots from the vicinity of the pit. The Jews still alive had been ordered to throw the corpses into the pit – then they had themselves to lie down in this to be shot in the neck.

I make the above statement at Wiesbaden, Germany, on 10th November 1945. I swear before God that this is the absolute truth.

– Hermann Friedrich Graebe
(Quoted in Arendt, 1962, pp. 1071–1073)

The Holocaust, the plague of hatred that culminated in the systematic murder of six million Jews by Nazi Germany, has come to stand as the central symbol for the multiple horrors of this, the 20th century. This has been so because the perpetrator could never be dismissed as a "backward" country. How could it have happened anywhere, let alone in a nation so central to the highest and most splendid creative achievements of Western civilization? In the sublime realm of music, for instance, Germany and Austria had given us the two giants of the early 18th century, Johann Sebastian Bach and Georg Friedrich Handel. From these societies also emerged the twin wonders of the late 18th century, Franz Josef Haydn and Wolfgang Amadeus Mozart. (Is anyone in the world so universally loved today as Mozart? Even reverence for Jesus cannot make a claim of universality equal to that for Mozart.) The transition to 19th-century Romanticism was shaped by Ludwig van Beethoven and Franz

Schubert, to be followed later in the century by such geniuses as Felix Mendelssohn, Robert Schumann, Richard Wagner, Johannes Brahms, Gustav Mahler, and a host of others. In philosophy, Germany had given the 19th-century world Goethe, Heine, Schiller, Schopenhauer, Hegel, Marx, Nietzsche, and Freud, among others. In the nightmare of Hitler's Germany, where does one begin to talk about human compassion, empathy, and emotional resonance? To ask such questions borders on obscenity, but we must note on its reverse side the ease with which hatred and fear can be spread.

Sad to say, Germany has not been alone in producing horrific events in our century on such a scale as to render irrelevant all issues excepting survival and the avoidance of torture and pain. Untold millions were murdered in the Soviet Union during the years of Stalin's rule. Millions more were obliterated during the tyrannies in China of both the right-wing Chiang Kai-shek and the Communist Mao Tse-tung. This century has also witnessed the unrelenting cruelty and bloodshed of two World Wars, the Korean and Vietnam wars, the Iran of both the Shah and the Ayatollah, the Iraq of Saddam Hussein, apartheid-ridden South Africa, the "disappeared" in Pinochet's Chile, Protestants' and Catholics' continued mutual destruction in Northern Ireland, tribal slaughter in Biafra, starvation and cynicism in Ethiopia, random bloodshed on the streets of most American cities, terrorism everywhere, and on and on and on. For billions of people, 20th-century life has been shaped by the omnipresence of dark emotions that grow quickly from a virus into a plague.

Historians have observed that, in many eras, fear, hysterical grief, and anger have swept through communities (Rude, 1981). Examining a few instances of emotional contagion on a mass scale in the past may further enrich our discussion of the phenomenon.

## The dancing manias of the Middle Ages

In the Middle Ages, in the wake of the Black Death, dancing manias, redolent of mass hysteria, swept throughout Europe. Harold Klawans (1990) set the scene of generalized "sorrow and anxiety" which drove people "to the point of hysteria":

> [The bubonic plague, the infamous Black Death,] appeared [in the 12th century,] an illness far worse than any of the others. . . .
> It was an epidemic of unprecedented proportions that broke

over Europe in a great wave. Entire villages were exterminated. Fields became neglected. Soon famine complicated the pestilence. And just as the plague receded and the population and economy began to recover, another wave struck.

From 1119 to 1340 – a period of 221 years – the plague ravaged Italy, for example, sixteen times. No words can fully describe its horrors, but the people who witnessed them, who lived in those days so full of the uncertainty of life, of sorrow, and of anxiety, were driven to the point of hysteria.

It was at that point that the dancing mania began and spread like a contagion. Today, most historians view this phenomenon as a form of mass hysteria. (pp. 236–237)

One writer (reported in Hecker, 1837/1970) described the 12th-century scene this way:

The effects of the *Black Death* had not yet subsided and the graves of millions of its victims were scarcely closed, when a strange delusion arose in Germany, which took possession of the minds of men, and, in spite of the divinity of our nature, hurried away body and soul into the magic circle of hellish superstition. It was a convulsion which in the most extraordinary manner infuriated the human frame, and excited the astonishment of contemporaries for more than two centuries, since which time it has never reappeared. It was called the dance of St. John or of St. Vitus, on account of the Bacchantic leaps by which it was characterized, and which gave to those affected, while performing their wild dance, and screaming and foaming with fury, all the appearance of persons possessed. It did not remain confined to particular localities, but was propagated by the sight of the sufferers, like a demoniacal epidemic, over the whole of Germany and the neighboring countries to the northwest, which were already prepared for its reception by the prevailing opinions of the times.

So early as the year 1374, assemblages of men and women were seen at Aix-la-Chapelle who had come out of Germany, and who, united by one common delusion, exhibited to the public both in the streets and in the churches the following strange spectacle. They formed circles hand in hand, and appearing to have lost all control over their senses, continued dancing, regardless of the by-standers, for hours together in wild delirium, until at length they fell to the ground in a state of exhaustion. They then complained of extreme oppression, and groaned as if in the agonies of death, until they were swathed in cloths bound tightly round their waists, upon which they again recovered, and remained free from complaint until the next attack. This practice of swathing was resorted to on account of the tympany which followed these spasmodic ravings, but the by-standers frequently relieved patients in a less artificial manner, by thumping and trampling upon the parts affected. While dancing they neither saw nor heard, being insensible to external impressions through the senses, but were haunted by visions, their fancies conjuring up spirits whose names they shrieked out; and some of them afterward asserted that they felt as if they had been immersed in a stream of blood, which obligated them to leap so high. Others, during the paroxysm, saw the heavens open and the Saviour enthroned with the Virgin Mary, according as the religious notions of the age were strangely and variously reflected in their imaginations.

Where the disease was completely developed, the attack commenced with epileptic convulsions. (pp. 1–2)

The dancing mania spread from town to town. In Cologne, 500 joined the wild revels; in Metz, 1,100 danced. Priests tried to exorcise the devils. Sufferers traveled to the Tomb of Saint Vitus in southern France to be cured. Paracelsus, a 16th-century physician and alchemist, devised a harsh but effective treatment for the dancing mania: He dunked the victims in cold water, forced them to fast, and condemned them to solitary confinement. The hysterical outbreaks began to subside.

The historical record abounds in descriptions of mass emotional effusions inspired by superstition and charismatic demagogues. (Modern-day tent and TV evangelists are masters of the art of contagion, as were such orators as Adolph Hitler.) However, even supposedly "reasonable" folk are not immune to the spread – as witness the next case from "The Age of Reason."

## The great fear of 1789

In the 18th century, the *philosophes* of the Enlightenment championed the cause of science and reason over ignorance, superstition, and tyranny. Much intellectual leadership came from such French writers as Voltaire, Montesquieu, Rousseau, and Diderot, who challenged the traditional legal, moral, hierarchical, and religious foundations of French society. By 1789, large sections of France's professional and middle classes had been converted to these revolutionary ideas, and they became active in trying to achieve the changes in French society that they thought necessary. In fact, some of these advocates of reason began to try to force social change.

Reason and persuasion soon gave way to hate and terror. Rumors began to circulate that the Royal Court and aristocracy were plotting to take over Paris by counterforce. People fled Paris in fear. As they trudged along country roads on their way to the French countryside, they spread rumors of an impending assault on the provinces by a mercenary army of criminals and foreigners in the pay of the aristocracy.

France became gripped by an almost universal panic. Fear bred fear. Local authorities and citizens became convinced that the criminal army was not just on the march, but was at the door. This led to the breakdown of local government, the arming of the poor, and food riots, and furnished a dramatic impetus to revolution in the provinces (Bernstein, 1990; Cook, 1974; Headley, 1971; Lefebvre, 1973).

After the storming of the Bastille in 1789, historians described the years which later ensued as the Reign of Terror – a term suggesting that emotional contagion may have a life well beyond the walls of the laboratory.

## The New York City riots of 1863

New York City in the hot summer of 1863 was a place of extremes. The Civil War had brought ever greater wealth to a few and increasing poverty to many. Wartime inflation eroded the buying power of the poor. The city's struggling immigrant population lived in rundown, crowded tenements. Immigrants, especially the Irish, were outraged at the use of blacks to replace striking Irish longshoremen.

New York was an antiwar city, controlled by a local Democratic political machine, which had lost power and influence to the national Republican "war" party. The city's Democratic press and politicians skillfully played up the theme that Northern white workers were betraying their own best interests by fighting to free slaves who would then compete for their jobs.

In the midst of this, a national military draft commenced during the summer of 1863. The new law permitted a commutation of military service for anyone who could pay a $300 fee. This set the stage for viewing the draft as a symbol of rich over poor, native over immigrant, Republican over Democrat, national over local government.

The first 1,236 names of New York City drafted men appeared in the morning papers at the same time that casualty lists from Gettysburg, the bloodiest battle ever fought on the North American continent, were posted around the city. Early the next morning, men, women, and boys began to move along streets carrying the weapons of the poor – crowbars and clubs. Mobs quickly formed and grew, caught up in and carried away with anger.

Four days of subsequent uncontrolled violence – including the lynching and burning of blacks – left 119 persons dead and 306 injured. Forty-three regiments of union troops had to be stationed in and around the city to ensure order (Church, 1964; McCague, 1968).

## The era of mass media

Research on emotional contagion has focused on the effect of interpersonal interactions; there is, however, historical evidence to suggest that the dissemination of emotions does not always require direct physical contact or proximity. As rumors spread, emotions may accompany them. Mass communications – films, newspapers, radio, and (particularly) television – can transmit people's emotions far beyond their geographical perimeters. Our very image of the mob is linked inextricably with notions of the spread of anger, leading to the out-of-control behaviors of murder, lynchings, and large-scale destruction. We see daily on television the pictures of weeping and angry crowds mourning the death of a Palestinian guerrilla or an Israeli child, a murdered leader and her mournful followers or the defiant and angry opposition. We replay the weekend of mourning by an entire nation (perhaps even the entire world) upon the assassination of John F. Kennedy. Are these instances of emotional contagion, or are these phenomena too complicated to be so labeled? Historical examples cannot be tested in the laboratory, but they do hint at the reality of emotional contagion and suggest that it may have occurred on a large scale in all historical eras. They also suggest that the mass media of our day may possess power even greater than generally realized because of their potential to precipitate the spread not just of information and entertainment, but of emotions as well.

## Summing up

In chapters 1–3, we have considered evidence in favor of three propositions: (1) that people tend to mimic others; (2) that emotional experience is affected by such feedback; and (3) that people therefore tend to "catch" others' emotions. In this chapter, we have reviewed evidence – from animal researchers, developmentalists, clinical researchers, social psychologists, and historians – suggesting that people may indeed catch the emotions of others in all times, in all societies, and, perhaps, on very large scales.

# 4. The ability to infect others with emotion

## Introduction

If we pursue the analogy, thinking of the transmission of moods as akin to the transmission of social viruses, it seems reasonable to suppose that some people (the Typhoid Marys of this world) may well possess a natural ability to infect others with the "virus" while others (the Marcel Prousts) stand especially vulnerable to contagion. Norman Mailer (1979), in *The Executioner's Song*, interviewed Nicole Baker, the girlfriend of condemned killer Gary Gilmore. While Gilmore was on death row, Nicole had a brief affair with two men. Nicole loved Tom because he was able to infect her with *his* cheerful emotions. She loved Cliff Bonnors because he was in tune with *her* deepest feelings:

> Cliff Bonnors was great because he always brought his mood around to meet hers. They could travel through the same sad thoughts never saying a word. Tom, she liked, for opposite reasons. Tom was always happy or full of sorrow, and his feelings were so strong he would take her out of her own mood. He wasn't dynamite but a bear full of grease. Always smelled full of hamburgers and french fries. He and Cliff were beautiful. She could like them and never have to worry about loving them one bit. In fact, she enjoyed it like a chocolate bar. Never thought of Gary when making love to them, almost never. (p. 329)

In this chapter, we consider the kinds of individual differences that affect men's and women's ability to shape an emotional climate. The factors that determine whether people will be susceptible or resistant to catching others' moods are considered in chapter 5.

## Theoretical background

When our father worried the energy he generated was
enormous. Waves of worry flowed from him – one could almost
see it playing round his head like forked lightening, and it
penetrated every corner of the cottage. As far as one could tell,
our mother was not affected by his mood, but my sister and I
soon succumbed, and crept out, each to her own pigsty, to worry
too.

                                        – Winifred Beechey

It doesn't take much in people's expressions, voices, or actions for
others to pick up on what they are feeling. Researchers have found
that teacher expectancies and affect toward students can be determined from brief clips of teachers' behavior; mothers' affect toward
their children can be guessed from a short snippet of behavior; and
judges' expectations for the trial outcome and the criminal history of
a defendant can be guessed based on brief excerpts of judges' instructions to the jurors (Ambady & Rosenthal, 1992). In an illustrative
study, Brian Mullen and his colleagues (1986) determined that ABC
newscaster Peter Jennings displayed more positive affect when referring to Reagan than to Mondale during the 1986 presidential campaign; Tom Brokaw (NBC) and Dan Rather (CBS) did not exhibit a
bias in facial expressions. These researchers conducted a follow-up
telephone survey of voters in Cleveland, Ohio; Rolla, Missouri; Wil-
liamstown, Massachusetts; and Erie, Pennsylvania. They found that
voters who watched ABC News were more likely to vote for Reagan
than those who watched the news on CBS or NBC. Subtle differences in Peter Jennings's facial and vocal expressions when talking
about the presidential candidates were apparently sufficient to influence viewers' preferences and voting behavior.

Newscasters are selected in part based on their on-camera charisma. When they are upbeat, viewers tend to be upbeat; when they are
somber, viewers tend to be somber. When we look around us, we
find that most of us simply disappear into the crowd; some individuals, however, are indeed able to draw others into their emotional
orbit. When they are happy, their laugh is infectious and they are
the "life of the party." When they are down, they are a "drag"; they
manage to bring everyone around them down. Why should some
people be more capable of infecting others with their emotions than
are their peers? These powerful "senders" probably possess at least
three characteristics:

> *Hypothesis 4.1. They must feel, or at least appear to feel, strong emotions.*
>
> *Hypothesis 4.2. They must be able to express (facially, vocally, and/or posturally) those strong emotions.*
>
> *Hypothesis 4.3. They must be relatively insensitive to and unresponsive to the feelings of those who are experiencing emotions incompatible with their own.*

It is the common wonder of all men, how among so many
millions of faces there should be none alike.
                                    – Sir Thomas Browne

As suggested by Peter Jennings's apparently inadvertent influence on the voting behavior of ABC viewers, a person's emotions can be socially perceptible (through voice, facial expressions, gestures, or postures) and transmittable even when the person has no such intention. What, then, are the processes that underlie the transmission of emotions? John Cacioppo and his colleagues (1992) have proposed that biological as well as social factors are important determinants of dispositional differences in emotional expressiveness. They noted, for instance, that people show wide variation in physical features (e.g., height, weight, eye color, hair color, skin pigmentation), in psychological attributes (e.g., sociability, temperament, intelligence, emotional expressivity, and vocal pitch [Buck, 1976a,b; Kagan, Reznick, & Snidman, 1988; Plomin, 1989]), and in deeper physiological structures (e.g., the size, shape, and specific location/orientation of the brain or heart [Gazzaniga, 1989]). There is even greater individual variability in the physiological structures that are less intimately involved in the maintenance of life (Anson, 1951; Bergman, Thompson, & Afifi, 1984). Studies of the facial muscles underlying expressivity have revealed that there are not just structural variations in the location and form of the muscles, but individual differences in their very existence. The corrugator supercilii and risorius muscles used for mimicry, for instance, have been estimated to be absent in approximately 20% and 50% of the population, respectively (Tassinary, Cacioppo, & Geen, 1989).

Reliable individual differences in physiological function – including somatic and sympathetic reactivity – have also been documented (Garwood, Engel, & Capriotti, 1982; Kasprowicz, Manuck, Malkoff, & Krantz, 1990; Sherwood, Dolan, & Light, 1990). *Individual re-*

*sponse stereotypy* is a generic term referring to variance in somatic and physiological activity attributable to the person or to person–situation interactions (e.g., reactivity measures; distinctive physiological responses attributable to idiosyncratic appraisals or coping strategies [Lacey, Bateman, & Van Lehn, 1953; Lacey & Lacey, 1958]). Early observations by Lacey and his colleagues (Lacey, 1959; Lacey, Kagan, Lacey, & Moss, 1963) of the effect of various kinds of stress (anticipation of cold pressor, cold pressor test, mental arithmetic, and tests of word fluency) on ANS responses (systolic and diastolic blood pressure, skin conductance, heart rate, heart rate variability, and pulse pressure) demonstrated two points:

1. Individuals show consistency in their patterns of physiological response across tasks.
2. Individuals show clear differences in the physiological systems that show relatively high or low reactivity across measures.

The concept of individual response stereotypy has been further differentiated since its introduction by Robert Malmo and Charles Shagass (1949) and John Lacey and his colleagues (Lacey et al., 1953). *Individual response hierarchy* refers to individual differences in the responses, showing maximal, second intermediate, and least maximal activation across stressors. Malmo and Shagass (1949), for instance, found that psychiatric patients who chronically complained of headaches showed relatively high reactivity to stressors in muscle tension in the forehead region, whereas those who chronically issued heart complaints (e.g., palpitations) showed relatively high reactivity in heart rate and heart rate variability.

*Individual response uniqueness* refers to differences across groups of individuals (e.g., hypertensives, normotensives) in response hierarchies. Hypertensives and their offspring, for instance, are more likely to exhibit high cardiovascular reactivity than are normotensives and their offspring (Fredrikson et al., 1985).

Finally, *individual response consistency* refers to the reliability of these physiological response profiles across time. John and Beatrice Lacey (1958) found vast individual differences in response consistency in their longitudinal study of children's response to stressors (see also Fahrenberg, Foerster, Schneider, Muller, & Myrtek, 1986). Some individuals show remarkably high individual response consistency across several different stressors; others show little response consistency.

John Cacioppo and his colleagues (1992) built on these principles by proposing that there are individual differences in (1) the system gain governing expressiveness, (2) the system gain governing sympathetic response, and (3) the stability of these gain parameters. *System gain* can be thought of as the volume on a radio. The radio signal is received, amplified, and outputted to the speakers; system gain in this instance thus refers to the amount of amplification of the signal en route to the speakers. Although you can change the volume on your radio, there are differences across radios in the amount of change achieved with each turn of the knob, and there are differences in the maximum volume that can be achieved. Cacioppo and co-workers suggested that these same kinds of differences exist across individuals in the amplification (or gain) applied to emotional signals en route to their output in facial, gestural/postural, and vocal responses, as well as in autonomic (e.g., internal organ) responses. They also posited that these differences in amplification were stable in some individuals but not in others. According to this framework, therefore, there is a subset of individuals who are inclined, by virtue of their physiology, to respond strongly, visibly, and consistently in emotional situations. All else constant, these individuals are thought to be particularly likely to initiate emotional contagion because they are especially expressive in emotional situations. There is another subset of individuals who are inclined, by virtue of *their* physiology, to respond strongly, but *not* visibly, in emotional situations. These individuals may feel their heart racing but show no socially perceptible signs of reacting emotionally to the stimulus. As indicated by Schachter and Singer's (1962) study (reviewed in chapter 3), physiological reactions of this sort increase the likelihood that a person's emotions will be influenced by the visible signs of another's emotional reaction. Thus, these are the individuals who may be especially "at risk" for emotional contagion. In this chapter, we focus on individual differences in how facially expressive people are to emotional stimuli, and thus how potent are the emotional messages they send to others.

## Individual differences in the ability to infect others with emotion

### Expressiveness and sympathetic arousal

Psychologists have found that there are individual differences in people's ability to experience and/or express emotion. For example, they have drawn a distinction between the way emotion is experienced/expressed by externalizers versus internalizers and by introverts versus extraverts.

*Externalizers and internalizers.* Personality researchers (Buck, 1980; Jones, 1935, 1950) have argued that some people are externalizers and others internalizers. *Externalizers* are those whose emotions can be read (externally) on their faces, yet who show little ANS sympathetic response. *Internalizers* are those whose faces are a blank, but whose ANS reactions tell a different (internal) story. Novelist Ruth Pewar Jhabvala (1986), in *Out of India,* describes a mother's hesitance to approach her son, Shammi. He is angry, but refuses to admit it. We would have no trouble labeling Shammi an internalizer.

> Shammi was packing his bag. He wouldn't talk to me and kept his head averted from me while he took neat piles of clothes out of the drawer and packed them neatly into his bag. He has always been a very orderly boy. I sat on his bed and watched him. If he had said something, if he had been angry, it would have been easier; but he was quite silent, and I knew that under his shirt his heart was beating fast. When he was small and something had happened to him, he would never cry, but when I held him close to me and put my hand under his shirt I used to feel his heart beating wildly inside his child's body, like a bird in a frail cage. And, now, too I longed to do this, to lay my hand on his suffering. (p. 10)

We use the term *generalizers* for those who are equally expressive (or inexpressive) facially and physiologically. In the scheme of Cacioppo and his colleagues (1992),

> externalizers would show relatively high gain on expressiveness and relatively low gain on sympathetic nervous reactions;
> internalizers would show relatively low gain on expressiveness and relatively high gain on sympathetic nervous reactions; and
> generalizers would show approximately equal increases in expressiveness and sympathetic activity (see also Jones, 1950).

Interesting studies by Tiffany Field (Field, 1982; Field & Walden, 1982) are consistent with the proposition that constitutional variations in physiological functions (e.g., system gains) contribute to individual differences in expressiveness and autonomic reactivity. Field and her colleagues recorded the facial expressiveness and heart rate reactivity of newborns (mean age, 36 hr) across a range of situations (e.g., during sleep, during facial and auditory discrimination tasks). They found the newborns differed considerably in their expressiveness, and that the expressive ones were characterized by lower heart rates than the relatively nonexpressive ones. This interesting research suggests that individual differences in expressiveness and autonomic reactivity are due, at least in part, to biological predispositions.

The existence of biological predispositions to respond in certain ways does *not* mean that people's personality and behaviors are bound by this biology. Social and learning processes also play an important role in shaping individual differences in expressiveness and physiological function, and in translating these physiologically based individual differences into personality and social behavior. For instance, the emotions of an expressive infant may be more evident, and more likely to infect caregivers, than the emotions of an inexpressive infant. Whether the expressive infant remains expressive, however, will depend on such factors as whether caregivers respond in a reinforcing or punishing manner when the infant shows signs of pleasure or distress. According to this reasoning, an expressive infant is likely to become an expressive adult (and a more potent carrier of emotional contagion) as long as the process of socialization does not produce a submissive individual. Though the necessary longitudinal research has yet to be conducted, the available evidence is consistent with this reasoning. For instance, Paul Ekman, Wallace Friesen, and Klaus Scherer (1976) found that adults judged by observers to be expressive also tended to score high on measures of sociability (defined by scales of *expressive–unexpressive, sociable–withdrawn,* and *outgoing–inhibited*) and dominance (defined by a scale of *dominant–submissive*).

*Introverts and extraverts.* Hans Eysenck (1967) proposed that individuals tend to fall into one of two basic personality types – introverts and extraverts. According to Eysenck, introverts are characterized by low thresholds for activating the reticular formation in the brain; consequently, they are easily aroused. Extraverts, in contrast, have a high threshold for arousal, in Eysenck's theory. One important implication of this constitutional difference is that introverts

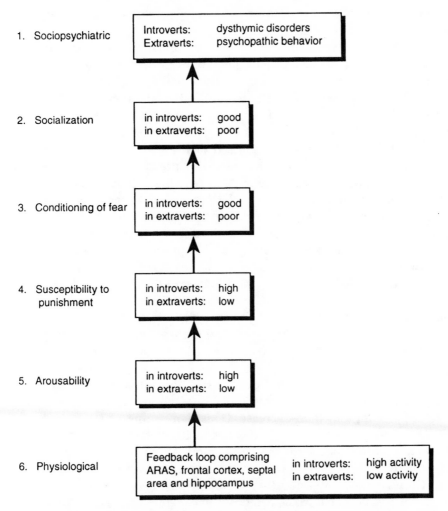

Figure 4.1: A proposed modification of Eysenck's theory of introversion–extraversion. *Source:* Gray, 1972, p. 197. Copyright © 1972 by Academic Press, Inc. Reprinted by permission.

are easier to condition than extraverts. As a consequence, introverts risk oversocialization, whereas extraverts court undersocialization. Jeffrey Gray (1971) offered a more elaborate model of how the two types should differ, especially in their relationships with other people (Figure 4.1). Both Hans Eysenck and Jeffrey Gray, of course, would surely assume that extraverts should be more powerful senders of emotion. Extraverts should also be better able to resist *others'* emotions.

There is some evidence that extraverts *are* unusually emotionally expressive. Ross Buck and his colleagues (Buck, Miller, & Caul, 1974) explored senders' ability to telegraph their feelings. First, subjects took a battery of personality tests, including the Extraversion–Introversion scale (Eysenck, 1967). Then, senders were asked to view 25 emotion-arousing slides (pictures of happy children, burned and disfigured bodies, etc.). As subjects discussed their reactions to the slides, hidden video cameras recorded their facial expressions (without audio) and electrodes recorded their ANS responses (heart rate and electrodermal responses). Some senders' emotional reactions were easy to "read"; others' reactions were opaque. Powerful senders differed in a number of ways from poor ones: They were extraverted, possessed a rich emotional language and expressive faces, and did *not* show strong ANS reactions to the slides. Weak senders were just the opposite: Introverts, they were unaware (or unwilling to admit) that they had been affected by the slides. Their emotional language was impoverished, and their faces showed little evidence of emotion. Inside, however, they were quite stirred up; in fact, they had a powerful internal physiological reaction to the emotionalizing slides.

Russell Geen (1983) suggested that, as stimulus intensity increases, the physiological reactions of both introverts and extraverts increase up to some point and then decrease. (This dampening of autonomic reactions to very intense stimuli may occur, for instance, because the intense stimuli activate both the sympathetic [excitatory] and parasympathetic [inhibitory] branches of the autonomic nervous system.) Geen further suggested that the difference between extraverts and introverts is that it takes a more intense emotional stimulus to evoke an autonomic response from an extravert than from an introvert, and it takes a more intense emotional stimulus to begin dampening the autonomic reactions of extraverts than it does those of introverts.

According to Geen's (1983) proposal, under moderate to high levels of stimulation extraverts should show an increase in autonomic reactivity, whereas introverts should show a decrease. This is precisely the pattern of results reported by Don Fowles and his colleagues (Fowles, Roberts, & Nagel, 1977). They gave subjects a paired-associate learning task that was either difficult or easy. (Working on the difficult paired-associate learning task was assumed to be more arousing than working on the simple one.) After working on this task, subjects were exposed to a series of tones that were either moderately (83 dB) or very (103 dB) loud. They found that the resultant skin conductance of extraverts was lowest when they had performed the easy paired-associate learning task and were exposed to moderately loud tones, and highest when they had performed the difficult paired-associate learning task and were exposed to the very loud tones; that is, their skin conductance increased with stimulus intensity. Introverts showed a different pattern of results: Their resultant skin conductance was highest when they had performed the easy paired-associate learning task but were exposed to very loud tones; that is, it was related to stimulus intensity in an inverted-U-shaped function.

In sum, extraverts appear to be characterized by a higher threshold for autonomic reactions, but also by lesser constraints on their autonomic reactions and their expressiveness, compared to introverts. Thus, extraverts show stronger expressive reactions and somewhat weaker autonomic reactions than introverts when the emotional stimulus is *not* intense, and stronger expressive *and* autonomic reactions when the stimulation *is* intense; they may therefore be more likely than introverts to be strong carriers of emotional contagion.

### Assessing the ability to infect others with emotion

*Assessing people's expressiveness.* Several researchers have developed scales designed to measure how charismatic or expressive men and women are. Howard Friedman and his colleagues (Friedman et al., 1980) observed:

> From common observation of slick and dull salespersons, charismatic and monotonous politicians, impassioned and muttering clergy, and eloquent and wearisome professors, it is clear that there are marked individual differences in expressiveness. Although some of these differences are in verbal fluency, the essence of eloquent, passionate, spirited communication seems to involve the use of facial expressions, voices, gestures, and body movements to transmit emotions. (p. 333)

The authors developed the Affective Communication Test (ACT), a 13-item self-report scale, to assess the extent of emotional charisma

Table 4.1. *The Affective Communication Test*

| | |
|---|---|
| 1. | When I hear good dance music, I can hardly keep still. |
| *2. | My laugh is soft and subdued. |
| 3. | I can easily express emotion over the telephone. |
| 4. | I often touch friends during conversations. |
| *5. | I dislike being watched by a large group of people. |
| *6. | I usually have a neutral facial expression. |
| 7. | People tell me that I would make a good actor or actress. |
| *8. | I like to remain unnoticed in a crowd. |
| *9. | I am shy among strangers. |
| 10. | I am able to give a seductive glance if I want to. |
| *11. | I am terrible at pantomime as in games like charades. |
| 12. | At small parties I am the center of attention. |
| 13. | I show that I like someone by hugging or touching that person. |

*Note:* Items marked with an asterisk (*) are scored in the reverse direction.
*Source:* Friedman et al. (1980), p. 335. Copyright © 1980, Howard S. Friedman. Adapted and reprinted by permission. No printing or other use of this test is permitted without written permission of Howard S. Friedman.

and expressiveness (Table 4.1). They found, as predicted, that people who scored high on this test were able to "move, inspire, and captivate others" (p. 337). They were charismatic, colorful, and entertaining; had often taught, lectured, or worked as salespersons; and shunned such careful, repetitive jobs as laboratory technician or computer expert. On the Personality Research Form (Jackson, 1974), the expressive scored high on dominance, affiliation, and exhibition. People who score high on exhibition are "colorful, spellbinding, noticeable, expressive, dramatic, and showy" (p. 340). On Hans Eysenck's (Eysenck & Eysenck, 1968a,b) Extraversion–Introversion scale, the expressive scored high on extraversion. (As we found in the preceding section, extraverts – outgoing, impulsive, and uninhibited – do not keep their feelings under tight control.) Physicians who score high on the Affective Communication Test even have more patient visits than those who score low!

More recently, David Klein and John Cacioppo (1993) developed the Facial Expressiveness Scale in order to measure individual differences in the tendency to express one's emotions (Table 4.2), that is, to gauge the extent to which individuals "wear their emotions on their sleeves." As would be expected, Klein and Cacioppo found that the Facial Expressiveness and ACT scales are moderately correlated

Table 4.2. *The Facial Expressiveness Scale*

---

How well do you know yourself?

The following items should be rated on a six-point scale ranging from 0 (*Not at all descriptive of me*) to 5 (*Very descriptive of me*). Please answer the following questions as accurately and honestly as possible.

1. I can't help but let other people know when I'm glad to see them.
2. People can tell I have a problem from my expression.
3. I tend to touch friends during conversation.
4. I laugh a lot.
5. People have told me that I am an expressive person.
6. I show that I like someone by hugging or touching that person.
7. I get excited easily.
8. People can tell from my facial expression how I am feeling.
9. When I am alone I can make myself laugh by remembering something from the past.
10. Watching television or reading a book can make me laugh out loud.

Subjects indicated their answers on the following scale:

  \_\_\_   0   Not at all descriptive of me
  \_\_\_   1   Rarely descriptive of me
  \_\_\_   2   Occasionally descriptive of me
  \_\_\_   3   Regularly descriptive of me
  \_\_\_   4   Frequently descriptive of me
  \_\_\_   5   Very descriptive of me

---

*Source:* Klein & Cacioppo (1993).

($r = +.32$, $N = 62$ in Study 1; $r = +.49$, $N = 33$ in Study 2), indicating that they are tapping related and not identical individual-difference variables. Consistent with the notion that the ACT measures charisma, scores on the ACT were found to be more predictive of the number of social contacts people had ($r = +.58$, Study 2) than were Facial Expressiveness Scale scores ($r = +.35$). Individuals' scores on the Facial Expressiveness Scale ($r = +.46$ in Study 1, $r = +.51$ in Study 2) were also found to be more predictive of their susceptibility to emotional contagion (as indexed by the Emotional Contagion Scale [Doherty, Orimoto, Hebb, & Hatfield, 1993]) than were scores on the ACT ($r = +.16$ in Study 1, $r = +.28$ in Study 2). Indeed, when the Facial Expressiveness and ACT scores were used simultaneously to predict those for emotional contagion, the results of both studies indicated that only Facial Expressiveness scores were significantly related to emotional contagion scores. These results are particularly interesting in light of the evidence reviewed in chapter 2 showing that the production of and/or feedback from facial expressions in emotional situations fosters emotional contagion. Thus, people who wear their emotions on their sleeves may be not only potent carriers of emotional contagion, but also particularly likely to mimic, express, and come to feel the emotions displayed by those around them. We return to the topic of susceptibility and resistance to emotional contagion in chapter 5.

*Assessing people's ability to infect others with emotion.* Self-report scales have been developed to index a person's tendency to be charismatic and emotionally expressive, and people who score relatively high on these scales may be particularly likely to infect others with emotion. It is unlikely, however, that all expressive or charismatic individuals are equally likely to infect others with emotion. Unfortunately, researchers have not yet crafted a scale designed specifically to assess people's ability to infect others with emotion. Researchers *have* developed experimental paradigms for studying emotional contagion, however, and we turn to the evidence from these paradigms in the next section.

## Evidence of variance in the ability to infect others with emotion

In Hypotheses 4.1–4.3, we proposed that if people are to be powerful senders, they (1) must feel (or at least appear to feel) strong emotion; (2) must be able to express (facially, vocally, and/or posturally) those emotions; and (3) must be relatively insensitive and unresponsive to the feelings of those who are experiencing emotions incompatible with their own. When people are in roughly the same mood, or when one person is experiencing a strong emotion and the other is not, senders need have only two "skills" if they are to transmit their own emotions – the abilities to feel emotion and to express it. For example, if two college students meet at a TGIF party, the evening is most likely to catch fire if *both* are expressive; it might even help if they can feed off of one another's excitement. Sometimes people are in very different moods, however. For example, someone might visit the hospital, hoping to cheer up a despondent friend; the manager of the complaint department might be assigned the job of calming irate customers; and a misogynist might be determined to make everyone as miserable as he. If these senders are to succeed, they must be able not only to transmit their own emotions, but to do so while simultaneously resisting getting caught up in the other's emotional swirl. Otherwise, the Good Samaritan would end up depressed, the manager would find himself screaming at customers, and the misogynist would end up having a good time. Finally, if people are *extremely* unemotional, oblivious to the feelings of themselves and others, they should not be very good at either sending or catching others' emotions.

There is some evidence in support of these hypotheses.

*Feeling and expressing emotion: The impact on the ability to infect others with emotion.* Howard Friedman and Ronald Riggio (1981) observed that expressive people tend to infect others with their fears, anxieties, and anger, while their "inexpressive" peers do not (at least, not to the same extent). To test this hypothesis, they invited college students to participate in a study of "fluctuations in moods." Subjects were asked how they felt "at this instant," and were told that "we want to see how your moods change during a period of two minutes when you sit quietly and let your thoughts wander" (p. 99). Three subjects were then seated in a circle. Each was allowed to look at, but not talk to, the others. Unbeknownst to them, the trios had been carefully set up: One member was always a highly expressive person (as measured by the ACT); the other two, inexpressive. After the two-minute get-acquainted session, subjects were asked how happy, bored, frightened, anxious, or angry they felt. As predicted, the mood with which the expressive subjects had entered the session prevailed, especially if they had been in a bad mood. Everyone (expressive or not) seemed capable of transmitting their happiness; but it was the expressives that infected the others with their fear, anxiety, or anger. Similar results were secured by Ellen Sullins (1991). She too found that, although everyone could pass on their happy moods, it was the expressive who were more likely to infect others with their *negative* emotions – sadness, anxiety, aggression, and fatigue.

*Possessing the ability to resist others' emotions.* Very little is known about how some people manage to keep their own emotional equilibrium in the face of others who are experiencing overwhelming emotion. Interviews with people who routinely deal with others in difficulty provide some hints. One prison guard with whom we conferred, a diminutive Filipino, told the following story: The day before he had been interviewing a very large, young, black man, who was in jail for peddling drugs to minors. The guard felt calm, but found himself looking at the prisoner who towered above him, his muscles rippling. Again and again he thought, "Most people would be afraid in this situation. Am I afraid? No. Well, *someone* is afraid here. What's going on?" Pausing to think about it, he had realized that, though the prisoner was trying to look "cool," fear seemed to be "sparking off of his skin." What could have happened to such a big man to make him so afraid? The tiny guard talked calmly to the prisoner for six hours! During this time he found that the prisoner had had a "gruesome" childhood and been abused both as a child and in other institutions. Co-workers mentioned that this guard just seemed to have a knack for dealing with prisoners: Everything stayed "cool" when he was around. He seems, then, somehow to avoid catching the emotions of prisoners, yet uses some kinds of emotional information in analyzing what is going on with them.

## Gender differences in the ability to infect others with emotion

Should men and women differ in their ability to infect others with their emotions? That is hard to say. Earlier, we observed that people who are able to infect others with their emotions must feel (or, at least, appear to feel) strong emotions, must be able to express (facially, vocally, and/or posturally) those emotions, and must be relatively insensitive and unresponsive to the feelings of others. According to gender stereotypes, men are less emotional than are women, and scientists asking questions in just the right way can get men and women to assert that their feelings are in accord with such stereotypes. For example, the more general the question ("How emotional are you?") and the longer the time frame ("How often did you get angry during the past year?"), the more the sexes will agree that they are very different. However, the minute scientists begin to get specific, asking not about one's emotionality but about one's feelings of joy, sadness, and anger – asking not how joyous one is generally but how joyous one is today – gender differences suddenly begin to disappear. Most recent reviews, then, end by concluding that there is no compelling evidence that men and women differ in how they *feel* (La France & Banaji, 1992; Shields, 1987); however, there is considerable evidence that women are more comfortable about *expressing* their emotions (Carlson & Hatfield, 1992; Hall, 1984). On the other hand, men may be more sympathetically reactive than women (La France & Banaji, 1992), and may also be less susceptible to catching others' emotions. Although the likelihood of gender as a factor in the ability to infect others with emotion is difficult to predict, let us consider the slight gender differences that have been found to exist.

*Gender and emotional expressiveness.* At birth, boys are often *more* emotionally expressive than girls. One study found, for example, that although infant girls expressed joy twice as often as boys, boys expressed fear, anger, and distress twice as often as girls. Soon, however, boys are taught to inhibit overt signs of emotion (Haviland & Malatesta, 1981).

By adulthood, women are generally far more emotionally expressive than men (Buck, 1984; Manstead, MacDonald, & Wagner, 1982). Judith Hall (1984) conducted a meta-analysis of 49 studies exploring gender differences in expressiveness, expression accuracy, and communication ability. The evidence was clear: Women are generally more open and expressive than are men. They are better encoders of friendly, unfriendly, and unpleasant affect, of happiness, love, fear, anger, surprise, and dominance. They spontaneously smile and laugh more, engage in more eye contact, touch more, and show more body movement, and are freer about expressing negative emotions as well. Even when men and women are both *trying* to communicate nonverbally, women are the far more effective senders.

Others second the conclusion that women are more nonverbally expressive than men. Women show a greater amount of facial activity (Buck, Baron, & Barette, 1982; Buck, Baron, Goodman, & Shapiro, 1980) and facial electromyographic activity (Dimberg, 1988; Schwartz, Brown, & Ahern, 1980). Not surprisingly, then, observers find it easier to read emotional states accurately from women's faces than from men's (Buck, Miller, & Caul, 1974; Fujita, Harper, & Wiens, 1980; Gallagher & Shuntich, 1981; Hall, 1984; Wagner, MacDonald, & Manstead, 1986).

In one experiment, for example, Ross Buck and his colleagues (1974) explored men's and women's emotional expressiveness and transmission accuracy. As senders viewed 25 emotionally loaded color slides, their facial expressions were secretly filmed and their ANS reactions (heart rate and skin conductance) recorded.

Previously, these researchers had found that women tend to be externalizers whereas men tend to be internalizers (see the section "Externalizers and Internalizers" earlier in this chapter). As predicted, in this experiment, too, judges found it easier to read women's facial expressions than men's. (Women also got *less* stirred up emotionally, as measured by their ANS reactions, than the men.)

In contrasting men's and women's tendency to express and "leak" emotions facially versus verbally, Hall proposed an interesting hypothesis:

> Women specialize in visual communication and behavior, men in vocal. What is intriguing is the research . . . that suggests that the visual modality (really the face) conveys degrees of positivity–negativity well, while the voice conveys degrees of dominance–submission particularly well.
>
> Putting these results together yields the hypothesis that the sexes specialize in the modalities that are most relevant to them. If women are attuned to degrees of interpersonal harmony and men to degrees of social dominance, then they could each profit from attention, skill, and a behavioral repertoire centered on the modalities most suited to their respective motives. (p. 140)

When men and women try to telegraph their feelings, it is women who find it easiest to do. Working with happily and unhappily married men and women, Patricia Noller (1987) tried to find out how effective they were in communicating with one another. How good were they at sending the emotional messages they wished to send? To find out, she gave the husbands or wives a script and asked them to do their best to let their mates know how they felt. (In the example in Table 4.3, the husband was given the script.) The catch? They could utter only one line: In this case, "Do you know what a trip like that costs?"

A husband, for instance, was supposed to make it clear (by saying, "Do you know what a trip like that costs?") either that he was (1) dead set against taking a trip, (2) eager to travel, or (3) without any particular feelings about the trip, one way or another. His wife was to listen to her husband and to try to gauge his intentions. Objective judges also viewed each marital interaction to decide what the husband (or wife) was trying to say. This procedure gave the experimenters a chance to classify people as "good" or "bad" senders, depending on whether or not judges could guess their intended messages. Noller found that men and women and happy and unhappy couples differed markedly in their communication skills.

Table 4.3. *Husband's script and wife's decoding card*

| Husband's script | (He must send the message.) |
|---|---|

*Situation:* Your wife tells you about the wonderful vacation that one of her friends just took with her husband. She says that she wishes you and she could also take a trip to the same place.

*Intention:* You feel that a trip to that place is unappealing and would hardly be worthwhile.

*Statement:* Do you know what a trip like that costs?

| Wife's decoding card | (She must guess what message he is trying to send.) |
|---|---|

*Situation:* You have told your husband about the wonderful trip that one of your friends just took with her husband. You say that you wish you and he could also take a trip to the same place.

*Your husband's intentions:*
  (a) He feels that a trip to that place is unappealing and would hardly be worthwhile.
  (b) He is pleased that you would want to go with him on such a trip and he would like to make serious inquiries about it.
  (c) He is interested in finding out if you know the approximate cost of their trip before committing himself one way or the other.

*Source:* Based on Noller (1987), p. 154.

1. Men and women in happy marriages were skilled at sending the messages they wanted to send. They were able – partly by facial expression (smiles or furrowed brows) or gestures, but mostly by their tone of voice – to make clear how they felt about the idea of the trip. Even in the shakiest of marriages, however, women were quite good at conveying their feelings; it was their husbands who had a communication problem. Unhappily married husbands were extremely inexpressive. When they attempted to send messages of encouragement, not even the objective judges could figure out what they were trying to say. These husbands did a slightly better job at signaling their disapproval. Other studies (Noller, 1982) demonstrated that unhappy wives got particularly upset about the lack of positive communications from their husbands; they longed for more affection, appreciation, and attention. It seems here that even when the men did try to send positive messages, they had trouble getting them across. Perhaps they intended to be rewarding, but just didn't know how, or perhaps even their most positive messages were contaminated by "leakage" from the anger and hostility they actually felt for their wives.

2. Noller (1982) also found gender differences in the ability to decode messages. (We consider this topic in more detail in chapter 5.) In successful marriages both men and women were very good at guessing how their partner felt about the various issues simply by attending to tone of voice. Women were also good at such detective work in faltering marriages (though, if anything, they tended to judge their husbands' messages as more positive than they actually were); but again, the husbands seemed to have a problem understanding their mates. Despite their confidence that they knew what their wives were feeling, they were wrong. They tended to interpret even the most positive messages as critical.

[As with love] so with fear, with indignation, jealousy,
ambition, worship. If they are there, life changes.
                                        – William James

If men are unaware of their own emotions and/or unable to express them, they are, of course, at a big disadvantage. People must possess an emotional vocabulary and emotional awareness if they are to understand themselves, others, and the world.

## Summing up

In this chapter, we reviewed evidence that some people are more potent at infecting others with their emotions than are their peers. We proposed (in Hypotheses 4.1–4.3) that powerful communicators should possess three traits:

1. They must feel (or at least appear to feel), strong emotions.
2. They must be able to express (facially, vocally, and/or posturally) those strong emotions.
3. When others are experiencing emotions incompatible with their own, they must be relatively insensitive to and unresponsive to the feelings of others.

We found some evidence in support of these hypotheses.

# 5. Susceptibility to emotional contagion

## Introduction

Blanche . . . could detect sorrow, could detect it a mile off. . . .
The gift of compassion is born in one or does not exist at all; the
artificial commodity, assumed or advertised, misses too many
clues.

– Anita Brookner

Does everyone have the capacity to share the joy, love, sadness, anger, and fear of others? Or do individuals differ markedly in their ability to get swept up in others' emotions? We assume that personality, self-construals, genetic heritage, and early experiences predispose some people to be unusually susceptible to emotional contagion and others to be unusually resistant to it.

## Theoretical background

A century ago, Gustave Le Bon (1896) wrote about the mysterious forces that operated when people congregated to form crowds. Feelings of membership within a crowd, Le Bon argued, contributed to an enlargement of the ego (a sense of power), the release of impulses, a *sense of contagion*, and heightened suggestibility. These psychological characteristics, Le Bon argued, derived from the absorption of an individual's identity into that of the crowd. The effective crowd leader, Le Bon reasoned, relied on the affirmation of simple, imagelike ideas that point directly to action, and on the repetition of these imagelike ideas: The affirmation evokes the image, the image evokes a sentiment, and the sentiment leads to action. Individuals in the crowd mimic the actions of the leader, and this mimicry, once initiated, infects all in attendance. Although Le Bon was not interested in emotional contagion per se, his observations of mob behavior may contain clues to some of the features of individuals most likely to be susceptible to emotional contagion. It seems logical that the following characteristics would make individuals especially susceptible to emotional contagion:

> *Hypothesis 5.1. People should be more likely to catch others' emotions if their attention is riveted on the others than if they are oblivious to others' emotions.*
>
> *Hypothesis 5.2. People should be more likely to catch others' emotions if they construe themselves in terms of their interrelatedness to the others rather than in terms of their independence and uniqueness.*
>
> *Hypothesis 5.3. Those able to read others' emotional expressions, voices, gestures, and postures should be especially vulnerable to contagion.*
>
> *Hypothesis 5.4. Those who tend to mimic facial, vocal, and postural expressions should be especially vulnerable to contagion.*
>
> *Hypothesis 5.5. Those who are aware of their own emotional responses (i.e., whose subjective emotional experience is tempered by facial, vocal, postural, and movement feedback) should be more vulnerable to contagion.*
>
> *Hypothesis 5.6. Emotionally reactive people should be more vulnerable to contagion.*

Conversely, people who do *not* attend to others, who construe themselves as distinct and unique from others, who are unable to read others' emotions, who fail to mimic, or whose subjective emotional experiences are unaltered by peripheral feedback should be fairly resistant to contagion.

Let us now consider the evidence in favor of Hypotheses 5.1–5.6.

## Individual differences in susceptibility to contagion

*Hypothesis 5.1: Attention and emotional contagion*

According to Hypothesis 5.1, people should be more likely to catch others' emotions if their attention is riveted on the others. Barbara Harrison (1989), in *Italian Days*, was struck by the Italians' stunning ability to read her feelings:

> "You are sad," Domenico says to me.
> He is absolutely right; and this is a statement that could pro-

ceed only from absolute simplicity, from immediacy; between stimulus – a look, a glance, a knotted shoulder – to response, no system or structure or ideology mediates or intervenes. Amerigo reads bodies – to this extent he has retained simplicity – and so does Domenico. (p. 420)

People who have little interest in other human beings, or who are momentarily preoccupied with their own problems and emotions, should, of course, be unlikely to perceive, much less catch, the emotions of others.

Every man has reminiscences which he would not tell to
everyone but only to his friends. . . . But there are other things
which a man is afraid to tell even to himself.
                              – Fyodor Dostoevsky

*Sensitizers and repressors.* Researchers point out that people differ in their willingness to attend to emotional messages, especially unpleasant ones. One of our clients reported that she and her girlfriend had teased her husband, Sam, mercilessly. When he would answer the telephone and hear a voice, choking back sobs, squeak, "Can I speak to Marcy?", he would hand the phone over with a cheerful "Marcy, it's for you." He was totally unaware that anyone was suffering on the other end of the line. A person so oblivious to others' emotional messages is not likely to catch them.

Sam was oblivious to emotional messages because he couldn't care less; others might avoid such messages because they fear they might care *too* much. Sigmund Freud (1904) proposed, of course, that the conscious mind possessed a variety of defense mechanisms that allowed it to shield itself from painful unconscious information. Today, social-psychophysiologists have renewed interest in the processing of information out of consciousness (Cacioppo & Petty, 1983; Wilson, 1985). Some researchers have begun to try to find out how the brain blocks out certain kinds of unsettling information. Galin (1974), for example, suggests that the left and right hemispheres may process different kinds of information about an emotional situation, and that the left may "block" the ability of the right to communicate the nonverbalizable information it possesses.

In any case, from the 1940s to the mid-1960s, social psychologists (Byrne, 1964; Gordon, 1957; Postman, Bruner, & McGinnies, 1948) became interested in personality differences in how people deal with threatening emotional material. People were classified as *sensitizers* if they were hypervigilant, alert to potential threats. They were sensitive to variations in their own emotions and in those of others, and tended to dwell on potential problems. *Repressors*, on the other hand, were eager to avoid, repress, or deny threatening material. They tended to deny that they were ever sad, frightened, or angry, even though their physiological reactions and overt behavior indicated the contrary. They tended to ignore as well evidence that others were upset (Byrne, 1964). Some can fall so out of touch with their own and others' feelings as to be labeled *alexithymic* (i.e., having no words for emotion). Neuroscientists have proposed various physiological explanations for alexithymia, including the blockage of impulses from the left hemisphere to the right at the corpus callosum and the disconnection between higher cortical centers and the limbic system (MacLean, 1949; Ten Houten, Hoppe, Bogen, & Walter, 1985, 1986).

We might expect sensitizers, who attend carefully to others' emotions, whether pleasant or not, to be more vulnerable to contagion; repressors, who are oblivious to others' unsettling feelings, should be more resistant. As yet, there is no evidence in support of these speculations.

*Mood and contagion.* Generally, novelist John Updike (1989) is the most gracious and generous of men. For many years, however, he suffered from psoriasis. When his suffering was most acute, he observed how insensitive he became to the suffering of others:

> So wrapped up in my skin, so watchful of its day-to-day permutations, I have, it might be, too little concern to spare for the homeless, the disenfranchised, and the unfortunate who figure so largely in the inner passions of smooth-pelted liberals like my first wife. *I* am unfortunate, is my prime thought: Nature played a quite unnecessary trick on me. Other disfigured or handicapped people annoy me, in reminding me of myself. How much hard heartedness is normal? I sometimes worry that my self-obsession on the epidermal level has deadened those feelers that sentimentally interact with the rest of mankind. (pp. 77–78)

Cognitive social psychologists have argued that mood should affect susceptibility to emotional contagion. Happy people should find it easy to pay full attention to others, to absorb and react to all that they say and do; thus, they should be quite vulnerable to contagion.

In contrast, people who are extremely depressed, anxious, or angry may have a great deal more trouble absorbing information. There is some evidence in support of this argument. It has been reported that happy people are more attentive to incoming stimuli and better able to process and recall it (Easterbrook, 1959; Mandler, 1984; Oatley & Jenkins, 1992; Sedikides, 1992); they are especially open and receptive to external stimulation (Bousfield, 1950), and their memories may be enhanced (Isen, 1987). Conversely, sad people seem to find it difficult to attend to, process, and recall incoming information. Researchers have observed that both sad and/or depressed people seem more preoccupied with themselves than with others or with the world around them; hence, not surprisingly, they show deficits in attention and performance (American Psychiatric Association, 1987; Beck, 1972; Oatley & Jenkins, 1992; Sedikides, 1992). People can only focus on a limited number of things at once; under stress, they are forced to devote at least some attention to their inner world – their throbbing heads, their pounding hearts, their upset stomachs (Carlson & Hatfield, 1992) – and to the events that seem to be causing stress; this, too, may make it hard to concentrate on peripheral events.

Elaine Hatfield and her colleagues in Hawaii (Hsee et al., 1991) conducted an experiment to ascertain whether happy subjects were indeed more likely than sad subjects to attend to and catch the emotions of target persons. First, college students were primed to experience a happy, neutral, or sad mood by being asked to recall a series of happy, neutral, or sad events. (Subjects in the neutral condition were asked to think of three classrooms and to recall various technical details of the rooms, such as their dimensions, number of windows, types of floor, and brands of equipment. The mood induction technique used – *autobiographic recollections,* developed by Harold Masak and Rudolf Dreikurs [1973] for use in clinical settings – has been found to be better than the oft-used Velton Mood Induction Procedures [Brewer et al., 1980].) After this standard mood manipulation, subjects were asked to observe the videotapes of the target person relating one of the happiest or saddest experiences in his life.

The authors found that subjects, regardless of their mood, did seem to catch the target person's emotions. This is clear both from their self-reports and from judges' ratings of subjects' facial expressions as they watched the happy or sad interview. There was also *some* suggestion, however, that preexisting mood may have affected subjects' receptivity to emotional contagion: Happy students were more attentive to the target person's expressions of emotion – simply knowing more about his emotional situation – and were somewhat more likely to mimic his happy *or* sad emotions than were sad subjects (although this difference was nonsignificant).

Such research suggests a dismal conclusion: It is happy people who are most receptive to others and most likely to catch their moods; the unhappy seem relatively oblivious to others' feelings and to contagion. Thus, when Good Samaritans venture out to cheer up the sad, anxious, and lonely, there looms the horrible possibility that they will make themselves miserable while accomplishing little for the suffering recipients of their good works.

## Hypothesis 5.2: Self-construals and contagion

Hypothesis 5.2 states that an individual whose self is construed as fundamentally interrelated with others should be more vulnerable to emotional contagion than one whose self is construed as distinct and unique from others. A therapist may become depressed while speaking with a depressed patient in part because the former is so attentive to and focused on what the latter is saying and doing. It may be precisely because a therapist is more absorbed in the patient than in herself that the therapist is at risk for being swept away in the client's emotions.

Hazel Markus and Shinobu Kitayama (1991) summarize evidence that self-construals do indeed have an impact on emotional experience and contagion. Western cultures, such as that of the United States, value individuality, independence, and uniqueness; socialization in these cultures, according to Markus and Kitayama, tends to produce individuals who construe themselves as distinct, independent, and unique. Other cultures, such as China's and Japan's, emphasize the fundamental relatedness of individuals to one another and value conformity and harmonious interdependence; socialization in these countries emphasizes the definition of self in relation to family, ancestors, and the others around one, so that the self tends to be construed as being part of a social collective. Markus and Kitayama (1991) review evidence that individuals from cultures that emphasize interdependence are especially vulnerable to the experience of other-focused emotions and contagion. Of course, individuals within a culture differ in the extent to which they construe the self as independent or interdependent. Kazuo Kato and Hazel Markus (1992) developed a scale, based on their work, by which to measure individual differences in these self-construals (Table 5.1).

# Table 5.1. *Interdependence–Independence Scale*

Please rate how well the following statements describe you, using the 10-point scale below (use integral numbers such as 1, not decimal numbers, such as 2.5). Put your rating on the line before each statement. Work as quickly as possible. Do not think too much of certain statements and do not worry about consistency of your responses.

| Doesn't describe me at all | 0—1—2—3—4—5—6—7—8—9 | Describes me very much |
|---|---|---|

\_\_ 1. When making a decision, I first consider how it will affect others before considering how it will affect me.[a]

\_\_ 2. How I behave depends upon the people around in the situation.[b]

\_\_ 3. I feel guilty when I say "No" to someone who asks me for help.[a]

\_\_ 4. I am special.[c]

\_\_ 5. Nothing can keep me from doing something if I want to do it.[c]

\_\_ 6. It is important to maintain harmony in the group.[a]

\_\_ 7. If someone helps me, I feel a strong obligation to return the favor sometime later.[a]

\_\_ 8. It is important to me that I remain in a group if the group needs me even though I am not happy with the group.[a]

\_\_ 9. It is better to follow tradition or authority than to try to do something in my way.[c]

\_\_ 10. It is important to me that I am liked by many others.[b]

\_\_ 11. It is important to me that I am a cooperative participant in group activities.[b]

\_\_ 12. I would rather not insist on it, if something I believe is right hurts other people's feelings.[c]

\_\_ 13. I am always myself. I do not act like other people.[d]

\_\_ 14. If other people do not like my idea, I tend to change it, even though I like it.[c]

\_\_ 15. I have difficulty saying "No" when someone asks me for help.[a]

\_\_ 16. I automatically tune myself into other people's expectations of me.[b]

\_\_ 17. If I like it, I do not care what other people around me think of my idea.[c]

\_\_ 18. When I am asked for help and I need to say "No," I may feel bad but not guilty because other people's business is not mine.[a]

\_\_ 19. Even though the people around me may hold a different opinion, I stick to what I believe in.[c]

\_\_ 20. No matter what the situation or setting is, I am always true to myself.[d]

\_\_ 21. It is important to me that I make a favorable impression on others.[b]

\_\_ 22. The most important thing to me is to have a sense of belonging to my own group(s).[b]

\_\_ 23. It is important to me to maintain a good relationship with everybody.[b]

\_\_ 24. I can take care of myself.[d]

\_\_ 25. I have planned my future.[d]

\_\_ 26. I know my weaknesses and strengths.[d]

\_\_ 27. I usually make my own decisions by myself.[d]

\_\_ 28. I always know what I want.[d]

\_\_ 29. I always care about what other people think of me.[b]

\_\_ 30. Before making a decision, I always consult with others.[b]

\_\_ 31. I am unique – different from others in many respects.[c]

[a]Maintaining self/other bonds (interdependence).
[b]Concern with others' evaluation (interdependence).
[c]Self–other differentiation (independence).
[d]Self-knowledge (independence).
*Source:* Adapted from Kato & Markus (1992).

Markus and Kitayama (1991) proposed that individual differences in interdependence–independence within cultures should also influence emotions and emotional contagion. Thus, someone whose self is construed as fundamentally interrelated to others should be more vulnerable to contagion of the emotions of others within this expanded self-construal than should an individual whose self is construed as distinct and unique from others.

### Hypothesis 5.3: Reading emotional expressions and contagion

Jeannette Haviland and Carol Malatesta (1981) observed that people differ in how well they can read others. According to Hypothesis 5.3, people who are able to read others' emotional expressions should be especially vulnerable to contagion. (Awareness of others' feelings is, we suspect, a predictor of sharing those feelings even if it is not a necessary condition for contagion.) According to Haviland and Malatesta, men and women differ in how interested they are in social stimuli, how carefully they attend to nonverbal cues to emotion, how good they are at interpreting emotional cues, and in their willingness to respond to those cues. These researchers also found that women were slightly more likely than men to catch others' emotions. (We discuss the research on gender differences later in this chapter.) Psychometricians have developed a number of psychological tests to measure what some regard as a prerequisite of emotional contagion – the ability to read (decode) others' emotional communications.

*Tests for the decoding of emotional communications.* Tests that evaluate one's ability to decode emotional communications include the following:

1. *The Affective Sensitivity Test* (Kagan, 1978). Subjects are shown videotapes of interactions between therapists and clients, physicians and patients, and teachers and students; they are then asked to guess what the clients, patients, and students were feeling.
2. *The Brief Affect Recognition Test* (Ekman & Friesen, 1974). Subjects view slides of people expressing happiness, sadness, fear, anger, surprise, disgust, or neutrality and are asked to guess which emotions are being expressed.
3. *The Communication of Affect Receiving Ability Test* (Buck, 1976b; Buck & Carroll, 1974). Subjects are asked to watch a silent

Table 5.2. *An early and brief emotional contagion scale*

| |
|---|
| * 1. I often find that I can remain cool in spite of the excitement around me. |
| 2. I tend to lose control when I am bringing bad news to people. |
| * 3. I tend to remain calm even though those around me worry. |
| 4. I cannot continue to feel O.K. if people around me are depressed. |
| * 5. I don't get upset just because a friend is acting upset. |
| 6. I don't become nervous if others around me are nervous. |
| 7. The people around me have a great influence on my moods. |

*Note:* Items marked with an asterisk are reversed in scoring.
*Source:* Stiff et al. (1988), p. 204. Copyright © 1988 by The Speech Communication Association. Reprinted by permission of the publisher.

videotape of 25 different target persons (who are themselves looking at slides that are sexual, scenic, unpleasant, or unusual) and to guess what sorts of slides the targets are viewing.

4. *Profile of Nonverbal Sensitivity* (Rosenthal et al., 1979c). Subjects view a videotape of a target person expressing a variety of emotions facially, vocally, and posturally.

5. *Social Interpretation Test* (Archer & Akert, 1977). Subjects watch 20 brief videotaped segments of two people talking. The segments contain visual and vocal cues as to what emotions the speakers feel. Respondents are asked a number of factual questions about the interaction (e.g., "Is the person on the telephone talking to a man or a woman?").

In each of these tests, respondents are credited for guessing correctly.

*Tests for emotional contagion.* Researchers have also developed two measures of emotional contagion:

1. *An early and brief emotional contagion scale.* James Stiff and his colleagues (Stiff, Dillard, Somera, Kim, & Sleight, 1988) developed a very brief measure of emotional contagion (Table 5.2). Individuals who score high on this scale should be especially vulnerable to emotional contagion; those who score low should be especially resistant.

2. *The Emotional Contagion Scale.* Recently, Elaine Hatfield and her students Lisa Orimoto and R. William Doherty (Doherty, Orimoto, Hebb, & Hatfield, 1993) developed the Emotional Contagion Scale, a measure of vulnerability to contagion (Table 5.3). This scale consists of 18 items designed to assess susceptibility to catching joy/

happiness, love, fear/anxiety, anger, and sadness/depression, as well as general susceptibility to emotional contagion. The items designed to tap susceptibility to each of these emotions are as follows (asterisks indicate reverse scoring):

| | | | | | |
|---|---|---|---|---|---|
| Joy/happiness | 7, *14, 18 | Fear/anxiety | 12, 15, 17 | Sadness/depression | 2, 4, *16 |
| Love | 3, 6, *8 | Anger | *1, 10, 12 | General category | 5, 9, *13 |

Nancy Stockert (1993) provided clear evidence as to the reliability and validity of the Emotional Contagion Scale. She found that men's and women's scores on the scale predicted the extent to which they were susceptible to catching positive and negative emotions.

The Emotional Contagion Scale is an important complement to the preceding scales because it is less dependent on the assumption that skill at decoding nonverbal communications is a prerequisite for emotional contagion. People who score high on this scale should be especially vulnerable to emotional contagion; those who score low should be especially resistant.

## Hypothesis 5.4: Mimicry/synchrony and contagion

According to Hypothesis 5.4, people who tend to mimic others' facial, vocal, and postural expressions should be especially vulnerable to contagion. Little attention has been paid to individual differences in the tendency to mimic emotional expressions, but Charles Osgood (1976) conducted a provocative study bearing on this hypothesis using no more than a window frame and shade on a table in front of the blackboard in a classroom. Students were seated at desks in the classroom, and Osgood wrote 44 emotion words (e.g., happy, sad) on the blackboard. He then selected a student to sit behind the window shade at the table. This student was given a sheet of paper with four emotion words written on it and was instructed to use his or her face to display the first emotion on the list to the rest of the students. When the student's facial display was ready, the window shade was raised to allow the others to see it. The shade was then drawn and the remaining students instructed to record which of the 44 listed emotions they thought they had just seen. Each of the remaining three emotions on the sheet of paper was displayed and rated in a similar fashion. Another student was then selected to display another four emotions, and so on, until all 44 emotions had been displayed and rated.

The purpose of the study, as described thus far, was to determine which facial expressions could be recognized accurately and which

Table 5.3. *The Emotional Contagion Scale*

This is a scale that measures a variety of feelings and behaviors in various situations. There are no right or wrong answers, so try very hard to be completely honest in your answers. Results are *completely confidential*. Read each question and indicate the answer which best applies to you. Please answer each question very carefully. Thank you.

Use the following key:
4. *Always* = Always true for me.
3. *Often*  = Often true for me.
2. *Rarely* = Rarely true for me.
1. *Never*  = Never true for me.

*1. It doesn't bother me to be around angry people.
2. I find myself nodding off when I talk with someone who is depressed.
3. I feel tender and gentle when I see a mother and child hugging each other affectionately.
4. Being around depressed people makes me feel depressed.
5. I pay attention to what other people are feeling.
6. I feel alive and vibrant when I am with the one I love.
7. When someone laughs hard, I laugh too.
*8. When people hug me affectionately, I get upset and I want to back away.
9. I'm very accurate in judging other people's feelings.
10. When I am around people who are angry, I feel angry myself.
11. I find myself clenching my fist when overhearing others quarrel.
12. I wince while observing someone flinching while getting a shot.
13. I'm very sensitive in picking up other people's feelings.
*14. I keep a straight face when those around me are laughing hard.
15. Listening to the shrill screams of a terrified child in a dentist's waiting room makes me feel nervous.
*16. Even if someone I'm talking with begins to cry, I don't get teary-eyed.
17. When someone paces back and forth, I feel nervous and anxious.
18. When someone smiles warmly at me, I smile back and feel happy inside.

*Note:* Items marked with an asterisk are reversed in scoring. The higher the score, the more susceptible to emotional contagion a person would be said to be.
*Source:* Doherty et al. (1993).

were confused with others. In addition, however, Osgood wanted to determine whether mimicry would make students more accurate in their judgments of facial expressions of emotion. He did this by instructing half the students in the class to mimic the facial displays they saw before trying to determine which of the 44 emotions the person was expressing. Of course, it is possible that the posers and/or the mimickers did not do a very good job, or that the students who had not been instructed to mimic what they saw nevertheless did so automatically. In addition, some expressions, such as a big smile for happiness, could be so identifiable as to produce high accuracy rates regardless of mimicry instructions. Nevertheless, Osgood found that students who had been instructed to mimic the posed expressions were more accurate in identifying expressions of pain than were those who had not been so instructed.

Osgood's relatively primitive procedures have been improved upon in recent research, and we found in reviewing this research in chapter 3 that mimicking facial, vocal, and postural expressions of emotion does indeed tend to arouse the emotion of individuals. If the mimicry produced as a result of experimental instructions enhances the transmission of an emotion, then we suspect individual differences in the production of spontaneous mimicry should have similar effects; that is, individuals who tend to mimic others' facial, vocal, and postural expressions should be especially vulnerable to contagion.

### Hypothesis 5.5: Feedback and contagion

According to Hypothesis 5.5, people whose conscious emotional experience is powerfully influenced by peripheral feedback should be most vulnerable to contagion.

There is some evidence that people differ markedly in the extent to which their inner emotional lives are affected by peripheral feedback. James Laird and Charles Bresler (1992) maintained that people can use two different kinds of information to pinpoint their own emotional states: *self-produced cues* and *situational cues*. Those who rely on self-produced cues are influenced by perceptions of their own expressive behaviors, levels of sympathetic arousal, and instrumental actions. Those who rely on situational cues to sort out what they must be feeling instead use their perceptions as to what most people would feel in such a situation. (They may take it for granted that they must be angry and offended when insulted because "anyone would be.") Laird and Bresler (1992) put it this way:

> For some people, the experience of an emotion is based on the patterning of bodily and instrumental activities, while for others it arises out of an appreciation of what is appropriate or customary in the particular situation. In James' classic example of the emotional events that link seeing a bear and feeling frightened, apparently some people would "know" they are afraid because they are screaming, fleeing, and their hearts are pound-

ing. Others would know they are afraid because anyone would be afraid when confronted with a large, potentially hungry carnivore. (p. 35, original MS)

Researchers have found that people vary greatly in the extent to which they rely on facial, vocal, and postural feedback in determining what they feel. When some subjects were induced to smile or frown, speak gently or harshly, stand proudly or stoop, they reported strong emotional responses; others were virtually uninfluenced by such peripheral feedback (Laird & Crosby, 1974; Bresler & Laird, 1983).

There is considerable evidence that persons who rely on self-produced cues for emotional information differ in a number of ways from those who use situational cues. The former tend to equate emotions with "sensations"; the latter, with "judgments," since they assume they must experience whatever emotions are appropriate in the given circumstances (Laird & Crosby, 1974, p. 57). Those who rely on self-produced cues for "decoding" their subjective emotional states are profoundly affected by facial feedback, gaze, and postural feedback (Duclos et al., 1989). They feel more romantic attraction for strangers into whose eyes they are induced to gaze than do people who rely on situational cues (Kellerman et al., 1989). When they are frightened (say, of snakes), their fear is not reduced by fake "tranquilizers" (Duncan & Laird, 1980; Ross & Olson, 1981; Storms & Nisbett, 1970); they are all too aware of what they feel – fear! They tend to remember emotional material better if it is associated with appropriate facial expressions (Laird et al., 1982), and can do better at identifying others' emotions if allowed first to imitate others' facial expressions and then to guess what these others are feeling (Wixon & Laird, 1981). The opposites are true of people who rely on situational cues to tell them what they feel.

We might thus expect people who rely on self-produced cues to be more vulnerable to emotional contagion than those who rely on situational cues.

*Hypothesis 5.6: Emotional responsiveness and contagion*

To foster study of constitutional differences in emotional reactivity, David Klein and John Cacioppo (1993) developed their Autonomic Reactivity Scale, which gauges individual differences in arousability in emotional situations. There are two parts to the questionnaire

(Table 5.4): In the first, individuals rate how well they are characterized by each of a list of autonomic reactions to arousing situations (e.g., "When I feel happy, I feel weak and shaky"). The second part, based on selected items from the Somatic Perception Questionnaire (Shields & Stern, 1979), requires that subjects indicate the degree to which they are aware that they react autonomically to arousing events in each of six different ways (e.g., sweating palms).

Hypothesis 5.6 posited that people who are emotionally responsive would find it easier to share others' emotional experiences. In two recent studies, David Klein and John Cacioppo (1993) administered the Autonomic Reactivity Scale and the Emotional Contagion Scale (Doherty et al., 1993) in addition to the Facial Expressiveness and ACT scales. As we noted in chapter 4, high scorers on the Facial Expressiveness Scale also scored high on the Emotional Contagion Scale. Results also indicated that people who scored high on the Autonomic Reactivity Scale scored high on the Emotional Contagion Scale ($r = +.51$, $N = 62$ in Study 1; $r = +.51$, $N = 33$ in Study 2). Importantly, the Autonomic Reactivity and Facial Expressivity scales were only weakly correlated ($r = +.32$ in Study 1; $r = +.11$ in Study 2), and each predicted significant and unique variance in people's scores on the Emotional Contagion Scale in both studies. Thus, people who tend to be physiologically responsive in emotional situations appear to be especially susceptible to emotional contagion.

## Gender differences in susceptibility to contagion

In chapter 4 we found evidence that, although infant girls are no more expressive than infant boys, by adulthood women are more expressive than men in Western cultures. There is also some evidence that women are slightly more likely than men to catch others' emotions.

Jeannette Haviland and Carol Malatesta (1981) explored the development of infant's and children's ability to read nonverbal communications. They found that, from birth, boys seemed to be far less effective than girls at decoding others' emotions. Let us review a bit of the evidence that led them to this conclusion.

First, in order to understand what others are feeling, one must pay attention to others (or risk missing cues). On all indicators, it appears that, from birth onward, females are more attentive than males to others' emotional expressions. For example, from age 1 *day*, females

Table 5.4. *The Autonomic Reactivity Scale*

*Part I: How Well Do You Know Yourself?*

The following items should be rated on a six-point scale ranging from 0 (*Not at all descriptive of me*) to 5 (*Very descriptive of me*). Please answer the following questions as accurately and honestly as possible.

1.  When I feel anxious, I experience accelerated heart rate.
2.  My hands get clammy before important dates.
3.  I tend to breathe irregularly before facing something unpleasant like telling someone something I know will disappoint them.
4.  Sudden changes of any kind produce an immediate emotional effect on me.
5.  When I feel anxious, I have difficulty talking.
6.  When I feel anxious, my breathing becomes more rapid.
7.  Working under a deadline makes me perspire.
8.  When I feel anxious, I get a sinking or heavy feeling in my stomach.
9.  Getting up in front of a group makes my stomach churn and/or my hands feel clammy.
10. When I feel anxious, I get a lump in my throat or a choked up feeling.
11. I get flustered when I have several things to do at once.
12. When I feel anxious, the intensity of my heart beat increases very much.
13. When I feel anxious, I am often aware of changes in my heart beat.
14. When I feel happy, I feel weak and shaky.

Subjects were asked to indicate their answers on the following scale:

\_\_\_ 0  Not at all descriptive of me
\_\_\_ 1  Rarely descriptive of me
\_\_\_ 2  Occasionally descriptive of me
\_\_\_ 3  Regularly descriptive of me
\_\_\_ 4  Frequently descriptive of me
\_\_\_ 5  Very descriptive of me

*Part II:* Below, you will find a list of six reactions to an arousing situation. On the same 0–5 scale as used in Part I, please indicate the degree to which you are aware of each of the following reactions in situations such as: (a) before an important interview, (b) before making a speech or presentation in front of strangers, (c) before going to or while waiting in a doctor's or dentist's office, or (d) any other situation that *you* find arousing.

1.  Sweating palms
2.  Lump in throat or dryness of mouth
3.  Awareness of heart beat
4.  Nervous stomach
5.  General body sweating
6.  Frequent urination or urge to urinate

*Source:* Klein & Cacioppo (1993).

establish and maintain eye contact better than do males (Haviland & Malatesta, 1981; Hittelman & Dickes, 1979). Girls and women establish eye contact faster and more frequently, maintain it for a longer duration, and spend a greater percentage of time so engaged. Boys and men, in contrast, are more likely to avert their gaze (Haviland & Malatesta, 1981). In addition, from at least age 4 years onward, females seem to be better at processing, storing, and retrieving social stimuli such as faces, names, or voices (Feldstein, 1976; Haviland & Malatesta, 1981).

Second, according to Haviland and Malatesta (1981), there is evidence that males are not as good as females at accurately interpreting others' nonverbal cues of emotion. Judith Hall (1978) conducted a meta-analysis of 125 studies exploring gender differences in the ability to read nonverbal expressions of emotion. She found that, at all ages, females were more accurate at judging emotional states, regardless of the emoter's gender and means of communication (face, voice, posture, or some combination thereof). (The stimuli had been presented in a variety of ways, including drawings, photos, films, videotapes, content-standard speech, randomized spliced speech, and electronically filtered speech.) Women had the advantage in 84% of the studies, men in only 16% of the studies where gender differences had been found, though these differences were moderate in magnitude. Women were simply better at reading what is meant by the awkward glance, superior smile, or hesitant speech. Their advantage was most pronounced for facial cues, less pronounced for bodily cues, and least pronounced for vocal cues.

Hall considered several possibilities for why women might be better than men at judging others' emotions: Perhaps they are "wired" from birth to be especially sensitive to others' feelings, or are taught to be this way by society; or perhaps their oppressed status makes them especially attuned to nonverbal communication – particularly if such cues allow them to anticipate the wishes of powerful others.

"She'd ne'er go away, I know, if Adam 'ud be fond on her an' marry her . . . ," said Lisbeth.

Seth paused a moment, and looked up, with a slight blush, at his mother's face. "What! has she said anything o' that sort to thee, mother?"

"Said? nay, she'll say nothin'. It's on'y the men as have to wait till folks say things afore they find them out."

– George Eliot, *Adam Bede*

In *Some Can Whistle*, Larry McMurtry (1989) depicted the unease of retired TV writer Dannie Deck with the fact that his old girlfriend Jeanie knew more about his emotional states than he did:

> As soon as it became morning in New York, I called Jeanie, an early riser. . . . From the tone of her hello I could tell that it must not be the best of times, that her outlook for the day was not really an optimistic outlook; but at the sound of my voice she immediately rose from her drift and raised her antenna. Just thinking of her raising her antenna made me nervous and hesitant, because Jeanie's receiving equipment – her brain and intuitive faculties – picked up far too much, even when she wasn't bothering to tune it, particularly. Even when she wasn't paying close attention she heard more than I really wanted her to hear, and when she *was* paying attention, as she was now, she not only heard more than I wanted her to hear, she heard more than I knew I was saying. (pp. 308–309)

He that has eyes to see and ears to hear may convince himself
that no mortal can keep a secret. If his lips are silent, he
chatters with his finger-tips; betrayal oozes out of him at
every pore.
                                                    – Sigmund Freud

Patricia Noller (1986) examined the array of theories that have been proposed to explain existing sex differences in decoding symbolic, intentional messages and spontaneous, nonverbal ones. Women seem to be equally good at decoding the messages of intimates, friends, and strangers. Men are more accurate at figuring out what people they know are trying to say; they are less good at decoding the messages of strangers. Both men and women find it hard to decode deceptive and discrepant communications (when, say, the face sends one message and the voice another). After considering a variety of possible explanations for these results, Noller concluded that the results were probably attributable to the fact that women understand the codes and usages of nonverbal communication better than do men. Women are more likely to know the social rules governing communications, to endorse the rules, and to be able to utilize them.

Robert Rosenthal and Bella DePaulo (1979a,b) offered additional evidence in support of this argument. They observed that interpersonal relations usually go better when people are sensitive to non-verbal cues. Sometimes, of course, if people knew everything their friends were thinking and feeling, their friendships would suffer. They tested the hypothesis that women are more "polite" than men (i.e., they learn not to "eavesdrop" on the conversations of others) in an intriguing series of experiments. Different nonverbal channels vary on the dimension of control versus "leakiness." How difficult it is for people to "fake it" depends on the channel of communication they use.

> [D]ifferent nonverbal channels can be ordered according to their leakiness, with the face being the most controlled and the least leaky; the body being more leaky than the face; tone of voice being more leaky than the body; very brief exposures of "micromomentary" facial/bodily cues being more leaky; and discrepancies between different channels being the more difficult to control and therefore the most leaky of all. (Buck, 1984, p. 266)

Rosenthal and DePaulo found that, as predicted, women's skills at decoding nonverbal messages get progressively worse as the nonverbal cues become leakier. (Women are better at reading faces than body language, better at reading body language than tone of voice, and worst of all at reading inconsistencies in messages.)

Some researchers (Fujita et al., 1980) have found that women are better than men in decoding posed but not spontaneous expressions. These findings make sense in terms of Rosenthal and De Paulo's analysis, for spontaneous expressions are more likely to contain leaky cues (Manstead et al., 1982).

If women do pay more attention to others, mimic their faces, voices, and postures more, and rely more on peripheral feedback than do men, it seems likely that they might also be more susceptible than men to emotional contagion. There is some evidence that girls and women are indeed more likely to catch the emotions of others. As Haviland and Malatesta (1981) observed, in reviewing 16 such studies of children from age 3 and up:

> When ability to share is measured by a matching emotional response, whether it be a matching facial or vocal expression, or a verbal report of matching feelings, girls "win" hands down. (pp. 192–193)

The authors concluded:

> 1. The trend is not always strong, nor totally consistent, but if we take together the results of all the studies reviewed thus far, we are forced to conclude that there is very definitely a female advantage in nonverbal sensitivity to emotional cues; in addition, there appears to be developmental continuity. Females of all ages gaze more, show greater facility at remembering faces and discriminating various affective expressions, and respond more emphatically (as measured by matching expressions) than do their male counterparts.
>
> 2. It is not clear whether the differences reflect initial motivational differences or differences in absolute ability. (p. 193)

Recently, Elaine Hatfield and her students (Doherty et al., 1993) explored gender and ethnic differences on the Emotional Contagion Scale. They interviewed 884 men and women from a variety of groups: college students (age range 18–53, avg. 22.8), physicians (24–80, avg. 40.9), and the United States Marines (18–44, avg. 24.7). The sample, representative of Hawaii's multicultural population, included subjects of African, Chinese, European, Filipino, Hawaiian, Japanese, Korean, Samoan, and other ancestry. In all groups, women reported being far more susceptible to emotional contagion than were men (Table 5.5). The researchers also compared men's and women's scores on the Emotional Contagion Scale's subscales. First, they divided the emotions into two categories: positive (joy and love) and negative (sadness, anger, and fear). Women said they were more susceptible to catching both the positive and negative emotions than were men. Finally, the study compared men's and women's susceptibility to catching each of the individual emotions. Women were found to be more likely to catch each of the emotions, and emotions in general, than were men.

## Susceptibility to contagion in various kinds of relationships

Recently, Elaine Hatfield and her colleagues (Hatfield, Cacioppo, & Rapson, 1992) proposed that people should be especially vulnerable to contagion in certain kinds of relationships:

> Couples passionately or companionately in love should be especially likely to catch the emotions of the beloved.

Table 5.5. *Gender and occupation in relation to susceptibility to emotional contagion*

| Emotional Contagion scores | Gender | | Occupation | | |
|---|---|---|---|---|---|
| | Men | Women | Student | Physician | Marine |
| *Total score* | 2.82$^a$ | 3.03$^b$ | 2.95$^a$ | 2.89$^{ab}$ | 2.81$^c$ |
| Positive items | 3.19$^a$ | 3.36$^b$ | 3.30$^a$ | 3.18$^b$ | 3.19$^{bc}$ |
| Negative items | 2.51$^a$ | 2.78$^b$ | 2.68$^a$ | 2.62$^{ab}$ | 2.48$^c$ |
| *Individual emotions* | | | | | |
| Joy | 3.14$^a$ | 3.31$^b$ | 3.27$^a$ | 3.11$^b$ | 3.08$^{bc}$ |
| Love | 3.28$^a$ | 3.46$^b$ | 3.35$^a$ | 3.30$^b$ | 3.37$^a$ |
| Fear | 2.61$^a$ | 2.96$^b$ | 2.83$^a$ | 2.70$^b$ | 2.59$^{bc}$ |
| Anger | 2.39$^a$ | 2.49$^b$ | 2.45$^a$ | 2.49$^{ab}$ | 2.35$^c$ |
| Sadness | 2.50$^a$ | 2.83$^b$ | 2.71$^a$ | 2.63$^{ab}$ | 2.46$^c$ |
| General | 2.94$^a$ | 3.08$^b$ | 3.00$^a$ | 3.03$^{ab}$ | 2.95$^b$ |

*Note:* Within each set ("Gender" or "Occupation"), means with different superscripts are significantly different.
*Source:* Doherty et al., 1993.

Mothers should be especially prone to share their infants' emotions. (In fact, the mother–infant relationship may be a prototype of the kind of relationship in which people "lose their boundaries.")

People who have a psychological investment in others' welfare should be vulnerable to contagion; thus, psychotherapists may be prone to catch their clients' emotions, teachers their students' moods, and caretakers their dependents' feelings.

Children of alcoholics ("co-dependents") may be especially sensitive to the changing moods of their troubled parents.

People who have power over others should be resistant to contagion; those they control should be more vulnerable to soaking up emotions.

In brief, men and women should be most vulnerable to contagion in two kinds of relationships: (1) love or other close relationships, and (2) those that involve power. Researchers have conducted a series of studies designed to document that subjects are most susceptible to contagion in such encounters. We review these next.

## The effect of loving and liking on emotional contagion

Where there are two, one cannot be wretched, and one not.
— Euripides

*The effect of loving on emotional contagion.* In the fifth century B.C., Plato, in his *Symposium* (1953), offered a wry theory about the origins of love. Originally, he contended, humanity was divided into three kinds of people: men/men, women/women, and the androgynous — a union of the two. Human beings were round: Their backs and sides formed a circle. They had one head with two faces (always looking in opposite directions), four ears, four hands, four feet, and two sets of genitalia. They could walk upright and go backward or forward, as they pleased; or they could roll over at a great pace, turning nimbly on their four hands and four feet like tumblers.

Eventually, the gods and humanity came into conflict. To punish them for their arrogance, the gods cut the men, women, and androgynous beings into two parts, "like a Sorb-apple which is halved for pickling." Since the division, the cleft parts have wandered the earth, each searching for its lost half. In the Platonic scheme, the halves of the once-complete men became "the best of the lot": These men were valiant and manly; they embraced that which was like themselves (other men). The androgynous halves, too, continued to seek *their* cleft portion: The men became lovers of women while the women became "adulterous women" who lusted after men. Finally, the halves of the once-complete women continued to seek their lost selves, yearning for lesbian attachments. Thus, humanity is always longing for completion, seeking to meld with another person. This, then, is the nature of love according to Plato: two deficient beings made whole by union with the other.

Literature echos the Platonic theme that, in love, we long to merge with our lost selves. For example, in Emily Brontë's (1847/1976) *Wuthering Heights*, Cathy pours out her heart to her nurse Nelly, explaining that she loves Heathcliff:

> It would degrade me to marry Heathcliff, now; so he shall never know how I love him; and that, not because he's handsome, Nelly, but because he's more myself than I am. Whatever our souls are made of, his and mine are the same. . . .
>
> I cannot express it; but surely you and everybody have a notion that there is, or should be, an existence of yours beyond

you. What were the use of my creation if I were entirely contained here? My great miseries in this world have been Heathcliff's miseries, and I watched and felt each from the beginning; my great thought in living is himself. If all else perished, and *he* remained, I should still continue to be; and, if all else remained, and he were annihilated, the Universe would turn to a mighty stranger. I should not seem a part of it. . . . Nelly, I *am* Heathcliff – he's always, always in my mind – not as pleasure, any more than I am always a pleasure to myself – but, as my own being – so, don't talk of our separation again. (pp. 100–102)

The Duke and Duchess of Windsor, in their love letters written before their marriage, referred to themselves as WE – the W standing for Wallis and the E for Edward. (Sometimes clients of Elaine Hatfield and Richard Rapson think of the two therapists as one, often calling them "Dickandelaine." This is especially unsettling when only one or the other is at the session: "Well, Dickandelaine, it was like this.") To the extent that lovers are "as one," we might expect them to be potent receivers of emotion.

No matter how much we love someone, our feelings may sometimes rise only to the level of pale reflections. C. S. Lewis (1961) wrote in *A Grief Observed* of being passionately in love with his new bride. When they discovered that she would soon die of cancer, they tried to cram a lifetime of joy into the time remaining:

It is incredible how much happiness, even how much gaiety, we sometimes had together after all hope was gone. How long, how tranquilly, how nourishingly, we talked together that last night!

And yet, not quite together. There's a limit to the 'one flesh'. You can't really share someone else's weakness, or fear or pain. What you feel may be bad. It might conceivably be as bad as what the other felt, though I should distrust anyone who claimed that it was. But it would still be quite different. When I speak of fear, I mean the merely animal fear, the recoil of the organism from its destruction; the smothery feeling; the sense of being a rat in a trap. It can't be transferred. The mind can sympathize; the body, less. In one way the bodies of lovers can do it least. All their love passages have trained them to have, not identical, but complementary correlative, even opposite, feelings about one another.

We both knew this. I had my miseries, not hers; she had hers, not mine. The end of hers would be the coming-of-age of mine. We were setting out on different roads. (pp. 14–15)

*The effect of liking on emotional contagion.* A number of researchers have pointed out that people are most likely to mimic those they like and to catch their emotions. One of my graduate students, who divorced a battering husband years ago, mentioned that she dreaded it when her adolescent son spent the summer with his father. He loved his dad so much that he came back with his haircut, dressed like him, and walking and talking like him. A strong advocate of the position that rapport, mimicry, and contagion are linked is Desmond Morris (1966). We shall let him speak for himself in this extended exerpt.

POSTURAL ECHO
When two friends meet and talk informally they usually adopt similar body postures. If they are particularly friendly and share identical attitudes to the subjects being discussed, then the positions in which they hold their bodies are liable to become even more alike, to the point where they virtually become carbon copies of each other. This is not a deliberate imitative process. The friends in question are automatically indulging in what has been called Postural Echo, and they do this unconsciously as part of a natural body display of companionship.

There is a good reason for this. A true bond of friendship is usually only possible between people of roughly equal status. This equality is demonstrated in many indirect ways, but it is reinforced in face-to-face encounters by a matching of the postures of relaxation or alertness. In this way the body transmits a silent message, saying: 'See, I am just like you'; and this message is not only sent unconsciously but also understood in the same manner. The friends simply 'feel right' when they are together.

The precision of the Postural Echo can be quite remarkable. Two friends talking in a restaurant both lean on the table with the same elbow, tilt their bodies forward to the same angle and nod in agreement with the same rhythm. Two other friends reclining in armchairs both have their legs crossed in exactly the same way and both have one arm across their lap. The two

friends chatting while standing by a wall both lean against it
with the same body slope and both have one hand thrust deep
into a pocket and the other hand resting on the hip.

More surprising is the fact that they frequently synchronize
their movements as they talk. When one uncrosses his legs,
the other soon follows suit, and when one leans back a little, so
does his companion. When one lights a cigarette or gets a
drink, he tries to persuade the other to join him. If he fails he is
disappointed, not because he really cares if his friend smokes a
cigarette or takes a drink, but because if they do not both smoke
or drink at the same time, there will be a slight loss of synchrony in their actions. In such situations we frequently see one
friend insisting that the other join him, even when it is obvious that he is not interested. 'I don't want to drink alone' and
'Am I the only one smoking?' are phrases often heard in this
context; and, quite often, the reluctant companion gives in, despite his wishes, in order to keep up the synchrony.

'Do come and sit down, you look so uncomfortable standing
there' is another common invitation that helps to increase the
chances for Postural Echo, and groups of friends usually try to
arrange themselves in such a way that they can lock in to one
another's body postures and movement rhythms. The subjective sensation gained in such cases is one of being 'at ease'. It is
simply enough for one person to destroy such ease, merely by
adopting an alien posture – stiff and formal, or jerky and anxious.

Similarly, an intensely active, excited gathering of friends
soon becomes critical if one of their number is slumped lethar-
gically in an unmatching posture. They will plead with him to
join in the fun and if, for some private reason, he cannot do so,
they will refer to him as having been a 'wet blanket' and spoil-
ing the evening. Again, the person in question has *said* nothing hostile and has done nothing that directly interfered with
the actions of the others. He has merely destroyed the group's
Postural Echo. . . .

Sometimes it is possible to observe two distinct sets of Postural Echoes in the same group. Usually this is related to 'taking sides' in a group argument. If three of the group are disput-
ing with the other four, the members of each sub-group will
tend to match up their body postures and movements by keep-

ing distinct from the other sub-group. On occasion, it is even possible to predict that one of them is changing sides before he has declared his change of heart verbally, because his body will start to blend with the postures of the opposing 'team'. A mediator, trying to control such a group, may take up an intermediate body posture as if to say 'I am neutral', folding his arms like one side and crossing his legs like the other . . .

Recent American slang includes the two terms 'good vibes' and 'bad vibes' . . . and it looks as if these expressions, referring to feeling at ease, or not at ease with someone, may reflect an intuitive recognition of the fundamental importance of Postural Echo and the unconscious synchrony of small body movements in everyday social life. (pp. 83–85)

Scientists have found considerable support for Morris's position. In chapter 1 we reviewed the evidence that rapport and vocal mimicry/synchrony are linked. There is also some evidence that people are more likely to "drink in" the emotions of those they like.

Norma Feshbach and Kiki Roe (1968) studied the effects of gender similarity on emotional contagion. They proposed that children would feel the most attraction and display the most empathy for targets of the same sex. Boys and girls in the first grade were told they were going to see pictures and hear stories about children their own age. They were shown a series of slides of children who were obviously happy, sad, frightened, or angry, and were told a bit about the situation in which the children found themselves (e.g., at a birthday party, having lost their dog, getting lost, having someone snatch their toy). After viewing each slide, the children were asked how *they* felt. They were also asked to guess how the target children felt. As predicted, the children were more likely to share the emotions if the targets were of their own gender.

In another typical experiment, Dennis Krebs (1975) explored the impact of liking and perceived similarity on emotional contagion. In an initial meeting, college men were given a series of personality and value tests. During the experimental session, half of the men were led to believe that they and their partners (experimental confederates) were very similar, the other half that they were very different. Then subjects observed their partners play roulette. Sometimes the confederate won, sometimes he lost. (The target signaled his distress by looking "concerned" and jerking his arm back in "pain" each time he was punished with electric shocks.) In the control conditions, subjects merely watched the confederate perform a series of innocuous perceptual and motor tasks. As predicted, it was the subjects who believed that they were similar to the confederate who felt the worst about his suffering. They showed the strongest physiological reactions (the greatest increases in skin conductance and heart rate acceleration) when they were anticipating his shock.

Defeat communicates itself, is handed on. Unlike euphoria. . . .
It was odd how glory could not be shared.
                                        – A. S. Byatt

People do not always share the emotions of others. William James (1890/1922) observed that people enjoy seeing those whom they admire prosper and share their misery when they suffer. Contrarily, they enjoy seeing those they dislike suffer and resent their pleasures. We can all think of examples when people do not reflect but contradict the emotions of others. A small boy may take intense pleasure in tormenting his little sister. A physics graduate student at the University of Iowa in 1991 was so envious of his ex-roommate, who had been nominated for a coveted physics prize, that he shot and killed his rival and four professors. The Germans even have a name for the pleasure we take in the suffering of our friends: *Schadenfreude*. We might predict, then, that when people are rivals or enemies they should be especially resistant to contagion.

*The effect of hatred and enmity on susceptibility to contagion.* There is some evidence that when we hate and dislike others it is unusually difficult to share their emotions. Dolf Zillmann and Joanne Cantor (1977) showed second and third graders a film in which a child behaved benevolently, neutrally, or malevolently.

> *Benevolent protagonist:* As the film opened, a little boy was shown in a cheerful mood, interacting with his chums in a friendly manner. Arriving home, he warmly greeted his dog, petting and hugging him. Later, when his little brother asked him for some lunch, he gave him half of his sandwich without hesitating. When his brother asked him to mend his toy airplane, he did so immediately and good-naturedly.
>
> *Malevolent protagonist.* The film opened as the boy was walking down the street with a group of boys his age. He behaved

aggressively, pushing and shoving one of the boys for no apparent reason. Upon arriving home, he hit and shoved his dog. In a later scene, he was shown fixing himself a peanut butter sandwich. When his younger brother asked for some, he refused to share his sandwich and gleefully taunted his brother with the fact that there was no more bread. Later, when his brother asked him to mend his broken airplane, he purposely damaged the toy further. (p. 158)

In the second half of the films, the boy's fate was systematically varied. Half the time, the boy's parents told him to come outside, where they presented him with a beautiful new bicycle. He was euphoric, and was last shown riding happily down the street. The other times the films ended with the boy going outside to ride his bike. While attempting to climb a steep curb, he lost his balance and fell off the bike, and was last seen crying and grimacing in pain. Schoolchildren were asked how happy or sad they had felt while watching the movie and while viewing various incidents therein. Children who had seen the boy behave benevolently or neutrally shared his happiness or pain. Those who had seen him behave malevolently, however, responded totally differently: They were unhappy at seeing him so happy, and happy to see him suffer. The experimenters also secretly videotaped the schoolchildren's faces as they watched the film, but were unable to read their reactions.

Dana Bramel and his colleagues (Bramel, Taub, & Blum, 1968), too, proposed that

[i]f we truly like someone, it pleases us to see him happy and hurts us to see him suffer. If we dislike him, our reaction is just the opposite. (p. 384)

In their test of this hypothesis, these authors invited men and women to serve as "clinicians" in a therapy project. While waiting for the experiment to begin, subjects had a chance to get acquainted with a fellow college student, who was also participating in the project. With half of them, the fellow student was polite and friendly; with the others, he was cocksure, domineering, and insulting.

The subjects were then told that their job as "a clinician" was to listen to a tape, presumably recorded six to nine months earlier: The student they had just met ("the client") had been injected with various kinds of drugs and asked to perform a series of tasks while under their influence. Subjects were to try to evaluate him "much as a therapist might respond to a real patient" (p. 386). They then listened to the tape. The drugs that the target had received presumably made him feel either euphoric, neutral, or miserable and markedly affected his task performance. On the euphoria tape, the confederate giggled wildly and spaced off, now and then, into flights of blissful fantasy. On the neutral tape, his reactions were slow, flat, and bland; presumably the drug blocked all strong emotions. On the misery tape, the confederate acted depressed, nauseated, assailed by unpleasant emotions, and physically miserable. Subjects were asked to indicate (confidentially) how happy and how interested *they* were in the tapes. Those who had been politely treated by the confederate shared his emotions, for good or ill: They were happier hearing his euphoric drug reactions than his misery. Subjects who had been insulted by the confederate did not sop up his emotions: They were equally happy or unhappy whether they heard him feeling euphoric or suffering, and seemed to have hardened their hearts against him, either way. People appeared more likely, then, to share the confederate's ups and downs when they liked him than when they did not.

*The effect of rivalry on emotional contagion.* Finally, there is some evidence that if people are feeling strong emotions, these emotions can swamp the little ripples of emotional contagion.

In an illustrative study, Basil Englis and his colleagues (1981) invited two students to play a stock market game. They were supposed to try to guess which market indicators would rise and which would fall. If they guessed right, they won money; if they guessed wrong, they suffered electric shock. During the game, subjects could presumably view one another on their TV monitors. (Actually, they viewed a videotape of another subject's reactions to learning he had won or lost.) Some subjects' winnings and losses were *linked* to those of the confederate: They soon found that when the confederate smiled, their own guesses had been correct; when he grimaced in pain, they had guessed badly and would themselves be shocked. Other subjects were *in competition* with the confederate: They soon learned that when their partner winced in pain, it was a telltale sign that their own guess had been correct and that they had won; when he smiled, they could anticipate that they had guessed wrong and would soon be receiving an electric shock. In the competition condition, subjects' faces and facial muscle activity (activity of the corrugator supercilii, masseter, and orbicularis oculi muscle regions, as well as heart rate and skin conductance activity) reflected *their own* pleasure or pain (which was directly opposite to that expressed by the confederate) rather than mimicking the confederate's facial displays of emotion.

Not surprisingly, when people are focusing primarily on their own interests, their emotions may well be shaped primarily by their own selfish interests, and their fellow feeling for others with competing interests pale in comparison.

## Power and emotional contagion

What impact does power have on susceptibility to emotional contagion? Elaine Hatfield and her colleagues (Hsee et al., 1990) and others have proposed that the powerless should be more likely to attend to and to experience/express the emotions of those who have power over them than vice versa. Theorists have offered several reasons why there might be an inverse relationship between power and sensitivity to others. First, powerful people have no particular reason to care about the thoughts and feelings of their subordinates; thus, they may pay little attention to them. Subordinates, on the other hand, have every reason to be interested in discovering what makes their superiors "tick": Because they must understand those with power over them if they are to win their favor, they pay close attention to them. At the time of the Selma marches, Martin Luther King expressed surprise that whites often had very little insight into the thoughts, feelings, and experiences of blacks. Blacks *had to* know a great deal about whites.

Second, because superiors may have little reason to care what impression they make on their subordinates, they can afford to be direct in expressing their thoughts and feelings. Hence, it should be fairly easy for subordinates to "read" and respond to them (Snodgrass, 1985). Subordinates, on the other hand, may pretend to think and feel what they think their superiors want them to; thus their superiors may have a great deal more trouble "reading" them (Hall, 1979; Miller, 1976; Thomas, Franks, & Calonico, 1972; Weitz, 1974). Researchers have assembled some evidence that possessing power and being sensitive to others' feelings are negatively correlated (Hall, 1979; Snodgrass, 1985).

Child development researchers have conducted some studies (Grusec & Abramovitch, 1982) to explore the impact that dominant or nondominant adults and children have on children (aged 2–5 years) in natural settings. They found that preschoolers imitated others even more than did older children. Dominant adults and children were more carefully observed, and their gestures, social behaviors, and instrumental behaviors often imitated; moreover, children were generally rewarded for such mimicry. Interestingly enough, however, these researchers also discovered that the dominant frequently imitated others' behavior. The imitation–counterimitation process appeared to foster social interaction, with the dominant seemingly "better" at both aspects – imitating and being imitated – than were their less dominant peers.

Elaine Hatfield and her colleagues (Hsee et al., 1990) tested the hypothesis that power and contagion would be negatively related. Teams of college students were assembled to participate in a learning experiment. Some subjects were assigned to be the teacher (i.e., powerful): It was their job to teach others a list of nonsense syllables, and they could administer severe jolts of electric shock if they thought it would help. Their partners were assigned to be learners (i.e., powerless): It was their job to try to learn the list of nonsense syllables.

The results were somewhat surprising. As predicted, subjects in all conditions did tend to catch the emotions of others. There was, however, no evidence that powerful people were any more resistant to emotional contagion than were their powerless counterparts! In fact, if anything, the powerful were even *more* susceptible to contagion! How can we account for this? First, it is possible that the authors had manipulated not power but *responsibility:* Those assigned to be teachers may have felt the same sort of responsibility that real teachers feel for their vulnerable charges, and may have been more sensitive to the learners than vice versa. Alternatively, perhaps subjects' emotions had been manipulated as well as their power: Teachers may have felt cool, calm, and collected; they may have found it easy to pay full attention to the task at hand and to absorb and react to all that their partners were saying. In contrast, the learners may have been extremely anxious and had a great deal more trouble absorbing information. Subsequent research (Hsee et al., 1991) found some support for this contention; more is needed to determine just how power and contagion are linked.

In spite of this paucity of evidence, applied psychologists certainly act as if there is strong evidence that the two are related. In an article in *Newsweek* (Reibstein & Joseph, 1988), for example, businesspeople were advised to mimic their way to success.

MIMIC YOUR WAY TO THE TOP*
*Employees make all the right moves – the boss's*

Here's the scene: the top executives of Microsoft Corp. are in a meeting and cofounder and CEO Bill Gates is talking. As he grows intense he starts rocking and bobbing back and forth in his chair, the rocking and bobbing speeding up as he continues. Seated around him, several of his lieutenants soon are rocking and bobbing, rocking and bobbing. Gates periodically pushes his glasses up on his nose; his associates push their glasses up.

What's wrong with this picture? Nothing, actually. Psychologists call the phenomenon "modeling," or "mirroring" or "patterning." The guy in the next office calls it sucking up to the boss. Whether done consciously or not, subordinates show a relentless tendency to copy their boss's mannerisms, gestures, way of speaking, dress and sometimes even choice of cars and homes. It's an acceptable mode of behavior – up to a point. Some people become so absorbed in their boss's identity that when the boss moves on, the subordinate may feel abandoned.

Experts say the motive to mimic derives from the same forces that lead children to imitate a parent. "We pay homage and show allegiance to the most powerful through mimicry," says Robert Decker, director of the Palo Alto Center for Stress Related Disorders. In groups, he notes, the real power is the person being mimicked, not the person with the biggest title.

When they do it intentionally, subordinates are trying to win the boss's approval. At one IBM office, corporate culture used to demand that the desks be steel and the chairs gray. But one top manager brought in a curvy, bright orange ashtray, and within days colorful objects materialized in offices. "When an executive believes he can evoke interest from the boss he'll fly the same airline, order the same cucumber salad at lunch, wear the same kind of cuff links," says Jean Hollands, a Silicon Valley consultant.

The danger is when such behavior slips into toadyism or steps on a boss's ego. Letitia Baldridge, an adviser on executive manners, recalls the young assistant who wore a plaid suit to please his boss, who always wore plaid. The boss promptly ordered him home to change clothes. The subordinate had diluted the boss's uniqueness. But most bosses bask in imitation. Hollands cites a California company whose top managers developed an interest in politics when their boss, a former Washington pol, took over.

*"Like a jerk"*: Lots of traits are picked up unintentionally, sometimes as a way to cope with stress. An Oakland lawyer who nodded like her boss says, "I felt like a jerk because I couldn't stand him." Yet unintentional traits are easily dropped. Maureen McNamara, media director at Emerson Lane Fortuna, a Boston advertising agency, says that she inherited a subordinate who gulped loudly to express surprise, a trait she picked up from the previous boss. Within a week, the aide dropped the gulp and picked up McNamara's way of saying "Really?!" It was a shrewd move. As McNamara puts it, "I tend to mimic up."

Mimicking's benefits – like career advancement – aren't necessarily available to all. Minorities and foreigners often find it puzzling to decipher the nonverbal traits of a boss of a different culture or sex, according to Jane Falk, a linguist. That reluctance to mirror the boss, Falk adds, may play at least a small role when minorities and foreigners are overlooked for top jobs. Says Falk, "They're not marching to the same drummer." (p. 50)

In his writings on postural echo, Desmond Morris (1966) reminds us that those who wish to ingratiate themselves with others should not mimic *everything* the others do – they cannot mimic the superiors' displays of power, for example. G. William Walster (personal communication), for example, recounts that when he was 5 years old, he observed his father and his friends greet one another with a hearty "How's it going, Jack?" and with playful cuffs and back slaps. Bill was crazy about his soccer coach, so the next time they met, he slapped *him* on the back with a cheery "How's it going?" All he got was a glacial stare: He had been friendly above his station. Morris (1966), too, observes that sometime superiors are freer to share their subordinates' emotions and mimic their behavior than vice versa:

Because acting in unison spells equal-status friendship, it can be used by dominant individuals to put subordinates at their ease. A therapist treating a patient can help him to relax by deliberately copying the sick person's body displays. If the patient sits quietly, leaning forward in his chair, with his arms folded across his chest and staring at the floor, the doctor who sits near him in a similar, quiet pose is more likely to be able to communicate successfully with him. If instead he adopts a more typical dominant posture behind his desk, he will find it harder to make contact.

Whenever a dominant and a subordinate meet, they signal their relationship by their body postures and it is a simple matter for a subordinate to manipulate such a situation. Just as the dominant doctor deliberately climbed down from his high status role by echoing the patient's body posture, so a subordinate can, if he wishes, unnerve a dominant individual by copying his body actions. Instead of sitting on the edge of his chair or leaning eagerly forwards, he can sprawl out his legs and recline his body in imitation of the high status posture he sees before him. Even if verbally he is politeness itself, such a course of action will have a powerful impact, and the experiment is best reserved for moments immediately prior to tendering one's resignation. (pp. 84–85)

## Careers that require sensitivity/resistance to contagion

- Newscasters do it nightly.
- Bankers do it with interest. Penalties for early withdrawal.
- Divers do it deeper.
- Lawyers always want to get into your briefs.
- Firemen are always in heat.
- Social psychologists are experimental.
- Psychiatrists are analytical.
- Sociologists do it in groups.
- Nurses do it with care.

– Bumper stickers

People, so says the folklore, are often drawn to occupations that fit their temperaments; of course, these occupations – once people get absorbed in them – further shape their characters and personalities.

It seems reasonable to argue that different careers require different skills. Bill Clinton confided to close friends that a childhood spent dealing with an alcoholic, abusive, volatile stepfather has caused him to shy away from conflict and feel most comfortable with consensus and negotiation. This combination worked well in the 1992 presidential election: He was able to resonate with people's feelings but resist getting caught up in their anger. Joe Klein (1992), a reporter who traveled with the Clinton campaign, provided this example:

The old couple was clearly around the bend. They sat in the front row at the senior-citizens center, screeching. The husband wanted to know why the government kept giving money to foreigners. "And *what about drugs?*" his wife bellowed. It was the Friday before the New Hampshire primary, and everything seemed to be spinning out of control. Bill Clinton was being pursued by a ravenous press horde – What about Gennifer? What about that letter you sent to the ROTC guy? What did you *mean* about preserving your political "viability"? – and now, even the civilians were beginning to seem loony. But Clinton lingered. He asked the woman, what concerns you about drugs? The price of them, she said. What sort of medication do you need and how much does it cost? he asked. How much does Medicare cover? he asked. And, how much do you get from social security? The woman – her name was Mary Davis – seemed calmer, talking about it. But then, as she was saying "We don't have enough [to pay] for drugs *and* food," she burst into tears. Immediately, Clinton was down, hunched over her, his arms around her, repeating "I'm so sorry, I'm so sorry . . ." for what seemed an eternity. Then he stood, wiped his eyes and continued on. (p. 14)

Of course, in some situations there are disadvantages in being too sensitive. Le Anne Schreiber (1990), in *Midstream*, points out that loving people sometimes makes us ineffective in helping them.

Last night, after learning Mom's tumor was malignant, I began packing for an indefinite stay in Minnesota.
. . . On the plane, I kept thinking of something that has worried me since Mike's first call last Tuesday. I have never been able to stand the sight of Mom in pain. I respond to it bodily. If she burns her hand on the iron, I wince. If she coughs, my chest heaves. Once, when we were shopping together in downtown Evanston, Mom tripped on a crack in the sidewalk and smashed headfirst into the pavement. My whole body started tingling, and when I saw the fright in her eyes, I almost fainted. The right half of her face looked broken, caved in, and I lied when she asked me if there was a mirror in the shoe store where we waited for an ambulance. I remember the effort I made to keep looking at her, as if there was nothing wrong, as if her beauty was intact.
I have witnessed only a few, rare accidents, spaced over dec-

ades of her healthy life. I have never had to repress, or even think about, my body's impulsive identification with hers. How will I react now that the threats to her are so much more extreme? What help will I be, what comfort can I give, if I am simply the mirror of her suffering? I wonder if all daughters feel this. (pp. 33–34)

Mikal Gilmore was always afraid of his brother, Gary (Mailer, 1979). While Gary was in prison, Mikal found it impossible even to visit him – the mood of menace reawakened all his old terrors:

Mikal began to feel steeped again in the dread he had always felt on those rare occasions he visited Gary in prison. It was not only Gary but the lost lives of the other prisoners in that visiting room, the depression, the apathy, the congealed rage, the bottomless potential for violence in those halls. After a while, Mikal stopped visiting. (p. 500)

In some careers, people must be able to share the most minute and fleeting changes in others' emotions. (Sidewalk mimes, who track passerby's facial expressions, postures, and emotional expressions, probably possess such skills.) Other careers require people to be able, when necessary, both to track others' emotions and to resist contagion. (Psychologists and physicians may belong in this career group.) Finally, some professionals, at least some of the time, must be able to harden their feelings and resist the emotions of their clients and adversaries alike. (Perhaps trial lawyers and military combat personnel are in such careers. Emergency room doctors may have to numb themselves even to dying.)

Elaine Hatfield and her students (Doherty et al., 1993) compared the extent to which men and women in various professions are susceptible to emotional contagion. (We touched upon this study in the section "Gender Differences in Susceptibility to Contagion.") Subjects were drawn from three groups: The first sample comprised 290 men and 253 women who were students at the University of Hawaii. The second consisted of 61 male and 24 female physicians from Queen's Medical Center, St. Francis West Hospital in Ewa Beach, and Tripler Military Hospital in Honolulu. Their medical specialities varied widely, though most specialized in internal medicine, radiology, or pediatrics, or were general practitioners. The third sample comprised 184 male and 71 female marines from the First Marine Expeditionary Brigade at Kaneohe Marine Corps Air Station in Honolulu. Marines ranged in rank from private first class to captain. All three groups included a wide variety of ethnic backgrounds.

The authors predicted:

> Students (who are just beginning their occupational training) will be undifferentiated in their susceptibility to emotional contagion. (They may be more or less susceptible to contagion than are members of various occupational groups.)
>
> Physicians and marines will differ significantly in susceptibility to contagion. They may differ little if at all in their susceptibility to catching positive emotions. Physicians should be far more susceptible than marines to catching negative emotions, however.

As can be seen in Table 5.5 (p. 166), these predictions received strong support. Students' total Emotional Contagion scores, as well as their scores on the positive and negative emotions, were higher than those of either other group. We also see that, as predicted, although physicians and marines did not differ in their susceptibility to catching positive emotions, physicians were more susceptible to catching negative emotions (fear, sadness, and anger) than were marines.

## Summing up

In this chapter we explored individual differences in susceptibility to emotional contagion. We reviewed the support for our hypotheses that people should be likely to catch others' emotions if they:

1. rivet their attention on the others;
2. construe themselves in terms of their interrelatedness to the others;
3. are able to read others' emotional expressions, voices, gestures, and postures;
4. tend to mimic facial, vocal, and postural expressions;
5. are aware of their own emotional responses; or
6. are emotionally reactive.

Conversely, it was hypothesized that those without the aforementioned attributes should be fairly resistant to contagion.

We saw that people seemed most likely to catch others' emotions in two kinds of relationships – those involving love or power – and that individuals in different occupations tended to possess different skills at sharing versus resisting the emotions of others.

# 6. Current implications and suggestions for future research

## Introduction

In this text we confront a puzzling incongruity: People seem capable of mimicking others' facial, vocal, and postural expressions with stunning rapidity and, consequently, are able to "feel themselves into" others' emotional lives to a surprising extent; however, they also seem oblivious to the importance of emotional contagion in social encounters, and unaware of how swiftly and completely they are able to track the expressions of others.

In one recent experiment, for example, Frank Bernieri and his students (Bernieri, Davis, Knee, & Rosenthal, personal communication) conducted a series of personal perception experiments. They compared how 45 judges *thought* they made decisions versus how they had *actually* made them. The judges viewed 50 one-minute clips of a social interaction between debating partners: It was their job to decide how much the partners liked one another. Afterward, the judges were asked what cues they had utilized in making their decisions. Those they *thought* most important in their decisions as to how much rapport debaters felt for one another are shown in Table 6.1. Judges assumed they had relied most heavily in their assessments on the targets' proximity, frequency of smiling, and expressiveness; they explicitly denied any influence of such factors as mutual silences, postural mirroring, or synchrony.

When we look at the cues judges *actually* used, however (Table 6.2), we see that, without knowing it, they were greatly influenced by synchrony. It is good that the judges (unbeknownst to them) used these factors, because measures of mimicry/synchrony turn out to be extremely good predictors of targets' actual rapport (Table 6.3).

Bernieri and his students concluded that although judges were

Table 6.1. *Cues people* think *they use in assessing rapport*[a]

| | |
|---|---|
| 1. Proximity | (22% ranked it as most influential.) |
| 2. Smiling | (33% ranked it as most influential.) |
| 3. Expressivity/general activity | |
| 4. Nervous behaviors | |
| 5. Speech turn-taking frequency | |
| 6. Mutual silences (not talking) | (38% reported not using it at all.) |
| 7. Postural mirroring | (64% reported not using it.) |
| 8. Synchrony | (71% reported not using it.) |

[a]In order of decreasing influence.
*Source:* Bernieri, Davis, Knee, & Rosenthal (personal communication).

Table 6.2. *Judgments of rapport as influenced by various factors*

| | |
|---|---|
| 1. Expressivity/activity | ($r = +.40$) |
| 2. Synchrony | ($r = +.37$) |
| 3. Proximity | ($r = +.33$) |

*Source:* Bernieri, Davis, Knee, & Rosenthal (personal communication).

fully aware that they were using traditional indicants of rapport – proximity, smiling, and so forth – they were unaware of how heavily they relied on mimicry/synchrony in making their judgments. They further concluded that the traditional indicants may actually be less important in establishing and communicating rapport than are mimicry and synchrony! (Often judges insisted they had ignored mimicry/synchrony because it is not important; see Table 6.4).

Why should this be? Why are people so oblivious to the importance of mimicry/synchrony in social encounters? Why are they unaware of how swiftly and how completely they are able to track the expressive behaviors and emotions of others? Our best bet is that people are probably most aware of the skills and processes requiring conscious awareness. Because primitive emotional contagion occurs automatically, they have previously been unaware of the power and ubiquity of this phenomenon.

## Implications of existing research

What practical implications might we draw from the research discussed in chapters 1–5?

Table 6.3. *Behavioral predictors of rapport*

| | |
|---|---|
| 1. Mutual eye contact | $(r = +.33)$ |
| 2. Mutual silence | $(r = -.33)$ |
| 3. Postural mirroring | $(r = +.30)$ |
| 4. Proximity | $(r = +.28)$ |
| 5. Synchrony | $(r = +.26)$ |

*Source:* Bernieri, Davis, Knee, & Rosenthal (personal communication).

Table 6.4. *Correlation of self-reported behavior cue with actual cue employment*[a]

| | |
|---|---|
| 1. Proximity | $(r = +.35)$ |
| 2. Nervous behaviors | $(r = +.16)$ |
| 3. Smiling | $(r = +.08)$ |
| 4. Mutual silences | $(r = +.07)$ |
| 5. Speech turn-taking frequency | $(r = +.05)$ |
| 6. Synchrony | $(r = -.13)$ |
| 7. Postural mirroring | $(r = -.14)$ |
| 8. Expressivity/general activity | $(r = -.23)$ |

[a]In order of decreasing positive correlation.
*Source:* Bernieri, Davis, Knee, & Rosenthal (personal communication).

*Implication 1: The better we understand ourselves – how we think, feel, and behave – the better the decisions we make about our lives.*

Rule your feelings, lest your feelings rule you.
– Publius Syrus

Scientists and artists have long disagreed about the value of emotions in making "the good life." Western thought has seesawed on whether to glorify rational man or to exalt creatures of passion. For example, the 18th century claimed to be the "Age of Reason." During the Enlightenment, Voltaire, John Locke, Thomas Jefferson, and a host of others struck back against the long dominion of what they regarded as superstition, ignorance, and Christian hysteria. Reason was enshrined and emotion disdained.

Inevitably, this obsession with rationality inspired a backlash. In the 19th century the passions were glorified. The Romantic era, associated with the emotional outpourings of such poets as Keats, Shelley, and Byron and the impassioned landscapes of Turner and Delacroix trumpeted the wonders of passion. It was a period alive with the turbulent sounds of Beethoven, the expressiveness of Chopin, Schumann, Brahms, and the tempestuousness of Verdi and Tchaikovsky. In the late 19th century, the teeterboard tipped again, and science and technology became the new messiahs. Western cultures became supremely confident that science, with the twin tools of reason and technology, could come to understand and control virtually everything – both the rational and the irrational.

Psychology, too, has been buffeted by a dialectic between sense and sensibility. In the first half of this century, psychologists emphasized reason, thinking, problem solving, and behavior; they ignored the nonrational, emotional, and impulsive. Today, of course, psychologists have become once again interested in emotion. Richard Lazarus (1984), for example, maintained that the "higher" mental processes of thought or reason are not superior to emotions. Emotions, he insists, are "a fusion of highly developed forms of cognitive appraisal with action impulse and bodily changes" (p. 213). More recently, Peter Salovey and John Mayer (1990) have argued that IQ researchers might wish to expand their definitions of intelligence, adding measures of social intelligence, in general, and emotional intelligence, in particular, to the mix. They defined *emotional intelligence* as

> the ability to monitor one's own and others' feelings and emotions, to discriminate among them and to use this information to guide one's thinking and actions. (p. 189)

An emotionally intelligent person would have to possess a trio of skills:

1. the ability to understand and express one's own emotions and recognize them in others;
2. the ability to regulate one's own and others' emotions; and
3. the ability to harness one's own emotions in order to motivate adaptive behaviors.

Of course, Salovey and Mayer (1990) conceptualized social and emotional intelligence as unrelated dimensions of general intelligence. Research on emotional contagion suggests that these dimensions may not be independent after all. Computer models of American Sign Language that accurately depict signing have been criticized by the handicapped for failing to include the emotional information so critical to social interactions. Such criticisms have resulted in biomedical engineers working to develop communication devices for ASL that include the facial expressions of the signaler.

Furthermore, Richard Rapson (1980) has argued that people must, often simultaneously, be able to take two very different perspectives on their lives: Sometimes they must be on "automatic pilot," caught up in life's swirl; now and then, however, they benefit from stepping back, carefully detaching themselves, and analyzing what is going on. It is when people are engaged in this latter process that both analytic intelligence and emotional intelligence matter.

Richard Lazarus (1991) reminded us that both cognitive and emotional information are critical in guiding us to sensible decisions:

> An emotion may also be *informative* to the person who experiences it . . . that is, a source of insight into oneself and what is happening. When we react with anxiety, anger, happiness, or whatever, there is usually awareness and understanding of how the emotion was precipitated as well as of the emotional reaction. We realize immediately, or later after reflection, that we are angry because someone has behaved toward us in a hostile, critical, or unresponsive way, or that we are anxious because the situation threatens us and we are vulnerable. This insight may be useful in helping us deal with recurrent emotional distress and is what clinicians want clients to have in order to better manage their emotional lives.
>
> There are also occasions in which a person is not aware of making an appraisal of harm or threat – which are the bases of negative emotions – either because the social relationship is ambiguous or because the person is engaging in ego-defense. We may not even be aware that we are reacting emotionally because we have misinterpreted our reaction or the conditions bringing it about. . . . I recently learned of an academic friend who was monitoring his heart rate because of a problem of ischemia (insufficient oxygen in the muscle tissues of the heart) when his heart rate would reach 150 beats per minute. He was amazed to discover that in departmental faculty meetings, when he had thought he was merely cynically detached from the faculty discussion, he was actually attaining heart rates that

approached the point of ischemia, presumably because he was strongly aroused emotionally (not happily, of course) by what was going on. The monitoring of his heart rate was useful because it made him attend to, and properly interpret, what was happening, giving him the opportunity to do something about the problem. (p. 18)

True vision is always twofold. It involves emotional comprehension as well as physical perception.

> – Ross Parmenter

*Implication 2: An understanding of the power and ubiquity of contagion helps us correctly assess the factors that shape social interactions, allowing us better to deal with those interactions.*

The research on contagion underscores the fact that we use multiple means to gain information about others' emotional states: Conscious analytic skills can help us figure out what makes other people "tick"; but if we pay careful attention to the emotions we experience in the company of others, we may well gain an extra edge into "feeling ourselves into" the emotional states of others. What we think and what we feel may provide valuable yet different information about others. Recall that Elaine Hatfield and her colleagues (1992) found that people's conscious assessments of what others "must be" feeling were heavily influenced by what the others said. Their own emotions, however, were more influenced by the others' nonverbal clues as to what they were really feeling.

Some examples: We began this text with a story of Elaine Hatfield's interactions with one of her colleagues at the University of Hawaii. Every time she talked with him she felt ill at ease; afterward, she always resolved to try harder next time. A recognition that she was picking up *his* panic allowed her to devise a more effective strategy: She could spend her energy subtly calming and reassuring her anxious friend. This worked much better, and everyone settled down.

In the last year, Richard Rapson and Elaine Hatfield have been invited to dinner at the home of Susan and Harry, local artists, on two occasions. The first dinner was horrid. Elaine, who had been working very hard, got so sleepy over the course of the two hours that she could barely hold her head up. The next day, she sent them a note of apology, promising that next time she would be more alert. A second dinner was arranged. Half an hour into the festivities, disaster struck again: Elaine began nodding off.

In replaying the evening in their minds, Elaine and Dick suddenly realized what had gone wrong, and would continue to go wrong if they tried to see this couple. Susan is filled with energy – and anxiety. Her conversation is a battery of long-stored-up grievances and complaints. She is not uninteresting, however: If one had only to listen to Susan, the dinner would probably have worked out. It is actually fairly interesting to listen to others' problems. It is slightly irritating when someone is not at all interested in you, and you might as well be a doorpost, but it is still bearable. Murmuring appreciative "uh-huh"s at appropriate intervals is not taxing. Dealing with Susan's husband, Harry, on his own would not have been a problem either, although he is profoundly depressed and says nothing: Elaine and Dick talk to depressed people all day, and would simply have questioned him about his life. The trouble was that there were two of them. When caught between the Scylla of hysteria and the Charybdis of depression, Elaine – busily sponging up both contradictory emotions – had nowhere to go but asleep. In this case, the problem was managed with a decision not to visit this couple again.

We might speculate that people would often do much better if they recognized how much of their mood was shaped by *others'* emotions. Then they could decide whether they wanted to try to soothe the others, wake them up, or avoid them.

Of course, there are some people who *never* blame themselves for anything. They tend to lash out at others any time things go wrong, and, not surprisingly, others snap back. You would think that this would be obvious, but it is not. Some people do not hear their own arrogant or sarcastic voices: They hear only others' replies, and are amazed at others' hostility. One client, a teenage boy, was actually surprised that after he told a girl she was ugly she said, "You're not so great looking yourself, you know." He was stunned that she could be so "mean." Such people would surely do better if they learned the opposite lesson – to focus more on their own contribution to problems.

Another example: When Elaine Hatfield first started teaching, she would occasionally think that teaching, research, writing, and therapy were simply too much. She would decide she and Richard Rapson should cut back their therapy practice; then, later, everything would fall back into place and she would decide the balance was just right. It took a few years before she realized there was a pattern to her feeling overwhelmed: Things always seemed to fall apart during the first week of school. So, for a while, she assumed that the problem was simply that she had not done enough preplanning – for some reason, there were too many emergencies the first week – but, somehow, no amount of preparation made things any better. It was not until she began her work on contagion that the whole process became explicable: *She* was prepared during the first week of class, but her students were not. Each day, the office was filled with frantic youths – students who had forgotten to preregister and could not get in classes, but who would not graduate without attending. They jostled with others whose scholarships hadn't come through: How would they pay their rents? What Elaine was reacting to was not *her* desperation but *theirs*. All she had to do was remind herself that in the forthcoming weeks all these problems could get sorted out, and the week's "burdens" suddenly diminished.

As suggested by these examples, social interactions are complex. We may believe we guide ourselves through our daily treks, but a moment's reflection shows we neither proceed alone nor have as much control as we might have thought over others or our interactions with them. (Control derives in large part from selecting the individuals with whom we interact and the situations in which the interactions occur, not from what we do once in a situation.) One need only recall the awkwardness of one's first day with unfamiliar classmates at a new school, one's first date with a relatively new acquaintance, or one's first speech to an audience to recall how helpless one can sometimes feel in the face of complex social situations. Just dealing with the social demands can be overwhelming; trying simultaneously to determine and respond to unexpected tasks, problems, or questions can be paralyzing if not personally embarrassing. However, once individuals begin to relax and stop monitoring consciously every move they are making, primitive emotional contagion is able to work its magic. We effortlessly "know" we are comfortable in some situations or with some new classmates but not others. The young couple on their first date may find conversation stilted when they first get in the car, but later find rapport between them to be established once their reactions are entrained by the loud and rhythmic beat of a rock band. Experienced public speakers are perhaps no less anxious about addressing an unfamiliar audience, but they have learned that the text of their talk must be so automatic that they have time to attend and be responsive to the individuals in the audience. In brief, each of these complex and awkward social situations can be transformed to a more pleasant interaction by allowing the subtle processes of emotional contagion to operate.

> *Implication 3: It is necessary for people to "feel themselves into" others' lives if they are to truly understand them.*

Sometimes, although someone is suffering, others act as if nothing has happened. Often, this is because the sufferers are not displaying the proper emotions. For example: Two of the present authors (Hatfield and Rapson) once treated a teenage girl who had been raped. In a monotone, and with great nonchalance, she said that a marine who had offered to give her a ride home had dragged her into a cane field, put a knife to her throat, and raped her. He had then driven her home and thrown her out of the car. In a state of shock, she had walked into the house and casually recounted what had happened. Her mother, with equal casualness, had said, "Well then, your dinner is in the oven. Why don't you try to eat something?" Thereafter, the matter of the rape had not been pursued.

We would have thought the mother was a monster had we not discovered, to our horror, that we had had to use our *minds* to realize the seriousness of what had happened. Usually, the faces, voices, and postures of teenagers who have been raped draw us into their experience. We feel parental, concerned, galvanized into action. In her case, we felt none of this: We felt nothing. We realized how important contagion is in allowing us to code the importance of events and do the right thing.

Such experiences are more common than one might think. Recently, Aloha Flight 243 took off from Hilo, Hawaii, on a routine 40-minute flight to Honolulu. Passengers and crew chatted during the uneventful takeoff and gradual ascent to cruising altitude. Twenty minutes after takeoff, passengers heard an explosion. It ripped off the top half of the cabin, which instantly decompressed. Deafening hurricanelike winds swept through the passenger area:

> "There was a blast . . . a whoosh, like someone popped a bag . . . and the air rushed out immediately," said Dan Dennin, a 31-year-old Honolulu salesman who was aboard the ill-fated flight.

"A third of the roof was gone . . . I looked up and saw blue sky."

In slow, measured tones Dennin painted a picture of heroism and despair aboard the crippled aircraft as the pilot struggled to control it and land on Maui. . . .

"We all thought we were going to die."

"One stewardess was crawling or walking up and down the aisle (afterward) . . ." said Dennin. "She almost got sucked out. A couple of passengers said they had a hold of her . . . passengers in aisle seats." (*Honolulu Advertiser*, April 29, 1988, p. A1)

A fight attendant, Clarabelle "C. B." Lansing, was sucked out of the plane. Debris swirled through the cabin. Suddenly, this everyday flight had turned into a nightmare of noise, terror, pain, and death. Thirteen minutes later, when the crippled plane touched down at the Maui airport in a perfect landing, the passengers were seriously shaken but alive. When the first paramedic arrived he observed:

"It was like walking into a convertible. There was just no roof, no walls. It was all open; looks like something ripped through there. The seats were all twisted and bent down." (p. A1B)

Sixty-one passengers were hospitalized with injuries: Two were critical, four in serious condition. A woman in Elaine Hatfield's class, Mimi Tomkins, was a pilot on that Aloha flight. She had been well briefed in how to deal with emergencies: Stay calm and slowly recite all the facts. The "black-box" recording of her report revealed how well trained she was. (She received a commendation for her heroism.) Her voice came over the microphone, casual, friendly, describing the accident. She returned the disabled airplane to Honolulu and it landed without further incident.

Later investigations criticized the Honolulu air traffic controllers, however, for failing to respond with sufficient vigor to the emergency. They had not even thought to arrange for appropriate firefighting equipment to meet the flight! Why had they been so cavalier? "She was so casual, that somehow we didn't fully realize the severity of the accident," one controller admitted. The board of inquiry failed to understand this "excuse"; perhaps we, who know what it takes for people to "feel themselves into" an emergency, can understand better. Had the pilot sounded more hysterical, more desperate, the tower would have "gotten it."

We see, then, that people who respond like "zombies" in emotionally charged situations may better understand why if they realize that some of the emotional cues they need to propel them into action are missing.

> *Implication 4: A knowledge of the power of contagion gives us a realistic perception as to how much we can expect to influence social situations.*

Earlier in the text, we pointed out that the very people who are most sensitive to other's moods are often also those most eager to improve social relations. What they may fail to recognize is that the same sensitivity that makes them good at perceiving the dynamics of a difficult situation sets limits on their ability to deal with that situation. Sensitive souls can spend only so much time with those who are depressed, angry, or anxious without getting swept up in the maelstrom themselves.

One of Hatfield and Rapson's clients, a dentist, recently came to see them. Usually, she was extraordinarily cheerful; this week she was depressed, and thought she might be coming down with the flu. As she recounted her week, however, it became clear that this nurturant woman was simply taking on too much. Her employees had been squabbling. With boundless energy, she had decided the "problem" was a structural one: No one was sure who was responsible for what; hence the squabbling. She had devised a new organizational plan and stayed up late at night to craft detailed job descriptions. To her amazement, after taking a cursory look at her carefully wrought plan, two of her workers, her hygienist and her secretary, had quit. As we stepped back to try to figure out what was going on, it became evident that her employees were simply upset and exhausted for reasons that had little to do with the work environment. The hygienist was having marital problems and arrived at the office each day in tears. The office manager, a single mother, was seething. She was trying to arrange a nice Christmas for her children to make up for her "neglect"; but she found it harder to delegate things to the new part-time secretary than to do them herself, and so was overwhelmed. The new part-time secretary was feeling humiliated: The office manager seemed to think she was capable of only the most menial of tasks. As we talked, it became clear to our client that she was being blown about by this whirlwind of feelings; she was catching not the flu virus, but the virus of distress. After a two-day vacation at a nearby resort she returned to work better natured. She took each of the employees out to dinner and talked about their real problems. Everyone cheered up. She had been able to short-circuit the spiral of contagion.

> *Implication 5: A knowledge of the power of contagion, then, reminds us: Don't take on too much.*

Arthur Miller (1987), in his autobiography, *Timebends*, admits that he fell in love with Marilyn Monroe, in part, because she was so trusting, so vulnerable, so needy; he had reacted physically to that need. One night she called him, terrified. He responded, in kind, to her fears:

> I kept trying to reassure her, but she seemed to be sinking where I could not reach, her voice growing fainter. I was losing her, she was slipping away out there, and with partner and friends so close by. "Oh, Papa, I can't make it, I can't make it!" Her suicide leapt up before me, an act I had never connected with her before. I tried to think of someone I knew in Hollywood who could go and see her, but there was no one, and suddenly I realized I was out of breath, a dizziness screwing into my head, my knees unlocking, and I felt myself sliding to the floor of the booth, the receiver slipping out of my hands. I came to in what was probably a few seconds, her voice still whispering out of the receiver over my head. After a moment I got up and talked her down to earth, and it was over; she would try not to let it get to her tomorrow, just do the job and get on with it. Lights were still revolving behind my eyes. We would marry and start a new and real life once this picture was done. "I don't want this anymore, Papa, I can't fight them alone, I want to live with you in the country and be a good wife, and if somebody wants me for a wonderful picture . . ." Yes and yes and yes and it was over, and the healing silence of the desert swept back and covered it all.
> I left the highway behind me and walked toward the two cottages and the low moon. I had never fainted before. A weight had fallen and my lungs felt scored, as if I had been weeping for a long time. I felt healed, as though I had crossed over a division within me and onto a plane of peace where the parts of myself had joined. I loved her as though I had loved her all my life; her pain was mine. (p. 380)

Miller thinks he will save Marilyn. Of course, after their marriage, he finds himself as desperate and despairing as she is.

When reporters call us to ask us about contagion, they inevitably end with a single question: "How, then, can people overcome the effects of contagion?" What they are wondering is this: How can we turn off our ability to share others' feelings so that we can deal with angry bosses, anxious fathers, or families in turmoil?

We would assume that, ideally, people would not try to alter their basic natures too much. Some people are extremely sensitive; others have to be hit over the head before they get the point. Each nature has its advantages and disadvantages. Sensitive people, susceptible to emotional contagion, are wonderful at understanding and dealing with others; but after a bit, they get tired. They can deal with the troubled for perhaps a few hours but, soon, enough is enough: They must go home, be absolutely quiet, and recover. Other, hardier individuals are more or less oblivious to the emotional climates in which they dwell. (You may recall our example in chapter 5 of the mellow client who, upon hearing a woman crying on the telephone, turned it over to his wife with a cheerful "It's for you.") Such people might not be aware of what is going on in emotionally charged situations, but they can stay in them and deal with them a lot longer.

People probably do best if they accept their own temperaments and the concomitant advantages and disadvantages. The very sensitive might be interpersonal experts or "angels of mercy," but only for short periods. When visiting the family, where woe and suffering are the norm, they had better plan to stay in a hotel and meet the relatives for dinner. Meanwhile, people who have become "turned off" to others' feelings often get overwhelmed when they begin to become more aware, feeling that they are somehow responsible for "fixing things." They do better if they remind themselves that probably the best they can do is to listen. Others should not expect them to be a miracle worker; those who demand too much attention cannot complain when the "oblivious" tune out for self-protection.

*Implication 6: A knowledge of the power of emotional contagion may shape public policy.*

Lynn Reynolds (personal communication) reports a powerful instance in which a failure to recognize the power of emotional communication posed a health hazard. She had had a baby by Caesarian section and her vital signs had been stabilized. Her doctor told her that in a few minutes she could be transferred to a regular hospital room. However, immediately thereafter, another woman, who had just had a Caesarian, was wheeled in. The new mother began to cry and moan in agony. Lynn began to relive her own recovery; she began to share the woman's suffering and to feel worse and worse herself. When the doctor returned, he found that her recovery had regressed: Her heart rate and blood pressure were now at the point where they had been more than six hours earlier. She had to wait an additional day to leave the hospital.

### Suggestions for future research

While writing this text, a number of glaring omissions became evident and basic questions arose. Let us now explore some of them.

*Are the emotions one catches always pale imitations of
the "real thing"?*

Usually, we have assumed that the emotions that people catch, second to second, are far less intense than those the target feels. Hatfield and Rapson once had a client who was quite narcissistic. He would say such things to his wife as, "I have the same cold as you do – only it's much worse." To some extent, most of us are like that man: We are the center of our universal drama, and the passions we observe often seem but pale reflections of our own. For theoretical as well as philosophical reasons, then, we might expect the emotions we catch to be tiny hints of the real thing. There is some evidence that this is so. Kenneth Craig (1968), for example, was interested in determining how similar were imagined arousal, vicarious arousal, and direct arousal in the emotions and physiological reactions they engendered. Subjects were assigned to one of three conditions: In one, men and women were asked to perform the cold pressor test, that is, to place one hand in ice water (2 °C) for two minutes. In another, subjects were asked to watch performers endure the cold pressor test. The third condition entailed only *imagining* having to endure this test:

> I want you to try to the best of your ability to imagine vividly and to think continuously that the water is as cold as ice and that it is very uncomfortable. In fact, cold enough to be very painful. Try as hard as you can to create the feelings and physiological sensations you would have if this were cold ice water. (p. 514)

Subjects' skin conductance responses and heart and respiration rates were assessed as they imagined, observed, or actually performed the stressful task. Not surprisingly, the authors found that imagined, vicarious, and direct experiences differed in the degree and pattern of autonomic arousal produced. Imagining or observing another's suffering was upsetting, but not as much as suffering oneself. Direct experience produced the strongest and longest-lasting physiological reactions. Furthermore, subjects sometimes showed different types of response in the various conditions: For example, a person's heart rate might decelerate when she was an observer but accelerate when she was imagining or actually performing the cold pressor task. This is consistent with psychophysiologists' observation that "cardiac deceleration accompanied and perhaps even facilitated ease of 'environmental intake,' whereas cardiac acceleration accompanied or facilitated 'rejection of the environment'" (Lacey et al., 1963, p. 165).

Generally, then, the data suggest that experiencing a stressor vicariously generates a similar but less intense emotional reaction than does direct experience of the stressor (Hygge & Ohman, 1976).

There are exceptions, of course: There are individuals whose powers of imagination, sensibility, kindness, or tendency to worry is greater than that of the person about whom they are worrying. Many mothers worry more about their teenagers who are experimenting with drugs than do the teenagers themselves. (That, in fact, is the problem.) The mothers are thrown into a panic when they observe the slightest hints of worry in their children. Some codependent women revel in how happy they are making the alcoholic or abusive husband by their momentous sacrifices, which he barely notices. We suspect they may well catch more emotion than he sends.

We would hope that subsequent research would provide some indication of how powerful the emotions we catch are compared to those we experience directly.

*When isthe emotion caught the same as, complementary to, or opposite from the emotion expressed?*

COMFORT, *n*. A state of mind produced by contemplation of a neighbor's uneasiness.
> – Ambrose Bierce, *The Devil's Dictionary*

Anything awful makes me laugh. I misbehaved once at a funeral.
> – Charles Lamb

Some emotions tend to evoke the same feeling; others evoke complementary or even contrary feelings. Angry faces sometimes stimulate fear as well as anger; another's fear may put us at ease. Mary McCarthy (1954), in *A Charmed Life,* presents such a situation. Martha Sinnott drops by to visit some old friends, Jane and Warren, and finds that her ex-husband, Miles, is already there.

> As he [Miles] took a step toward the door, a knock sounded. There was a stark moment of silence; no one moved. The conviction that it must be the Sinnotts was graven, Miles saw, on every face. "It *can't* be them," whispered Jane. "It might be," whispered back Warren. Another knock came. "They know we're here because of the cars," whispered Jane, "Answer it man," said Miles, in his normal voice. As Warren skipped to the door, Miles turned aside, steadying himself. Very likely, he said to himself, it was not Martha at all.
>
> But it was Martha, in a gray cloak, accompanied by her husband ...
>
> It was, as they said, a situation. Martha was shaking all over. Miles could feel it, as he lifted the cloak from her shoulders; he remembered that she had trembled, the first time he saw her, on the stage of a hapless summer theater production, so badly that the scenery shook.
>
> Her nervousness put him at ease. (pp. 71–72)

Cynthia Clement (personal communication) reports that, when she was a girl in England, schoolgirls played a game guaranteed to drive them into paroxysms of giggles. They would sit in a circle and try to think of a "profoundly sad event." Then, they would try to arrange their brows and mouths into excruciatingly sad expressions. For some reason, this exercise inevitably engendered falling-down hilarity. She labeled this phenomenon "paradoxical emotional contagion."

Emotions are inevitably mixed. Our own selfish concerns meld with the emotions we catch. Daniel McIntosh (1991) observed:

> [I]t is critical to note that the socially induced emotion may not be the entirety of what the observer feels. Inasmuch as the observer's situation is necessarily different from the performer's, a perfect match in emotion cannot be expected. For example, after my wife has ridiculed me for warning her that her vegetable-

cutting technique is dangerous, I may simultaneously feel both socially induced distress and self-generated satisfaction when she nicks her thumb with the knife. (p. 17)

In this text, it has been all we could manage to explore the simple process of primitive emotional contagion. In subsequent work, researchers may well wish to explore the far more complex question of when the emotions we observe produce identical, complementary, or opposite emotions in ourselves. A few communication researchers who have spent decades exploring this question provide some hints as to the variables one might wish to explore.

*Social norms.* Joseph N. Cappella and his colleagues (Cappella & Flagg, 1992) have explored automatic interaction patterns in adults. They provide a convenient terminology for discussing the question of when people experience similar, complementary, or opposite emotions:

> One pattern of interaction between partners is called *mutual influence.* Mutual influence usually refers to the similarity (or reciprocity) and complementarity (or compensation) in *aggregate* behaviors exhibited by partners. (p. 2)

Communication researchers have long been interested in conversational interactions. In their decades of their research, they have developed a good idea of when speakers and listeners will show reciprocal mutual influence and when they will exhibit complementary behavior. For example, when a professor lectures, her students will probably exhibit both similar and complementary behaviors. Social norms dictate that when when a professor or others are speaking, others are supposed to listen. When students raise their hands and begin to ask questions, the professor is supposed to wait until they have finished posing a question before she formulates her answer. Joseph Cappella and Mary Flagg (1992) provided a clear demonstration of this point. They pointed out that when people hold the floor, they tend to vocalize (rather than pause), avert their eyes (rather than gaze), and gesture in support of their speech. (They label this cluster of behaviors the *Floor Index.*) As you might guess, in formal speech settings, speakers and listeners tend to exhibit complementarity in the display of such floor behaviors. If we look at other less scripted behaviors, however, we find that participants are still imitating one another's speech behaviors. Cappella and Flagg observe:

> In adult interactions, reciprocal mutual influence has been observed among various speech behaviors including accents, speech rate, pauses, latency to respond, vocal intensity, fundamental voice frequency, and turn durations. A range of kinesic behaviors exhibit mutual influence as well including postural and gestural behaviors, illustrators, movement synchrony, gaze, head nods and facial affect, facial displays of emotion, smiles and laughter, and more generalized hostile affect. The evidence certainly supports the existence of mutual influence for a variety of behaviors (see Cappella, 1981, 1985, 1991 for summaries). (1992, p. 3)

*People's comfort with intimate conversations.* Social psychologists point out that people prefer an optimal level of intimacy: Too much or too little intimacy makes everyone uncomfortable. Miles Patterson (1976) proposed that when people get close to us, we become physiologically aroused. If we feel positive about this arousal, we move closer; if it is "too much," we back off. Michael Argyle and Janet Dean (1965) tested this equilibrium model of social interaction. They found that people literally back up when someone gets too close too fast, and move forward when others seem to be slipping away. In one study, for example, they found that people unconsciously signal "come closer" by making eye contact, smiling, moving closer, or starting to talk about very intimate things. If an acquaintance begins to get too close, however, people unconsciously signal that she should "back up" by looking away, looking stone-faced, moving away, or changing the subject to a less intimate topic. Such intricate ballets ensure that equilibrium is continually maintained. To test their model, the scientists asked subjects to stand "as close as is comfortable to see well" and to slowly approach either a life-sized photograph of a person or the same person (in the flesh), whose eyes were either open or shut. (Presumably, it is most intimate to stare at someone who is staring back.) As predicted, subjects stood 11 in. closer to the photograph than to a living person and 8½ in. closer to a person whose eyes were shut than one whose eyes were open. The authors also studied the flip side of the equilibrium process. Students were seated either 10, 6, or 2 ft from one another. As they talked, one student (an experimental confederate) gazed into the other's eyes for three minutes during the conversation. As soon as the confederate began to stare, most subjects immediately reduced eye contact. They looked away or down – anywhere but right at him. The closer they were, the more they averted their eyes. Perhaps you have seen the same sort of intimacy regulation operating in elevators. When people are forced to stand much too close to strangers, they tend to look nervously up at the ceiling or down at the floor, anywhere, avoiding one another's eyes.

Two features of Argyle and Dean's model are worth noting. First, they view intimacy from a dialectical perspective, seeing people as constantly adjusting the level of their intimate encounters. Second, they point out that once the intimacy equilibrium has been disturbed, any of several different techniques can be used to restore it.

Joseph Cappella (1981) reviewed the research designed to test the equilibrium hypothesis, examining such behaviors as breadth and depth of intimate disclosures, eye contact, smiling, touch, bodily orientation, and proximity. He concluded that whether a person reciprocates another's intimate gestures or tries to restore equilibrium depends on how much intimacy they prefer and on how much they think is appropriate. His general conclusion: "When the other's behavior is outside the expected range, compensation results; when it is in the expected range, matching results" (p. 112). In other words, if someone stands too close, most people will tend to back up. If they begin to confide too much too soon, most people tend to "set a good example" by drawing back a bit. In a review of 36 different studies of the effects of proximity on others' reactions, Cappella (1981) concluded that

> [i]ncreasing proximity by one member of the dyad seems to lead the other to reintroduce normal social distances, to gaze less, to adopt less direct body postures, to move more, to have faster reactions, to leave or to compensate, and in general to speak less. (p. 111)

On the other hand, so long as people behave "appropriately," most people match their behavior – smiling more and standing closer to those who treat them more warmly. In a review of 25 studies, Cappella (1981) also found that people's intimate overtures tend to be matched in the breadth and depth of information exchanged. Of course, when things go too far and people begin to spill secrets that are too personal too soon, compensation occurs: People become wary and clam up themselves or leave.

*People's desire to control or manage situations.* Sometimes people intentionally avoid matching others' emotions in order to "keep a lid" on things. They try to be polite in the face of rudeness, calm in the face of hysteria, and smile sweetly when others are reeling in anger. An example: Recently, we (Hatfield & Rapson) walked up to the counter at Bernie's Deli and started to place our order with one of the three waiters who were just standing around, smiling pleasantly, ready to serve customers. As we started to place our order, a very large and very angry customer glared at us and said, "Excuse me!" He was clearly furious. Totally perplexed, Dick smiled and said, "Is something wrong?" In fury, the man shouted: "I here first. You all wait until I figure out what I want and order; wait your turn!" All of the waiting customers glanced at one another. No one ordered. Furious, he slowly proceeded to read through the menu, following item by item with his finger. All the customers remained frozen. All waiting, all perplexed. If they felt as we did, we had indeed caught his anger. (I had vague fantasies of stabbing him with my fork. Two of a kind!) On all our faces, however, were fake pleasant smiles, which certainly did not match his scowl. However, our fury surely wiped out the normal ballet of movements. We were all awkward and wooden.

*What are the advantages/disadvantages of being able to infect
others with your emotions?*

There are times when people may wish to transmit their own emotions to others. When we try to distract an irritable child, when we go to the hospital to "cheer up" a friend, when we try to liven up a dull party, we are trying to dominate an interpersonal encounter.

Theorists might attempt systematically to analyze when it is to people's advantage to make their feelings known and when it is a distinct disadvantage to do so.

*What are the advantages/disadvantages of catching others'
emotions?*

Sometimes people benefit from being able to read and share others' feelings. At other times, however, contagion is too much of a good thing. People may well wish to build a glass wall around their feelings when they must act coolly in a "hot" situation or respond with verve and energy in a cool, dead environment. They may not wish to share others' feelings when their interests are opposed. In such situations, it may be a good thing to be able to resist.

One of Elaine's students referees volleyball at the University of Hawaii. Last week he made a controversial call and both sides booed him. He got so angry and upset from absorbing *their* anger and upset that he could hardly carry on. He kept wanting to tell them off, to punish both teams. How do you stop yourself from catching others' emotions? he asked. He knows that he will have to figure out how to toughen his hide if he hopes to keep coaching.

Theorists might attempt systematically to analyze when it is to people's advantage to catch others' emotions and when it is a distinct disadvantage to do so.

## Can you teach people to mimic/synchronize with others' movements?

Most authors seem to take it for granted that people can voluntarily mimic or refrain from mimicking others' postures. Since Richard Bandler and John Grinder's (1975) book *The Structure of Magic*, which described techniques of "neurolinguistic programming," many business people have been teaching employees to mimic clients' movements. For example, one of my graduate students, who works in the complaint department of Liberty House, an upscale department store, was taught to mimic the faces, voices, and postures of irate clients, hoping to calm them. (Personally, we wouldn't expect this to be a very good idea: The potential for violence seems greater than the potential for calming.) In chapter 5, we saw that Desmond Morris (1966) took it for granted that therapists could put clients at ease by modeling their movements. There is a question as to just how effective such self-conscious mimicry might be, however. As was discussed in chapter 1 (in the section "Movement Coordination"), some researchers (e.g., Davis, 1985) have speculated that people are probably *not* able consciously to improve their ability to track others' expressive behavior and emotions: It took even Muhammad Ali at least 190 milliseconds to spot a light and another 40 ms to punch in response, whereas college students could synchronize their movements within 21 ms (Condon & Ogston, 1966). Davis, you'll recall, argued that such microsynchrony is mediated by basal brain structures, and that people who try consciously to mirror others are doomed to look phony.

Marianne LaFrance and William Ickes (1981), too, found that if subjects mirrored one another's posture too much at a first meeting, they ended up feeling self-conscious and evaluated the encounter as forced, awkward, and strained. Early attempts to teach therapists to be empathic failed dismally. According to clinical lore, therapists can best display empathy by leaning forward in their chairs, periodically nodding their heads, and saying "uh-huh" now and then. Raymond Birdwhistell observed that psychotherapy interns who were instructed to use these techniques failed. Instead of nodding when their *clients* needed support, they nodded each time *they* became anxious and desperate to do something. Thus, they ended up telegraphing not empathy but panic (Davis, 1985, pp. 66–67).

In spite of such discouraging possibilities, one would want to explore the possibilities for making people more sensitive to contagion and/or better able to resist it.

## Summing up

We have attempted in this book to assemble evidence from a multitude of sources and a variety of disciplines that the phenomenon of emotional contagion exists. In so doing, we hope to have signaled its importance and sketched out some promising paths for future research and application. Contagion clearly enters into *interpersonal* encounters in assorted ways. Recognizing this may be useful for psychotherapists in reading their clients, doctors their patients, lawyers their adversaries, teachers their students, husbands their wives, mothers their children, and so on.

> Human beings have one faculty which, though it is of the greatest utility for collective purposes, is most pernicious for individuation, and that is the faculty of imitation. Collective psychology cannot dispense with imitation, for without it all mass organizations, the State and the social order, are impossible. Society is organized, indeed, less by law than by the propensity to imitation, implying equally suggestibility, suggestion, and mental contagion.
> – Carl Gustav Jung

Equally suggestive is the contagion that may occur in larger *social* interactions. Groups of individuals often appear to catch the emotions of others, whether it be laughter in a movie theater or hatred in a lynch mob. Did Hitler employ contagion in stirring up the crowds with his inflammatory oratory? Would it be possible for someone trained in the art of emotional contagion to exert a similar influence? Do totalitarian regimes or religious revival meetings or antiwar (or prowar) or prochoice (or antiabortion) rallies exploit the phenomenon? Can emotions be spread by the mass media, as suggested by the study of Mullen and his colleagues (1986) on the influence of the facial displays of newscasters on voting behavior? With the expansion and increased power of new communications, should we attend more carefully to the way this phenomenon functions? What is the effect on social bonds and relations of technologies (i.e., personal computers, electronic mail) that facilitate the transmission of information but diminish the parallel transmission of emotional communications?

We end with questions and with the hope that the emotions implicit in the last paragraph may spread to others.

# References

Adelmann, P. K., & Zajonc, R. [B.] (1989). Facial efference and the experience of emotion. *Annual Review of Psychology, 40,* 249–280.

Allport, G. W. (1937/1961). *Pattern and growth in personality.* New York: Holt, Rinehart, & Winston.

Ambady, N., & Rosenthal, R. (1992). Thin slices of expressive behavior as predictors of interpersonal consequences: A meta-analysis. *Psychological Bulletin, 111,* 256–274.

American Psychiatric Association. (1987). *Diagnostic and statistical manual of mental disorders* (3rd ed.). Washington, DC: Author.

Anson, B. J. (1951). *Atlas of human anatomy.* Philadelphia: W. B. Saunders.

Archer, D., & Akert, R. M. (1977). Words and everything else: Verbal and nonverbal cues in social interpretation. *Journal of Personality and Social Psychology, 35,* 443–449.

Arendt, H. (1962). The Graebe memorandum. In Contemporary Civilization Staff of Columbia College. Columbia University (Eds.), *Man in contemporary society* (pp. 1070–1073). New York: Columbia University Press.

Argyle, M., & Dean, J. (1965). Eye-contact, distance and affiliation. *Sociometry, 28,* 289–304.

Arnold, M. B. (1960). *Emotion and personality: Vol. 1. Psychological aspects.* New York: Columbia University Press.

Aronfreed, J. (1970). The socialization of altruistic and sympathetic behavior: Some theoretical and experimental analyses. In J. Macaulay & L. Berkowitz (Eds.), *Altruism and helping behavior* (pp. 103–126). New York: Academic Press.

Ax, A. F. (1953). The physiological differentiation between fear and anger in humans. *Psychosomatic Medicine, 15,* 433–442.

Babad, E., Bernieri, F., & Rosenthal, R. (1989). Nonverbal communication and leakage in the behavior of biased and unbiased teachers. *Journal of Personality and Social Psychology, 56,* 89–94.

Bandler, R., & Grinder, J. (1975). *The structure of magic: I. A book about language and therapy.* Palo Alto, CA: Science & Behavior Books.

Bandura, A. (1969) *Principles of behavior modification.* New York: Holt, Rinehart & Winston.

   (1973). *Aggression: A social learning analysis.* Englewood Cliffs, NJ: Prentice–Hall.

Bavelas, J. B., Black, A., Chovil, N., Lemery, C. R., & Mullett, J. (1988). Form and function in motor mimicry: Topographic evidence that the primary function is communication. *Human Communication Research, 14,* 275–299.

Bavelas, J. B., Black, A., Lemery, C. R., & Mullett, J. (1987). Motor mimicry as primitive empathy. In N. Eisenberg & J. Strayer (Eds.), *Empathy and its development* (pp. 317–338). New York: Cambridge University Press.

Bayer, E. (1929). Beitrage zur zweikomponententheorie des hungers. *Zeitschrift für Psychologie und Physiologie der Sinnesorgane, 112,* 1–54.

Beaumont, W. (1833). *Experiments and observations on the gastric juice and the physiology of digestion.* Plattsburgh, NY: F. P. Allen.

Beck, A. T. (1972). *Depression: Causes and treatment.* Philadelphia: University of Pennsylvania Press.

Beebe, B., Gerstman, L., Carson, B., Dolins, M., Zigman, A., Rosensweig, H., Faughey, K., & Korman, M. (1982). Rhythmic communication in the mother–infant dyad. In M. Davis (Ed.), *Interaction rhythms: Periodicity in communicative behavior* (pp. 77–100). New York: Human Sciences Press.

Bem, D. J. (1972). Self-perception theory. In L. Berkowitz (Ed.), *Advances in experimental social psychology* (Vol. 6, pp. 1–62). New York: Academic Press.

Berger, S. M., & Hadley, S. W. (1975). Some effects of a model's performance on an observer's electromyographic activity. *American Journal of Psychology, 88,* 263–276.

Bergman, R. A., Thompson, S. A., & Afifi, A. K. (1984). *Catalog of human variation.* Baltimore: Urban & Schwarzenberg.

Berghout-Austin, A. M., & Peery, J. C. (1983). Analysis of adult–neonate synchrony during speech and nonspeech. *Perceptual and Motor Skills, 57,* 455–459.

Bernieri, F. J. (1988). Coordinated movement and rapport in teacher–student interactions. *Journal of Nonverbal Behavior, 12,* 120–138.

Bernieri, F. J., Davis, J. M., Knee, C. R., & Rosenthal, R. (1991). *Interactional synchrony and the social affordance of rapport: A validation study.* Unpublished manuscript, Oregon State University, Corvallis.

Bernieri, F. J., Reznick, J. S., & Rosenthal, R. (1988). Synchrony, pseudosynchrony, and dissynchrony: Measuring the entrainment process in mother–infant interactions. *Journal of Personality and Social Psychology, 54,* 243–253.

Bernstein, I. (1990). *The New York City draft riots.* New York: Oxford University Press.

Berscheid, E. (1983). Emotion. In H. H. Kelley, E. Berscheid, A. Christensen, J. H. Harvey, T. L. Huston, G. Levinger, E. McClintock, L. A. Peplau, & D. R. Peterson (Eds.), *Close relationships* (pp. 110–168). New York: Freeman.

Bloch, S., Orthous, P., & Santibanez-H, G. (1987). Effector patterns of basic emotions: a psychophysiological method for training actors. *Journal of Social and Biological Structures, 10,* 1–19.

Bloom, K. (1975). Social elicitation of infant vocal behavior. *Journal of Experimental Child Psychology, 20,* 51–58.

Bousfield, W. A. (1950). The relationship between mood and the production of affectively toned associates. *Journal of General Psychology, 42,* 67–85.

Bower, G. H. (1981). Mood and memory. *American Psychologist, 36,* 129–148.

Bramel, D., Taub, B., & Blum, B. (1968). An observer's reaction to the suffering of his enemy. *Journal of Personality and Social Psychology, 8,* 384–392.

Bresler, C., & Laird, J. D. (1983). Short-term stability and discriminant validity of the "self-situational" cue dimension. Paper presented at the Eastern Psychological Association Meeting, Philadelphia, PA.

Brewer, D., Doughtie, E. B., & Lubin, B. (1980). Induction of mood and mood shift. *Journal of Clinical Psychology, 36,* 215–226.

Brontë, E. (1847/1976). *Wuthering Heights.* Oxford, England: Clarendon Press.

Brookner, A. (1987). *A friend from England.* New York: Harper & Row.

Brothers, L. (1989). A biological perspective on empathy. *American Journal of Psychiatry, 146,* 10–19.

Buck, R. (1976a). *Human motivation and emotion.* New York: Wiley.

———(1976b). A test of nonverbal receiving ability: Preliminary studies. *Human Communication Research, 2,* 162–171.

———(1980). Nonverbal behavior and the theory of emotion: The facial feedback hypothesis. *Journal of Personality and Social Psychology, 38,* 811–824.

———(1984). *The communication of emotion.* New York: Guilford Press.

———(1985). Prime theory: An integrated view of motivation and emotion. *Psychological Review, 92,* 389–413.

Buck, R., Baron, R., & Barette, D. (1982). Temporal organization of spontaneous emotional expression. *Journal of Personality and Social Psychology, 42,* 506–517.

Buck, R., Baron, R., Goodman, N., & Shapiro, B. (1980). Unitization of spontaneous nonverbal behavior in the study of emotion communication. *Journal of Personality and Social Psychology, 39,* 522–529.

Buck, R., & Carroll, J. (1974). *CARAT and PONS: Correlates of two tests of nonverbal sensitivity.* Unpublished manuscript, Carnegie–Mellon University, Pittsburgh.

Buck, R., Miller, R. E., & Caul, W. F. (1974). Sex, personality and physiological variables in the communication of emotion via facial expression. *Journal of Personality and Social Psychology, 30,* 587–596.

Buder, E. (1991). *Vocal synchrony in conversations: Spectral analysis of fundamental voice frequency.* Unpublished doctoral dissertation, Department of Communication Arts, University of Wisconsin–Madison.

Bugental, D. B., Blue, J., & Lewis, J. (1990). Caregiver beliefs and dysphoric affect directed to difficult children. *Developmental Psychology, 26,* 631–638.

Bull, N. (1951). The attitude theory of emotion. *Nervous and Mental Disease Monographs, 81,* New York: Coolidge Foundation.

Bush, L. K., Barr, C. L., McHugo, G. J., & Lanzetta, J. T. (1989). The effects of facial control and facial mimicry on subjective reactions to comedy routines. *Motivation and Emotion, 13,* 31–52.

Byatt, A. S. (1985). *Still life.* New York: MacMillan.

Byers, P. (1976). Biological rhythms as information channels in communication behavior. In P. P. G. Bateson and P. H. Klopfer (Eds.), *Perspectives in ethology* (Vol. 2, pp. 135–164). New York: Plenum Press.

Byrne, D. (1964). Repression–sensitization as a dimension of personality. In B. A. Maher (Ed.), *Progress in experimental personality research* (pp. 169–220). New York: Academic Press.

Cacioppo, J. T., Bush, L. K., & Tassinary, L. G. (1992). Microexpressive facial actions as a function of affective stimuli: Replication and extension. *Personality and Social Psychology Bulletin, 18,* 515–526.

Cacioppo, J. T., Klein, D. J., Berntson, G. G., & Hatfield, E. (1993). The psychophysiology of emotion. In M. Lewis & J. Haviland (Eds.), *The handbook of emotion.* New York: Guilford Press.

Cacioppo, J. T., & Petty, R. E. (1983). *Social psychophysiology: A sourcebook.* New York: Guilford Press.

Cacioppo, J. T., Priester, J. R., & Berntson, G. G. (in preparation). Rudimentary determinants of attitudes: Collateral somatic activity influences attitude formation.

Cacioppo, J. T., Tassinary, L. G., & Fridlund, A. J. (1990). Skeletomotor system. In J. T. Cacioppo & L. G. Tassinary (Eds.), *Principles of psychophysiology: Physical, social, and inferential elements* (pp. 325–384). New York: Cambridge University Press.

Cacioppo, J. T., Uchino, B. N., Crites, S. L., Snydersmith, M. A., Smith, G., Berntson, G. G., & Lang, P. J. (1992). Relationship between facial expressiveness and sympathetic activation in emotion: A critical review, with emphasis on modeling underlying mechanisms and individual differences. *Journal of Personality and Social Psychology, 62,* 110–128.

Campos, J. J., & Sternberg, C. R. (1981). Perception, appraisal and emotion: The onset of social referencing. In M. Lamb & L. Sherrod (Eds.), *Infant social cognition* (pp. 273–314). Hillsdale, NJ: Erlbaum.

Candland, D. K. (1977). The persistent problems of emotion. In D. K. Candland, J. P. Fell, E. Keen, A. I. Leshner, R. Plutchik, & R. M. Tarpy (Eds.), *Emotion* (pp. 1–84). Monterey, CA: Brooks/Cole.

Cannon, W. B. (1929). *Bodily changes in pain, hunger, fear, and rage, on account of recent researches into the function of emotional excitement* (2nd ed.). New York: Appleton.

Cantril, H. (1940). *The invasion from Mars.* Princeton, NJ: Princeton University Press.

Cappella, J. N. (1981). Mutual influence in expressive behavior: Adult–adult and infant–adult dyadic interaction. *Psychological Bulletin, 89,* 101–132.

(1985). The management of conversations. In M. L. Knapp & G. R. Miller (Eds.), *The handbook of interpersonal communication* (pp. 393–438). Beverly Hills, CA: Sage.

(1991). The biological origins of automated patterns of human interaction. *Communication Theory, 1,* 4–35.

Cappella, J. N., & Flagg, M. E. (1992, July 23–28). Interactional adaptation, expressiveness, and attraction: Kinesic and vocal responsiveness patterns in initial liking. Paper presented at the VIth International Conference on Personal Relationships, University of Maine, Orono.

Cappella, J. N., & Palmer, M. T. (1990). Attitude similarity, relational history, and attraction: The mediating effects of kinesic and vocal behavior. *Communication Monographs, 57,* 161–183.

Cappella, J. N., & Planalp, S. (1981). Talk and silence sequences in informal conversations: III. Interspeaker influence. *Human Communication Research, 7,* 117–132.

Carlson, J. G., & Hatfield, E. (1992). *Psychology of emotion.* Fort Worth, TX: Harcourt, Brace, Jovanovich.

Chapple, E. D. (1982). Movement and sound: The musical language of body rhythms in interaction. In M. Davis (Ed.), *Interaction rhythms: Periodicity in communicative behavior* (pp. 31–52). New York: Human Sciences Press.

Charney, E. J. (1966). Psychosomatic manifestations of rapport in psychotherapy. *Psychosomatic Medicine, 28,* 305–315.

Chen, S. C. (1937). Social modification of the activity of ants in nest-building. *Physiological Zoology, 10,* 420–436.

Chew, P. K., Phoon, W. H., & Mae-Lim, H. A. (1976). Epidemic hysteria among some factory workers in Singapore. *Singapore Medical Journal, 17,* 10–15.

Church, W. F. (Ed.), (1964). *The influence of the enlightenment on the French revolution: Creative, disastrous or non-existent?* Lexington, MA: D. C. Heath.

Clark, K. (1969). *Civilisation.* New York: Harper & Row.

Clynes, M. (1980). The communication of emotion: Theory of sentics. In R. Plutchik & H. Kellerman (Eds.), *Emotion: Theory, research, and experience: Vol. 1. Theories of emotion* (pp. 271–304). New York: Academic Press.

Colby, C. Z., Lanzetta, J. T., & Kleck, R. E. (1977). Effects of the expression of pain on autonomic and pain tolerance responses to subject-controlled pain. *Psychophysiology, 14,* 537–540.

Condon, W. S. (1982). Cultural microrhythms. In M. Davis (Ed.), *Interaction rhythms: Periodicity in communicative behavior* (pp. 53–76). New York: Human Sciences Press.

Condon, W. S., & Ogston, W. D. (1966). Sound film analysis of normal and pathological behavior patterns. *Journal of Nervous and Mental Disease, 143,* 338–347.

(1967). A method of studying animal behavior. *Journal of Auditory Research, 7,* 359–365.

Condon, W. S., & Sander, L. W. (1974). Neonate movement is synchronized with adult speech: Interactional participation and language acquisition. *Science, 183,* 99–101.

Cook, A. (1974). *The armies of the streets: The New York City draft riots of 1863.* Lexington, KY: University of Kentucky Press.

Coyne, J. C. (1976). Depression and the response of others. *Journal of Abnormal Psychology, 85,* 186–193.

Craig, K. D. (1968). Physiological arousal as a function of imagined, vicarious, and direct stress experiences. *Journal of Abnormal Psychology, 73,* 513–520.

Crown, C., & Feldstein, S. (in press). Coordinated interpersonal timing of vision and voice as a function of interpersonal attraction.

Cummings, E. M. (1987). Coping with background anger in early childhood. *Child Development, 58,* 976–984.

Cupchik, G. C., & Leventhal, H. (1974). Consistency between expressive behavior and the evaluation of humorous stimuli: The role of sex and self-observation. *Journal of Personality and Social Psychology, 30,* 429–442.

Czaplicka, M. A. (1914). *Aboriginal Siberia: A study in social anthropology.* Oxford, England: Clarendon Press.

Darnton, R. (1984). *The great cat massacre.* New York: Basic Books.

Darwin, C. (1872/1965). *The expression of the emotions in man and animals.* Chicago: University of Chicago Press.

Davis, M. R. (1985). Perceptual and affective reverberation components. In A. B. Goldstein & G. Y. Michaels (Eds.), *Empathy: Development, training, and consequences* (pp. 62–108). Hillsdale, NJ: Erlbaum.

DiMascio, A., Boyd, R. W., & Greenblatt, M. (1957). Physiological correlates of tension and antagonism during psychotherapy: A study of "interpersonal physiology." *Psychosomatic Medicine, 19,* 99–104.

DiMascio, A., Boyd, R. W., Greenblatt, M., & Solomon, H. D. (1955). The psychiatric interview: A sociophysiologic study. *Diseases of the Nervous System, 26,* 4–9.

Dimberg, U. (1982). Facial reactions to facial expressions. *Psychophysiology, 19,* 643–647.

(1988). Facial electromyography and the experience of emotion. *Journal of Psychophysiology, 3,* 277–282.

(1990). Facial electromyography and emotional reactions. *Psychophysiology, 27,* 481–494.

Doctorow, E. L. (1985). *World's fair.* New York: Random House.

Doherty, R. W., Orimoto, L., Hebb., J., & Hatfield, E. (1993). *Emotional contagion: Gender and occupational differences.* Unpublished manuscript, University of Hawaii, Honolulu.

Downey, G., & Coyne, J. C. (1990). Children of depressed parents: An integrative review. *Psychological Bulletin, 108,* 50–76.

Douglas, K. (1988). *The ragman's son: An autobiography.* New York: Pocket Books.

Douglis, C. (1989, April 14). We've got rhythm. *Pacific Sun,* pp. 3–6.

Doyle, A. C. (1917/1967). The adventure of the cardboard box. In W. S. Baring-Gould (Ed.), *The Annotated Sherlock Holmes* (Vol. II, pp. 193–208). New York: Clarkson N. Potter.

Drabble, M. (1939/1972). *The needle's eye, a novel.* New York: Knopf.

Duclos, S. E., Laird, J. D., Schneider, E., Sexter, M., Stern, L., & Van Lighten, O. (1989). Emotion-specific effects of facial expressions and postures on emotional experience. *Journal of Personality and Social Psychology, 57,* 100–108.

Duncan, J. W., & Laird, J. D. (1977). Cross-modality consistencies in individual differences in self-attribution. *Journal of Personality, 45,* 191–206.

(1980). Positive and reverse placebo effects as a function of differences in cues used in self-perception. *Journal of Personality and Social Psychology, 39,* 1024–1036.

Dysinger, D. W. (1931). A comparative study of affective responses by means of the impressive and expressive methods. *Psychological Monographs, 41,* 14–31.

Easterbrook, J. A. (1959). The effect of emotion on cue-utilization and the organization of behavior. *Psychological Review, 66,* 183–201.

Ebrahim, G. J. (1968). Mass hysteria in school children: Notes on three outbreaks in East Africa. *Clinical Pediatrics, 7,* 437–438.

Eisenberg, N., & Miller, P. (1987). Empathy, sympathy, and altruism: Empirical and conceptual links. In N. Eisenberg & J. Strayer (Eds.), *Empathy and its development* (pp. 292–316). New York: Cambridge University Press.

Eisenberg, N., & Strayer, J. (1987). *Empathy and its development.* New York: Cambridge University Press.

Ekman, P. (1985). *Telling lies.* New York: Berkeley Books.

(1992). Are there basic emotions? A reply to Ortony and Turner. *Psychological Review, 99,* 550–553.

Ekman, P., & Friesen, W. V. (1974). Nonverbal behavior and psychopathology. In R. J. Friedman & M. M. Katz (Eds.), *The psychology of depression: Contemporary theory and research* (pp. 203–224). New York: John Wiley & Sons.

Ekman, P., Friesen, W. V., & Scherer, K. (1976). Body movement and voice pitch in deceptive interaction. *Semiotica, 16,* 23–27.

Ekman, P., Levenson, R. W., & Friesen, W. V. (1983). Autonomic nervous system activity distinguishes among emotions. *Science, 221,* 1208–1210.

Emde, R. N., Gaensbauer, T., & Harmon, R. J. (1981). Using our emotions: Some principles for appraising emotional development and intervention. In M. Lewis & L. T. Taft (Eds.), *Developmental disabilities: Theory, assessment and intervention* (pp. 409–424). New York: SP Medical & Scientific Books.

Englis, B. G., Vaughan, K. B., & Lanzetta, J. T. (1981). Conditioning of counterempathic emotional responses. *Journal of Experimental Social Psychology, 18,* 375–391.

Eysenck, H. J. (1967). *The biological basis of personality.* Springfield, IL: Thomas.

Eysenck, H. [J.], & Eysenck, S. (1968a). *Manual for the Eysenck Personality Inventory.* San Diego: Educational Testing Service.

(1968b). *Personality structure and measurement.* San Diego, CA: Knapp.

Fahrenberg, J., Foerster, F., Schneider, H. J., Muller, W., & Myrtek, M. (1986). Predictability of individual differences in activation processes in field setting based on laboratory measures. *Psychophysiology, 23,* 323–333.

Feiffer, J. (1982). Introduction. In S. Heller (Ed.), *Jules Feiffer's America: From Eisenhower to Reagan.* New York: Alfred Knopf.

Feldstein, J. H. (1976). Sex differences in social memory among preschool children. *Sex Roles, 2,* 75–79.

Feldstein, S., & Welkowitz, J. (1978). A chronography of conversation: In defense of an objective approach. In A. W. Siegman & S. Feldstein (Eds.), *Nonverbal behavior and communication* (pp. 435–499). Hillsdale, NJ: Erlbaum.

Feshbach, N. D., & Roe, K. (1968). Empathy in six- and seven-year-olds. *Child Development, 39,* 133–145.

Field, T. (1982) Individual differences in the expressivity of neonates and young infants. In R. W. Feldman (Ed.), *Development of nonverbal behavior in children* (pp. 279–298). New York: Springer–Verlag.

Field, T., & Walden, T. A. (1982). Perception and production of facial expressions in infancy and early childhood. In H. Reese & L. Lipsett (Eds.), *Advances in child development and behavior* (Vol. 16, pp. 169–211). New York: Academic Press.

Field, T., Woodson, R., Cohen, D., Garcia, R., & Greenberg, R. (1982). Discrimination and imitation of facial expressions by term and preterm neonates. *Infant Behavior Development, 6,* 485–490.

Fischer, K. W., Shaver, P. R., & Carnochan, P. (1990). How emotions develop and how they organize development. *Cognition and Emotion, 4,* 81–127.

Fowles, D. C., Roberts, R., & Nagel, K. (1977). The influence of introversion/ extraversion on the skin conductance responses to stress and stimulus intensity. *Journal of Research in Personality, 11,* 129–146.

Fraiberg, S. (1974). Blind infants and their mothers: An examination of the sign system. In M. Lewes & L. A. Rosenblum (Ed.), *The effect of the infant on its caregiver* (pp. 215–232). New York: Wiley.

Fredrikson, M., Danielssons, T., Engel, B. T., Frisk-Holmberg, M., Strom, G., & Sundin, O. (1985). Autonomic nervous system function and essential hypertension: Individual response specificity with and without beta-adrenergic blockade. *Psychophysiology, 22,* 167–174.

Freud, S. (1904/1959). *Psychopathology of everyday life.* New York: New American Library.

    (1912/1958). Recommendations to physicians practising psycho-analysis. In J. Strachey (Ed.) (Trans. J. Reviene), *The standard edition of the complete psychological works of Sigmund Freud* (Vol. 12, p. 115). London: Hogarth Press.

Friedman, H. S., Prince, L. M., Riggio, R. E., & DiMatteo, M. R. (1980). Understanding and assessing non-verbal expressiveness: The Affective Communication Test. *Journal of Personality and Social Psychology, 39,* 333–351.

Friedman, H. S., & Riggio, R. E. (1981). Effect of individual differences in nonverbal expressiveness on transmission of emotion. *Journal of Nonverbal Behavior, 6,* 96–101.

Frodi, A. M., Lamb, M. E., Leavitt, L. A., Donovan, W. L., Neff, C., & Sherry, D. (1978). Fathers' and mothers' responses to the faces and cries of normal and premature infants. *Developmental Psychology, 14,* 490–498.

Fromm-Reichmann, F. (1950). *Principles of intensive psychotherapy.* Chicago: University of Chicago Press.

Fujita, B. N., Harper, R. G., & Wiens, A. N. (1980). Encoding–decoding of nonverbal emotional messages: Sex differences in spontaneous and enacted expressions. *Journal of Nonverbal Behavior, 4,* 131–145.

Gadlin, H. (1977). Private lives and public order: A critical view of the history of intimate relationships in the United States. In G. Levinger & H. L. Rausch (Eds.), *Perspectives on the meaning of intimacy* (pp. 33–72). Amherst: University of Massachusetts Press.

Galin, D. (1974). Implications for psychiatry of left and right cerebral specialization: A neurophysiological context for unconscious processes. *Archives of General Psychiatry, 31*, 572.

Gallagher, D., & Shuntich, R. J. (1981). Encoding and decoding of nonverbal behavior through facial expressions. *Journal of Research in Personality, 15*, 241–252.

Galton, F. (1884). Measurement of character. *Fortnightly Review, 42*, 179–185.

Garwood, M., Engel, B. T., & Capriotti, R. (1982). Autonomic nervous system function and aging: Response specificity. *Psychophysiology, 19*, 378–385.

Gazzaniga, M. S. (1985). *The social brain: Discovering the networks of the mind.* New York: Basic Books.

(1989). Organization of the human brain. *Science, 245*, 947–952.

Geen, R. G. (1983). The psychophysiology of extraversion–introversion. In J. T. Cacioppo & R. E. Petty (Eds.), *Social psychophysiology: A sourcebook* (pp. 391–416). New York: Guilford Press.

Gellhorn, E. (1964). Motion and emotion: The role of proprioception in the physiology and pathology of emotions. *Psychological Review, 71*, 457–572.

Gewirtz, J. L., & Boyd, E. F. (1976). Mother–infant interaction and its study. In H. W. Reese (Ed.), *Advances in child development and behavior* (Vol. 11, pp. 153–159). New York: Academic Press.

(1977). Experiments on mother–infant interaction underlying mutual attachment acquisition: The infant conditions the mother. In T. Alloway, P. Pliner, & L. Krames (Eds.), *Attachment behavior: Advances in the study of communication and affect* (Vol. 3, pp. 109–143). New York: Plenum Press.

Giles, H., & Powesland, P. F. (1975). *Speech style and social evaluation.* London: Academic Press.

Givner, J. (1982). *Katherine Anne Porter: A life.* New York: Simon & Schuster.

Goldfried, M. R., & Robins, C. (1983). Self-schema, cognitive bias, and the processing of therapeutic experiences. In P. C. Kendall (Ed.), *Advances in cognitive-behavioral research and therapy* (pp. 33–80). New York: Academic Press.

Goleman, D. (1989, March 28). The roots of empathy are traced to infancy. *New York Times,* pp. B1, B10.

(1991, October 15). Happy or sad, a mood can prove contagious. *New York Times,* pp. B5–7.

Gordon, J. E. (1957). Interpersonal predictions of repressors and sensitizers. *Journal of Personality, 25*, 686–698.

Gornick, V. (1987). *Fierce attachments.* New York: Simon & Schuster.

Gottman, J. M. (1979). *Marital interaction: Experimental investigations.* New York: Academic Press.

Gray, J. A. (1971). *The psychology of fear and stress.* New York: McGraw–Hill.

(1972). The psychophysiological nature of introversion–extraversion: A modification of Eysenck's theory. In V. D. Neylitsyn & J. A. Gray (Eds.), *Biological basis of individual behavior* (pp. 182–205). New York: Academic Press.

Grusec, J. E., & Abramovitch, R. (1982). Imitation of peers and adults in a natural setting: A functional analysis. *Child Development, 53*, 636–642.

Haggard, E. A., & Isaacs, K. S. (1966). Micromomentary facial expressions as indicators of ego mechanisms in psychotherapy. In L. A. Gottschalk & A. H. Auerbach (Eds.), *Methods of research in psychotherapy* (pp. 154–165). New York: Appleton–Century–Crofts.

Hall, J. A. (1978). Gender effects in decoding nonverbal cues. *Psychological Bulletin, 85*, 845–857.

——— (1979). Gender, gender roles, and nonverbal communication skills. In R. Rosenthal (Ed.), *Skill in nonverbal communication: Individual differences* (pp. 32–67). Cambridge, MA: Oelgeschlager, Gunn & Hain.

——— (1984). *Nonverbal sex differences: Communication accuracy and expressive style.* Baltimore: Johns Hopkins University Press.

Harlow, H. F., & Harlow, M. K. (1965). The affectional systems. In A. M. Schrier, H. F. Harlow, & F. Stollnitz (Eds.), *Behavior of nonhuman primates* (Vol. 2, pp. 287–334). New York: Academic Press.

Harrison, B. G. (1989). *Italian days.* New York: Ticknor & Fields.

Hatfield, E., Cacioppo, J., & Rapson, R. L. (1992). Emotional contagion. In M. S. Clark (Ed.), *Review of personality and social psychology: Vol. 14. Emotion and social behavior* (pp. 151–177). Newbury Park, CA: Sage.

Hatfield, E., Hsee, C. K., Costello, J., Schalenkamp, M., & Denney, C. (in press). The impact of vocal feedback on emotional experience and expression. *Journal of Nonverbal Behavior.*

Hatfield, E., & Rapson, R. (1990). Emotions: A trinity. In E. A. Bleckman (Ed.), *Emotions and the family: For better or worse* (pp. 11–33). Hillsdale, NJ: Erlbaum.

Hatfield, E., & Sprecher, S. (1986). *Mirror, mirror: The importance of looks in everyday life.* Albany, NY: SUNY Press.

Haviland, J. M., & Lelwica, M. (1987). The induced affect response: 10-week-old infants' responses to three emotion expressions. *Developmental Psychology, 23,* 97–104.

Haviland, J. M., & Malatesta, C. Z. (1981). The development of sex differences in nonverbal signals: Fallacies, facts, and fantasies. In C. Mayo & N. M. Henley (Eds.), *Gender and nonverbal behavior* (pp. 183–208). New York: Springer–Verlag.

Headley, J. T. (1971). *The great riots of New York 1712 to 1873.* New York: Dover.

Hebb, J. (1992). On measuring emotional contagion. Unpublished honors thesis. University of Hawaii, Honolulu.

Hecker, J. F. (1837/1970). *The dancing mania of the middle ages* (B. G. Babington, Trans.). New York: Burt Franklin.

Hirt, E. R. (1990). Do I see only what I expect? Evidence for an expectancy-guided retrieval model. *Journal of Personality and Social Psychology, 58,* 937–951.

Hittelman, J. H., & Dickes, R. (1979). Sex differences in neonatal eye contact time. *Merrill–Palmer Quarterly, 25,* 171–184.

Hoffman, M. L. (1973). Empathy, role-taking, guilt, and the development of altruistic motives. *Developmental Psychology Report No. 30,* Ann Arbor: University of Michigan.

——— (1978). Toward a theory of empathic arousal and development. In M. Lewis & L. A. Rosenblum (Eds.), *The development of affect* (pp. 227–256). New York: Plenum.

——— (1987). The contribution of empathy to justice and moral judgement. In N. Eisenberg & J. Strayer (Eds.), *Empathy and its development* (pp. 47–80). New York: Cambridge University Press.

Hohmann, G. W. (1966). Some effects of spinal cord lesions on experienced emotional feelings. *Psychophysiology, 3,* 143–156.

Howes, M. J., Hokanson, J. E., & Lowenstein, D. A. (1985). Induction of depressive affect after prolonged exposure to a mildly depressed individual. *Journal of Personality and Social Psychology, 49,* 1110–1113.

Hsee, C. K., Hatfield, E., Carlson, J. G., & Chemtob, C. (1990). The effect of power on susceptibility to emotional contagion. *Cognition and Emotion, 4,* 327–340.

(1991). *Emotional contagion and its relationship to mood.* Unpublished manuscript, University of Hawaii, Honolulu.

Hsee, C. K., Hatfield, E., & Chemtob, C. (1991). Assessment of the emotional states of others: Conscious judgments versus emotional contagion. *Journal of Social and Clinical Psychology, 11,* 119–128.

Hugo, V. (1831/1928). *The hunchback of Notre-Dame.* New York: Dodd, Mead.

Humphrey, G. (1922) The conditioned reflex and the elementary social reaction. *Journal of Abnormal and Social Psychology, 17,* 113–119.

Hygge, S., & Ohman, A. (1976). The relation of vicarious to direct instigation and conditioning of electrodermal responses. *Scandanavian Journal of Psychology, 17,* 217–222.

Ickes, W., Patterson, M. L., Rajecki, D. W., & Tanford, S. (1982). Behavioral and cognitive consequences of reciprocal versus compensatory responses to pre-interaction expectancies. *Social Cognition, 1,* 160–190.

Isen, A. M. (1987). Positive affect, cognitive processes, and social behavior. *Advances in Experimental Social Psychology, 20,* 203–253.

Izard, C. E. (1971). *The face of emotion.* New York: Appleton–Century–Crofts.

(1990). Facial expressions and the regulation of emotions. *Journal of Personality and Social Psychology, 58,* 487–498.

(1992). Basic emotions, relations among emotions, and emotion–cognition relations. *Psychological Review, 99,* 561–565.

Jackson, D. N. (1974). *Personality Research Form manual.* New York: Research Psychologists Press.

James, W. (1890/1922). *The principles of psychology,* Vol. 2. New York: Dover.

(1890/1984a). Emotions. In *Psychology: Briefer course* (pp. 324–338). Cambridge, MA: Harvard University Press.

(1890/1984b). What is an emotion? In C. Calhoun and R. C. Solomon (Eds.), *What is an emotion?* (pp. 125–142). New York: Oxford University Press.

Jelalian, E., & Miller, A. G. (1984). The perseverance of beliefs: Conceptual perspectives and research developments. *Journal of Social and Clinical Psychology, 2,* 25–56.

Jhabvala, R. P. (1986). *Out of India.* New York: William Morrow.

Jochelson, W. I. (1900). The Yukaghir and Yukaghirized Tungus. *Materials for the study of the Yukaghir language and folk-lore, collected in the Kolyma district* (p. 34). St. Petersburg, Russia: IRAS.

Jones, H. E. (1935). The galvanic skin reflex as related to overt emotional expression. *American Journal of Psychology, 47,* 241–251.

(1950). The study of patterns of emotional expression. In M. L. Reymert (Ed.), *Feelings and emotions.* (pp. 161–168). New York: McGraw–Hill.

Jung, C. G. (1968). Lecture five. *Analytical psychology; Its theory and practice* (pp. 151–160). New York: Random House.

Kagan, J., Reznick, J. S., & Snidman, N. (1988). Biological bases of childhood shyness. *Science, 240,* 167–171.

Kagan, N. I. (1978). Affective sensitivity test: Validity and reliability. Paper presented at the meeting of the American Psychological Association, San Francisco.

Kasprowicz, A. L., Manuck, S. B., Malkoff, S. B., & Krantz, D. S. (1990). Individual differences in behaviorally evoked cardiovascular response. *Psychophysiology, 27,* 605–619.

Kato, K., & Markus, H. (1992). *Interdependence and culture: Theory and measurement.* Unpublished manuscript, University of Michigan, Ann Arbor.

Kellerman, J., Lewis, J., & Laird, J. D. (1989). Looking and loving: the effects of mutual gaze on feelings of romantic love. *Journal of Research in Personality, 23,* 145–161.

Kendon, A. (1970). Movement coordination in social interaction: Some examples described. *Acta Psychologica, 32,* 1–25.

Kerckhoff, A. C., & Back, K. W. (1968). *The June bug: A study of hysterical contagion.* New York: Appleton–Century–Crofts.

Klawans, H. L. (1990). *Newton's madness: Further tales of clinical neurology.* London: Headline Book Publ.

Kleck, R. E., Vaughan, R. C., Cartwright-Smith, J., Vaughan, K. B., Colby, C. Z., & Lanzetta, J. T. (1976). Effects of being observed on expressive, subjective, and physiological responses to painful stimuli. *Journal of Personality and Social Psychology, 34,* 1211–1218.

Klein, D. J., and Cacioppo, J. T. (1993). *The Facial Expressiveness Scale and the Autonomic Reactivity Scale.* Unpublished manuscript, Ohio State University, Columbus.

Klein, J. (1992, November/December). The year of the voter. *Newsweek,* special issue, pp. 14–15.

Kleinke, C. L., & Walton, J. H. (1982). Influence of reinforced smiling on affective responses in an interview. *Journal of Personality and Social Psychology, 43,* 557–565.

Klinnert, M. D., Campos, J. J., Sorce, J. F., Emde, R. N., & Sveida, M. (1983). Emotions as behavior regulators: Social referencing in infants. In R. Plutchik & H. Kellerman (Eds.), *Emotion: Theory, research, and experience: Vol. 2. Emotions in early development* (pp. 57–86). New York: Academic Press.

Kohler, W. (1927). *The mentality of apes* (2nd ed.) (E. Winter, Trans.). New York: Harcourt.

Kopel, S., & Arkowitz, H. S. (1974). Role playing as a source of self-observation and behavior change. *Journal of Personality and Social Psychology, 29,* 677–686.

Kraut, R. E. (1982). Social pressure, facial feedback, and emotion. *Journal of Personality and Social Psychology, 42,* 853–863.

Krebs, D. (1975). Empathy and altruism. *Journal of Personality and Social Psychology, 32,* 1134–1146.

Lacey, J. I. (1959). Psychophysiological approaches to the evaluation of psychotherapeutic process and outcome. In E. A. Rubinstein & M. B. Parloff (Eds.), *Research in psychotherapy* (Vol. 1, pp. 160–208). Washington, DC: American Psychological Association.

——— (1967). Somatic response patterning and stress: Some revisions of activation theory. In M. H. Appley & R. Trumbull (Eds.), *Psychological stress: Issues in research* (pp. 14–42). New York: Appleton–Century–Crofts.

Lacey, J. I., Bateman, D. E., & Van Lehn, R. (1953). Autonomic response specificity: An experimental study. *Psychosomatic Medicine, 15,* 8–21.

Lacey, J. I., Kagan, J., Lacey, B. C., & Moss, H. A. (1963). The visceral level: Situational determinants and behavioral correlates of autonomic response patterns. In P. H. Knapp (Ed.), *Expression of the emotions in man* (pp. 161–196). New York: International Universities Press.

Lacey, J. I., & Lacey, B. C. (1958). Verification and extension of the principle of autonomic response-stereotypy. *American Journal of Psychology, 71*, 50–73.

Lachman, R., Lachman, J. L., & Butterfield, E. C. (1979). *Cognitive psychology and information processing: An introduction.* Hillsdale, NJ: Erlbaum.

Ladurie, E. L. R. (1979). *Montaillou: The promised land of error.* New York: Vintage Press.

La France, M. (1979). Nonverbal synchrony and rapport: Analysis by the cross-lag panel technique. *Social Psychology Quarterly, 42*, 66–70.

(1982). Posture mirroring and rapport. In M. Davis (Ed.), *Interaction rhythms: Periodicity in communicative behavior* (pp. 279–298). New York: Human Sciences Press.

La France, M., & Banaji, M. (1992). Toward a reconsideration of the gender–emotion relationship. In M. S. Clark (Ed.), *Review of personality and social psychology: Vol. 14. Emotion and social behavior* (pp. 178–201). Newbury Park, CA: Sage.

La France, M., & Broadbent, M. (1976). Group rapport: Posture sharing as a nonverbal indicator. *Group and Organization Studies, 1*, 328–333.

La France, M., & Ickes, W. (1981). Posture mirroring and interactional involvement: Sex and sex typing effects. *Journal of Nonverbal Behavior, 5*, 139–154.

Laird, J. D. (1974). Self-attribution of emotion: The effects of expressive behavior on the quality of emotional experience. *Journal of Personality and Social Psychology, 33*, 475–486.

(1984). The real role of facial response in the experience of emotion: A reply to Tourangeau and Ellsworth, and others. *Journal of Personality and Social Psychology, 47*, 909–917.

Laird, J. D., & Bresler, C. (1992). The process of emotional experience: A self-perception theory. In M. S. Clark (Ed.), *Review of personality and social psychology: Vol. 13. Emotion* (pp. 213–234). Newbury Park, CA: Sage.

Laird, J. D., & Crosby, M. (1974). Individual differences in the self-attribution of emotion. In H. London and R. E. Nisbett (Eds.), *Thought and feeling: Cognitive alteration of feeling states* (pp. 45–59). Chicago: Aldine.

Laird, J. D., Wagener, J. J., Halal, M., & Szegda, M. (1982). Remembering what you feel: Effects of emotion and memory. *Journal of Personality and Social Psychology, 42*, 646–675.

Lang, P. J. (1985). The cognitive psychophysiology of emotion: Fear and anxiety. In A. H. Tuma & J. D. Maser (Eds.), *Anxiety and the anxiety disorders* (pp. 131–170). Hillsdale, NJ: Erlbaum.

Lange, C. (1885/1922). The emotions (I. A. Istar Haupt, Trans.). In K. Dunlap (Ed.), *The emotions* (pp. 33–90). Baltimore: Williams & Wilkens.

Lanzetta, J. T., Biernat, J. J., & Kleck, R. E. (1982). Self-focused attention, facial behavior, autonomic arousal and the experience of emotion. *Motivation and Emotion, 6*, 49–63.

Lanzetta, J. T., Cartwright-Smith, J., & Kleck, R. E. (1976). Effects of nonverbal dissimulation on emotional experience and autonomic arousal. *Journal of Personality and Social Psychology, 33*, 354–370.

Lanzetta, J. T., & McHugo, G. J. (1986, October). The history and current status of the facial feedback hypothesis. Paper presented at the 26th annual meeting of the Society for Psychophysiological Research, Montréal, Québec, Canada.

Lanzetta, J. T., & Orr, S. P. (1980). Influences of facial expression on the classical conditioning of fear. *Journal of Personality and Social Psychology, 39*, 1081–1087.

(1981). Stimulus properties of facial expressions and their influence on the classical conditioning of fear. *Motivation and Emotion, 5*, 225–234.

(1986). Excitatory strength of expressive faces: Effects of happy and fear expressions and context on the extinction of a conditioned fear response. *Journal of Personality and Social Psychology, 50,* 190–194.

Larsen, R. J., Kasimatis, M., & Frey, K. (1992). Facilitating the furrowed brow: An unobtrusive test of the facial feedback hypothesis applied to negative affect. *Cognition and emotion, 6,* 321–338.

Lazarus, R. S. (1984). Thoughts on the relations between emotion and cognition. In K. Scherer & P. Ekman (Eds.), *Approaches to emotion* (pp. 247–257). Hillsdale, NJ: Erlbaum.

(1991). *Emotion and adaptation.* New York: Oxford University Press.

Le Bon, G. (1896). *The crowd: A study of the popular mind.* London: Ernest Benn, Ltd.

Le Doux, J. E. (1986). Sensory systems and emotion: A model of affective processing. *Integrative Psychiatry, 4,* 237–248.

Lefebvre, G. (1973). *The great fear of 1789* (J. White, Trans.). New York: Pantheon.

Lehmann-Haupt, C. (1988, August 4). How an actor found success and himself. *New York Times,* p. B2.

Levenson, R. W., Carstensen, L. L., Friesen, W. V., & Ekman, P. (1991). Emotion, physiology, and expression in old age. *Psychology and Aging, 6,* 28–35.

Levenson, R. W., Ekman, P., & Friesen, W. V. (1990). Voluntary facial action generates emotion-specific autonomic nervous system activity. *Psychophysiology, 27,* 363–384.

Levenson, R. W., & Gottman, J. M. (1983). Marital interaction: Physiological linkage and affective exchange. *Journal of Personality and Social Psychology, 45,* 587–597.

Levenson, R. W., & Ruef, A. M. (1992). Empathy: A physiological substrate. *Journal of Personality and Social Psychology, 63,* 234–246.

Leventhal, H., & Mace, W. (1970). The effect of laughter on evaluation of a slapstick movie. *Journal of Personality, 38,* 16–30.

Lewicki, P. (1986). *Nonconscious social information processing.* New York: Academic Press.

Lewis, C. S. (1961). *A grief observed.* London: Faber and Faber.

Lipps, T. (1903). XIV. Kapitel: Die einfühlung. In *Leitfaden der psychologie* [Guide to psychology] (pp. 187–201). Leipzig: Verlag von Wilhelm Engelmann.

Luria, A. R. (1902/1987). *The mind of a mnemonist* (L. Solotaroff, Trans.). Cambridge, MA: Harvard University Press.

Maak, R. (1883–1887). *The Viluysk district of the Yakutsk territory* (Vol. 3., pp. 28). St. Petersburg, Russia.

McArthur, L. A., Solomon, M. R., & Jaffee, R. H. (1980). Weight and sex differences in emotional responsiveness to proprioceptive and pictorial stimuli. *Journal of Personality and Social Psychology, 39,* 308–319.

McCague, J. (1968). *The second rebellion: The story of the New York City draft riots of 1863.* New York: Dial Press.

McCarthy, M. (1954). *A charmed life.* New York: New American Library.

McCaul, K. D., Holmes, D. S., & Solomon, S. (1982). Voluntary expressive changes and emotion. *Journal of Personality and Social Psychology, 42,* 145–152.

McCurdy, H. G. (1950). Consciousness and the galvanometer. *Psychological Review, 57,* 322–327.

McHugo, G. J., Lanzetta, J. T., Sullivan, D. G., Masters, R. D., & Englis, B. G. (1985). Emotional reactions to a political leader's expressive displays. *Journal of Personality and Social Psychology, 49,* 1513–1529.

McIntosh, D. N. (1991). *The social induction of affect.* Unpublished manuscript, University of Michigan, Ann Arbor.

MacLean, P. D. (1949). Psychosomatic disease and the "visceral brain." *Psychosomatic Medicine, 11,* 338–353.

(1975). Sensory and perceptive factors in emotional function of the triune brain. In R. G. Grenell & S. Gabay (Eds.), *Biological foundations of psychiatry* (Vol. 1, pp. 177–198). New York: Raven Press.

McMurtry, L. (1989). *Some can whistle.* New York: Pocket Books.

Mailer, N. (1979). *The executioner's song.* Boston: Little, Brown.

Malatesta, C. Z., & Haviland, J. M. (1982). Learning display rules: The socialization of emotion expression in infancy. *Child Development, 53,* 991–1003.

Malmo, R. B., & Shagass, C. (1949). Physiologic study of symptom mechanisms in psychiatric patients under stress. *Psychosomatic Medicine, 11,* 25–29.

Mandler, G. (1975). *Mind and emotion.* New York: Wiley.

(1984). *Mind and body: Psychology of emotion and stress.* New York: Norton.

Mann, T. (1965). *Death in Venice.* New York: Alfred A. Knopf.

(1969). *The magic mountain.* New York: Vintage.

Manstead, A. S. R. (1988). The role of facial movement in emotion. In H. L. Wagner (Ed.), *Social psychophysiology and emotion: Theory and clinical applications* (pp. 105–130). New York: Wiley.

Manstead, A. S. R., MacDonald, C. J., & Wagner, H. L. (1982). *Nonverbal communication of emotion via spontaneous facial expressions.* Unpublished manuscript, University of Manchester, England.

Marcia, J. (1987). Empathy and psychotherapy. In N. Eisenberg & J. Strayer (Eds.), *Empathy and its development* (pp. 81–102). New York: Cambridge University Press.

Markus, H. (1977). Self-schemata and processing information about the self. *Journal of Personality and Social Psychology, 35,* 63–78.

Markus, H. R., & Kitayama, S. (1991). Culture and self: Implications for cognition, emotion, and motivation. *Psychological Review, 98,* 224–253.

Marshall, G., & Zimbardo, P. (1979). The affective consequences of inadequately explained physiological arousal. *Journal of Personality and Social Psychology, 37,* 970–988.

Maslach, C. (1979). Negative emotional biasing of unexplained arousal. *Journal of Personality and Social Psychology, 37,* 953–969.

Matarazzo, J. D., Weitman, M., Saslow, G., & Wiens, A. N. (1963). Interviewer influence on durations of interviewee speech. *Journal of Verbal Learning and Verbal Behavior, 1,* 451–458.

Matarazzo, J. D., & Wiens, A. N. (1972). *The interview: Research on its anatomy and structure.* Chicago: Aldine–Atherton.

Matsumoto, D. (1987). The role of facial response in the experience of emotion: More methodological problems and a meta-analysis. *Journal of Personality and Social Psychology, 52,* 769–774.

Meltzoff, A. N. (1988). Infant imitation after a 1-week delay: Long-term memory for novel acts and multiple stimuli. *Developmental Psychology, 24,* 470–476.

Meltzoff, A. N., & Moore, M. K. (1977). Imitations of facial and manual gestures by human neonates. *Science, 198,* 75–78.

Miller, A. (1987). *Timebends.* New York: Harper & Row.

Miller, J. B. (1976). *Towards a new psychology of women.* Boston: Beacon Press.

Miller, R. E. (1967). Experimental approaches to the physiological and behavioral concomitants of affective communication in rhesus monkeys. In S. A. Altmann

(Ed.), *Social communication among primates* (pp. 125–134). Chicago: University of Chicago Press.

Miller, R. E., Banks, J. H., & Ogawa, N. (1963). Role of facial expression in "cooperative–avoidance conditioning" in monkeys. *Journal of Abnormal and Social Psychology, 67,* 24–30.

Miller, R. E., Murphy, J. V., & Mirsky, I. A. (1959). Non-verbal communication of affect. *Journal of Clinical Psychology, 15,* 155–158.

Mirsky, I. A., Miller, R. E., & Murphy, J. V. (1958). The communication of affect in rhesus monkeys: I. An experimental method. *Journal of the American Psychoanalytic Association, 6,* 433–441.

Moore, S. (1960). *The Stanislavski system.* New York: Viking Press.

Morgan, T. (1980). *Maugham.* New York: Simon & Schuster.

Morgenstern, J. (1990, November 11). Robin Williams: More than a shtick figure. *New York Times Magazine,* pp. 33–108.

Morris, D. (1966). Postural echo. *Manwatching* (pp. 83–85). New York: Henry N. Abrahams.

Mosak, H. H., & Dreikurs, R. (1973). Adlerian psychology. In R. Corsini (Ed.), *Current psychotherapies* (pp. 35–83). Itasca, IL: F. E. Peacock.

Mullen, B., Futrell, D. E., Stairs, D., Tice, D. M., Baumeiser, R. F., Dawson, K. E., Riordan, C. A., Radloff, C. E., Goethals, G. R., Kennedy, J. G., & Rosenfeld, P. (1986). Newscasters' facial expressions and voting behavior of viewers: Can a smile elect a president? *Journal of Personality and Social Psychology, 51,* 291–295.

Murphy, G. (1947). *Personality: A biosocial approach to origins and structure.* New York: Harper.

Natale, M. (1975). Convergence of mean vocal intensity in dyadic communication as a function of social desirability. *Journal of Personality and Social Psychology, 32,* 790–804.

Nisbett, R. E., & Wilson, T. D. (1977). Telling more than we can know: Verbal reports on mental processes. *Psychological Review, 84,* 231–259.

Noller, P. (1982). Couple communication and marital satisfaction. *Australian Journal of Sex, Marriage and Family, 3,* 69–75.

(1986). Sex differences in nonverbal communication: Advantage lost or supremacy regained? *Australian Journal of Psychology, 38,* 23–32.

(1987). Nonverbal communication in marriage. In D. Perlman & S. Duck (Eds.), *Intimate relationships: Development, dynamics, and deterioration* (pp. 149–175). London: Sage Publications.

Oatley, K., & Jenkins, J. M. (1992). Human emotions: Function and dysfunction. *Annual Review of Psychology, 43,* 55–85.

O'Brien, D. (1985). *Two of a kind: The Hillside stranglers.* New York: New American Library.

Ohman, A. (1988). Nonconscious control of autonomic responses: A role for Pavlovian conditioning? *Biological Psychology, 27,* 113–135.

Ohman, A., & Dimberg, U. (1978). Facial expressions as conditioned stimuli for electrodermal response: A case study of "preparedness"? *Journal of Personality and Social Psychology, 36,* 1251–1258.

Orr, S., & Lanzetta, J. (1980). Facial expressions of emotion as conditioned stimuli for human autonomic responses. *Journal of Personality and Social Psychology, 38,* 278–282.

(1984). Extinction of an emotional response in the presence of facial expressions of emotion. *Motion and Emotions, 8,* 55–66.

Ortony, A., & Turner, T. J. (1990). What's basic about basic emotions? *Psychological Review, 97,* 315–331.

Osgood, C. (1976). *Focus on meaning.* Paris: Mouton.

O'Toole, R., & Dubin, R. (1968). Baby feeding and body sway: An experiment in George Herbert Mead's "taking the role of the other." *Journal of Personality and Social Psychology, 10,* 59–65.

Panksepp, J. (1986). The anatomy of emotions. In R. Plutchik & H. Kellerman (Eds.), *Emotion: Theory, research, and experience. Vol. 3: Biological foundations of emotion* (pp. 91–124). New York: Academic Press.

(in press). A critical role for "affective neuroscience" in resolving what is basic about basic emotions: Response to Ortony and Turner. *Psychological Review.*

Papez, J. W. (1937). A proposed mechanism of emotion. *Archives of Neurology and Psychiatry, 38,* 725–743.

Perper, T. (1985). *Sex signals: The biology of love.* Philadelphia: ISI Press.

Patterson, M. L. (1976). An arousal model of interpersonal intimacy. *Psychological Review, 83,* 235–245.

Plato (1953). *Symposium* (B. Jowett, Trans.). *The dialogues of Plato* (pp. 479–555). Oxford, England: Clarendon Press.

Plomin, R. (1989). Environment and genes: Determinants of behavior. *American Psychologist, 44,* 105–111.

Poe, E. A. (1915). The purloined letter. *The tales and poems of Edgar Allan Poe: Vol. III. Tales and poems* (pp. 84–113). New York: G. P. Putnam's Sons.

Posner, M. I., & Snyder, C. R. R. (1975). Attention and cognitive control. In R. L. Solso (Ed.), *Information processing and cognition: The Loyola symposium* (pp. 55–87). Hillsdale, NJ: Erlbaum.

Postman, L., Bruner, J. S., & McGinnies, E. (1948). Personal values as selective factors in perception. *Journal of Abnormal and Social Psychology, 43,* 142–154.

Priklonski, V. L. (1890). *Three years in the Yakutsk territory* (p. 34). St. Petersburg, Russia: LAT.

Provine, R. R. (1986). Yawning as a stereotyped action pattern and releasing stimulus. *Ethology, 72,* 109–122.

(1989). Contagious yawning and infant imitation. *Bulletin of the Psychonomic Society, 27,* 125–126.

(1992). Contagious laughter: Laughter is a sufficient stimulus for laughs and smiles. *Bulletin of the Psychonomic Society, 30,* 1–4.

Provine, R. R., & Fischer, K. R. (1989). Laughing, smiling, and talking: Relation to sleeping and social context in humans. *Ethology, 83,* 295–305.

Rapson, R. L. (1980). *Denials of doubt: An interpretation of American history.* Lanham, MD: University Press of America.

Reay, M. (1960). "Mushroom madness" in the New Guinea Highlands. *Oceania, 31,* 135–139.

Reibstein, L., & Joseph, N. (1988, August 8). Mimic your way to the top. *Newsweek,* p. 50.

Reich, W. (1933/1945). *Character analysis* (3rd ed.; V. R. Carfagno, Trans.). New York: Simon & Schuster.

Reik, T. (1948). *Listening with the third ear: The inner experience of a psychoanalyst.* New York: Farrar, Straus & Giroux.

Reissland, N. (1988). Neonatal imitation in the first hour of life: Observations in rural Nepal. *Developmental Psychology, 24,* 464–469.

Rhodenwalt, F., & Comer, R. (1979). Induced–compliance attitude change: Once more with feeling. *Journal of Experimental Social Psychology, 15,* 35–47.

Riskind, J. H. (1983). Nonverbal expressions and the accessibility of life experience memories: A congruency hypothesis. *Social Cognition, 2,* 62–86.

(1984). The stoop to conquer: Guiding and self-regulatory functions of physical posture after success and failure. *Journal of Personality and Social Psychology, 47,* 479–493.

Riskind, J. H., & Gotay, C. C. (1982). Physical posture: Could it have regulatory or feedback effects on motivation and emotion? *Motivation and Emotion, 6,* 273–298.

Rodgers, R., & Hammerstein, O. (1943). *Oklahoma!* New York: Random House.

Rooney, A. A. (1989). *Not that you asked.* New York: Random House.

Rosenthal, R., & DePaulo, B. M. (1979a). Sex differences in eavesdropping on nonverbal cues. *Journal of Personality and Social Psychology, 37,* 273–285.

(1979b). Sex differences in accommodation in nonverbal communication. In R. Rosenthal (Ed.), *Skill in nonverbal communication: Individual differences* (pp. 68–103). Cambridge, MA: Oelgeschlager, Gunn, & Hain.

Rosenthal, R., Hall, J. A., DiMatteo, M. R., Rogers, P. L., & Archer, D. (1979). *Sensitivity to nonverbal communication: The PONS test.* Baltimore: Johns Hopkins University Press.

Ross, M., & Olson, J. M. (1981). An expectancy–attribution model of the effects of placebos. *Psychological Review, 88,* 408–437.

Rude, G. P. E. (1981). *The crowd in history: A study of popular disturbances in France and England.* London: Lawrence & Wishart.

Rutledge, L. L., & Hupka, R. B. (1985). The facial feedback hypothesis: Methodological concerns and new supporting evidence. *Motivation and Emotion, 9,* 219–240.

Sackett, G. (1966). Monkeys reared in isolation with pictures as visual input: Evidence for an innate releasing mechanism. *Science, 154,* 1468–1473.

Sacks, O. (1987). *The man who mistook his wife for a hat.* New York: Harper Perennial.

Salovey, P., & Mayer, J. D. (1990). Emotional intelligence. *Imagination, Cognition and Personality, 9,* 185–211.

Schachter, S., & Singer, J. (1962). Cognitive, social, and physiological determinants of emotional state. *Psychological Review, 69,* 379–399.

Schachter, S., & Wheeler, L. (1962). Epinephrine, chlorpromazine, and amusement. *Journal of Abnormal and Social Psychology, 65,* 121–128.

Scheflen, A. E. (1964). The significance of posture in communication systems. *Psychiatry, 27,* 316–331.

Scherer, K. (1982). Methods of research on vocal communication: Paradigms and parameters. In K. R. Scherer & P. Ekman (Eds.), *Handbook of methods in nonverbal behavior research* (pp. 136–198). New York: Cambridge University Press.

Schmeck, H. M. (1983, Sept. 9). Study says smile may indeed be an umbrella. *New York Times,* pp. A1, A16.

Schreiber, L. (1990). *Midstream.* New York: Viking.

Schwartz, G. E., Brown, S., & Ahern, G. L. (1980). Facial muscle patterning and subjective experience during affective imagery: Sex differences. *Psychophysiology, 17,* 75–82.

Sedikides, C. (1992). Mood as a determinant of attentional focus. *Cognition and Emotion, 6,* 129–148.

Shepard, R. N. (1990). *Mind sights.* San Francisco: W. H. Freeman.

Sherwood, A., Dolan, C. A., & Light, K. C. (1990). Hemodynamics of blood pressure during active and passive coping. *Psychophysiology, 27,* 656–668.

Shields, S. A. (1987). Women, men, and the dilemma of emotion. In P. Shaver & C. Hendrick (Eds.), *Review of personality and social psychology: Vol. 7. Sex and gender* (pp. 229–250). Newbury Park, CA: Sage.

Shields, S. A., & Stern, R. M. (1979). Emotion: The perception of bodily change. In P. Pliner, K. R. Blankstein, & I. M. Spigel (Eds.), *Perception of emotion in self and others* (pp. 85–106). New York: Plenum Press.

Shiffrin, R. M., & Schneider, W. (1977). Controlled and automatic human information processing: II. Perceptual learning, automatic attending and a general theory. *Psychological Review, 84,* 127–190.

Siegman, A. W., Anderson, R. A., & Berger, T. (1990). The angry voice: Its effects on the experience of anger and cardiovascular reactivity. *Psychosomatic Medicine, 52,* 631–643.

Siegman, A. W., & Reynolds, M. (1982). Interviewer–interviewee nonverbal communications: An interactional approach. In M. Davis (Ed.), *Interaction rhythms: Periodicity in communicative behavior* (pp. 249–278). New York: Human Sciences Press.

Simner, M. L. (1971). Newborn's response to the cry of another infant. *Developmental Psychology, 5,* 136–150.

Smith, A. (1759/1976). *The theory of moral sentiments.* Oxford, England: Clarendon Press.

Snodgrass, S. E. (1985). Women's intuition: The effect of subordinate role on interpersonal sensitivity. *Journal of Personality and Social Psychology, 49,* 146–155.

Snyder, M. (1984). When beliefs create reality. In L. Berkowitz (Ed.), *Advances in experimental social psychology* (Vol. 18, pp. 247–305). New York: Academic Press.

Snyder, M., Tanke, E. D., & Berscheid, E. (1977). Social perception and interpersonal behavior: On the self-fulfilling nature of social stereotypes. *Journal of Personality and Social Psychology, 35,* 656–666.

Stein, E. (1917/1964) *On the problem of empathy* (W. Stein, Trans.). The Hague: Marinus Nyhoff.

Stepper, S., & Strack, F. (1992). Proprioceptive determinants of affective and non-affective feelings. Manuscript under review.

Stiff, J. B., Dillard, J. P., Somera, L., Kim, H., & Sleight, C. (1988). Empathy, communication, and prosocial behavior. *Communication Monographs, 55,* 198–213.

Stockert, N. (1993). *Perceived similarity and emotional contagion.* Unpublished Ph.D. dissertation, University of Hawaii, Honolulu.

Stone, L. (1977). *The family, sex, and marriage: In England 1500–1800.* New York: Harper & Row.

Storms, M. D., & Nisbett, R. E. (1970). Insomnia and the attribution process. *Journal of Personality and Social Psychology, 16,* 319–328.

Stotland, E. (1969). Exploratory investigations of empathy. In L. Berkowitz (Ed.), *Advances in experimental social psychology* (Vol. 4, pp. 271–314). New York: Academic Press.

Strack, F., Martin, L. L., & Stepper, S. (1988). Inhibiting and facilitating conditions of the human smile: A nonobtrusive test of the facial feedback hypothesis. *Journal of Personality and Social Psychology, 54,* 768–776.

Street, R. L., Jr. (1984). Speech convergence and speech evaluation in fact-finding interviews. *Human Communication Research, 11,* 139–169.

Sullins, E. S. (1991). Emotional contagion revisited: Effects of social comparison and expressive style on mood convergence. *Personality and Social Psychology Bulletin, 17,* 166–174.

Swann, W. B., & Read, S. J. (1981). Self-verification process: How we sustain our self-conceptions. *Journal of Experimental Social Psychology, 17,* 351–372.

Tansey, M. J., & Burke, W. F. (1989). *Understanding counter-transference: From projective identification to empathy.* Hillsdale, NJ: Analytic Press.

Tassinary, L. G., Cacioppo, J. T., & Geen, T. R. (1989). A psychometric study of surface electrode placements for facial electromyographic recording: I. The brow and cheek muscle regions. *Psychophysiology, 26,* 1–16.

Taylor, C. (1989). *Sources of the self: The making of the modern identity.* Cambridge, MA: Harvard University Press.

Ten Houten, W. D., Hoppe, K. D., Bogen, J. E., & Walter, D. O. (1985). Alexithymia and the split brain: IV. Gottschalk–Gleser content analysis, an overview. *Psychotherapy and Psychosomatics, 44,* 113–121.

    (1986). Alexithymia: An experimental study of cerebral commissurotomy patients and normal control subjects. *American Journal of Psychiatry, 143,* 312–316.

Teoh, J. I., Soewondo, S., & Sidharta, M. (1975). Epidemic hysteria in Malaysian schools: An illustrative episode. *Psychiatry, 38,* 258–269.

Termine, N. T., & Izard, C. E. (1988). Infants' response to their mother's expressions of joy and sadness. *Developmental Psychology, 24,* 223–229.

Theroux, P. (1988). *Riding the iron rooster: By train through China.* London: Hamish Hamilton.

Thomas, D. L., Franks, D. D., & Calonico, J. M. (1972). Role-taking and power in social psychology. *American Sociological Review, 37,* 605–614.

Thompson, R. A. (1987). Empathy and emotional understanding: The early development of empathy. In N. Eisenberg & J. Strayer (Eds.), *Empathy and its development* (pp. 119–145). New York: Cambridge University Press.

Tickle-Degnen, L., & Rosenthal, R. (1987). Group rapport and nonverbal behavior. *Review of Personality and Social Psychology, 9,* 113–136.

Titchener, E. (1909). *Experimental psychology of the thought processes.* New York: Macmillan.

Tomkins, S. S. (1962, 1963). *Affect, imagery, consciousness,* 2 vols. New York: Springer.

    (1980). Affect as amplification: Some modifications in theory. In R. Plutchik & H. Kellerman (Eds.), *Emotion: Theory, research, and experience: Vol. 1. Theories of emotion* (pp. 141–164). New York: Academic Press.

Tourangeau, R., & Ellsworth, P. C. (1979). The role of facial response in the experience of emotion. *Journal of Personality and Social Psychology, 37,* 1519–1531.

Tronick, E. D., Als, H., & Brazelton, T. B. (1977). Mutuality in mother–infant interaction. *Journal of Communication, 27,* 74–79.

Trout, D. L., & Rosenfeld, H. M. (1980). The effect of postural lean and body congruence on the judgment of psychotherapeutic rapport. *Journal of Nonverbal Behavior, 4,* 176–190.

Tseng, W-S., & Hsu, J. (1980). Minor psychological disturbances of everyday life. In H. C. Triandis & J. D. Draguns (Eds.), *Handbook of cross-cultural psychology: Vol. 6. Psychopathology* (pp. 61–97). Boston: Allyn & Bacon.

Uchino, B. C., Hatfield, E., Carlson, J. G., & Chemtob, C. (1991). *The effect of cognitive expectations on susceptibility to emotional contagion.* Unpublished manuscript, University of Hawaii, Honolulu.

Updike, J. (1989). *Self-consciousness.* New York: Fawcett Crest.

Vaughan, K. B., & Lanzetta, J. T. (1980). Vicarious instigation and conditioning of facial expressive and autonomic responses to a model's expressive display of pain. *Journal of Personality and Social Psychology, 38,* 909–923.

Voglmaier, M. M., & Hakeren, G. (1989, August) Facial electromyography (EMG) in response to facial expressions: Relation to subjective emotional experience and trait affect. Paper presented at the meetings of the Society for Psychophysiological Research, New Orleans, LA.

Wagner, H. L., MacDonald, C. J., & Manstead, A. S. R. (1986). Communication of individual emotions by spontaneous facial expressions. *Journal of Personality and Social Psychology, 50,* 737–743.

Wallbott, H. G. (1991). Recognition of emotion from facial expression via imitation? Some indirect evidence for an old theory. *British Journal of Social Psychology, 30,* 207–219.

Ward, G. C. (1989). *A first-class temperament.* New York: Harper & Row.

Warner, R. [M.] (1990). *Interaction tempo and evaluation of affect in social interaction: Rhythmic systems versus causal modeling approaches.* Unpublished manuscript, University of New Hampshire, Durham.

Warner, R. M., Waggener, T. B., & Kronauer, R. E. (1983). Synchronized cycles in ventilation and vocal activity during spontaneous conversational speech. *Journal of Applied Physiology: Respiratory, Environmental and Exercise Physiology, 54,* 1324–1334.

Watson, L. (1976). *Gifts of unknown things.* New York: Simon & Schuster.

Webb, J. T. (1972). Interview synchrony: An investigation of two speech rate measures in an automated standardized interview. In B. Pope & A. W. Siegman (Eds.), *Studies in dyadic communication* (pp. 115–133). New York: Pergamon.

Webster, R. L., Steinhardt, M. H., & Senter, M. G. (1972). Changes in infants' vocalizations as a function of differential acoustic stimulation. *Developmental Psychology, 7,* 39–43.

Wegner, D. M., Lane, J. D., & Dimitri, S. (1991). Secret liaisons: *The allure of covert relationships.* Unpublished manuscript, University of Virginia, Charlottesville.

Weitz, S. (1974). *Nonverbal communication: Readings with commentary.* New York: Oxford University Press.

Wells, G. L., & Petty, R. E. (1980). The effects of overt head movement on persuasion: Compatibility and incompatibility responses. *Basic and Applied Social Psychology, 1,* 219–230.

Wenger, M. A. (1950). Emotion as a visceral action: An extension of Lange's theory. In M. L. Raymert (Ed.), *Feelings and emotions* (pp. 3–10). New York: McGraw–Hill.

Wheeler, L. (1966). Toward a theory of behavioral contagion. *Psychological Review, 73,* 179–192.

Wilson, T. D. (1985). Strangers to ourselves: The origins and accuracy of beliefs about one's own mental status. In J. N. Harvey & G. Weary (Eds.), *Attribution: Basic issues and applications* (pp. 9–36). New York: Academic Press.

Wispé, L. (1991). *The psychology of sympathy.* New York: Plenum Press.

Wixon, D. R., & Laird, J. D. (1981). Effects of mimicry on the judgment of facial expressions in others. Paper presented at the Annual Meeting of the Eastern Psychological Association.

Yalom, I. D. (1989). *Love's executioner.* New York: Harper Perennial.

Young, R. D., & Frye, M. (1966). Some are laughing; some are not – Why? *Psychological Reports, 18,* 747–752.

Zahn-Waxler, C., & Radke-Yarrow, M. (1990). The origins of empathic concern. *Motivation and Emotion, 14,* 107–130.

Zajonc, R. B. (1965). Social facilitation: A solution is suggested for an old unresolved social psychological problem. *Science, 149,* 269–274.

(1984). On the primacy of affect. *American Psychologist, 39,* 117–123.

Zajonc, R. B., & Markus, H. (1982). Affective and cognitive factors in preferences. *Journal of Consumer Research, 9,* 123–131.

(1984). Affect and cognition: The hard interface. In C. E. Izard, J. Kagan, & R. B. Zajonc (Eds.), *Emotions, cognition, and behavior* (pp. 73–102). Cambridge, England: Cambridge University Press.

Zajonc, R. B., Murphy, S. T., & Inglehart, M. (1989). Feeling and facial efference: Implications of the vascular theory of emotion. *Psychological review, 96,* 395–416.

Zillman, D., & Cantor, J. R. (1977). Affective responses to the emotions of a protagonist. *Journal of Experimental Social Psychology, 13,* 155–165.

Zuckerman, M., Klorman, R., Larrance, D. T., & Speigel, N. H. (1981). Facial, autonomic, and subjective components of emotion: The facial feedback hypothesis versus the externalizer–internalizer distinction. *Journal of Personality and Social Psychology, 41,* 929–944.

# Index

229

238 *Index*